# A Guide to Experimental Algorithmics

Computational experiments on algorithms can supplement theoretical analysis by showing what algorithms, implementations, and speed-up methods work best for specific machines or problems. This book guides the reader through the nuts and bolts of the major experimental questions: What should I measure? What inputs should I test? How do I analyze the data?

Answers to these questions draw on ideas from algorithm design and analysis, operating systems and memory hierarchies, and statistics and data analysis. The wide-ranging discussion includes a tutorial on system clocks and CPU timers, a survey of strategies for tuning algorithms and data structures, a cookbook of methods for generating random combinatorial inputs, and a demonstration of variance reduction techniques. Numerous case studies and examples show how to apply these concepts.

All the necessary concepts in computer architecture and data analysis are covered so that the book can be used by anyone who has taken a course or two in data structures and algorithms. A companion website, AlgLab (www.cs.amherst.edu/alglab) contains downloadable files, programs, and tools for use in projects.

DR. CATHERINE C. MCGEOCH is the Beitzel Professor of Technology and Society in the Department of Computer Science at Amherst College. Professor McGeoch was co-founder (with David S. Johnson) in 1990 of the Discrete Mathematics and Theoretical Computer Science (DIMACS) Implementation Challenges. In 1999 she co-founded (with Michael Goodrich) the annual Workshop on Algorithm Engineering and Experimentation (ALENEX), sponsored by SIAM. She was Editor-in-Chief of the ACM *Journal of Experimental Algorithmics* from 2003 to 2008 and currently serves on the ACM Publications Board.

# A Guide to Experimental Algorithmics

CATHERINE C. MCGEOCH

*Amherst College*

CAMBRIDGE
UNIVERSITY PRESS

CAMBRIDGE
UNIVERSITY PRESS

Shaftesbury Road, Cambridge CB2 8EA, United Kingdom

One Liberty Plaza, 20th Floor, New York, NY 10006, USA

477 Williamstown Road, Port Melbourne, VIC 3207, Australia

314–321, 3rd Floor, Plot 3, Splendor Forum, Jasola District Centre, New Delhi – 110025, India

103 Penang Road, #05–06/07, Visioncrest Commercial, Singapore 238467

Cambridge University Press is part of Cambridge University Press & Assessment,
a department of the University of Cambridge.

We share the University's mission to contribute to society through the pursuit of
education, learning and research at the highest international levels of excellence.

www.cambridge.org
Information on this title: www.cambridge.org/9780521173018

First published 2012

*A catalogue record for this publication is available from the British Library*

ISBN    978-1-107-00173-2    Hardback
ISBN    978-0-521-17301-8    Paperback

Additional resources for this publication at www.cs.amherst.edu/alglab

To my parents, Jim and Nancy Cole

# Contents

# Preface

This guidebook is written for anyone – student, researcher, or practitioner – who wants to carry out computational experiments on algorithms (and programs) that yield correct, general, informative, and useful results. (We take the wide view and use the term "algorithm" to mean "algorithm or program" from here on.)

Whether the goal is to predict algorithm performance or to build faster and better algorithms, the experiment-driven methodology outlined in these chapters provides insights into performance that cannot be obtained by purely abstract means or by simple runtime measurements. The past few decades have seen considerable developments in this approach to algorithm design and analysis, both in terms of number of participants and in methodological sophistication.

In this book I have tried to present a snapshot of the state-of-the-art in this field (which is known as *experimental algorithmics* and *empirical algorithmics*), at a level suitable for the newcomer to computational experiments. The book is aimed at a reader with some undergraduate computer science experience: you should know how to program, and ideally you have had at least one course in data structures and algorithm analysis. Otherwise, no previous experience is assumed regarding the other topics addressed here, which range widely from architectures and operating systems, to probability theory, to techniques of statistics and data analysis

A note to academics: The book takes a nuts-and-bolts approach that would be suitable as a main or supplementary text in a seminar-style course on advanced algorithms, experimental algorithmics, algorithm engineering, or experimental methods in computer science. Several case studies are presented throughout; a companion website called *AlgLab – Open Laboratory for Experiments on Algorithms* makes the files, programs, and tools described in the case studies available for downloading. Suggestions for experimental problems and projects appear at the end of each chapter.

This book wouldn't exist without the "number of participants" alluded to earlier, members of the research community who have worked to develop this new methodology while contributing a huge body of experiment-based research on design and analysis of algorithms, data structures, heuristics, and models of computation. I am grateful for all those collegial conversations during break-out sessions, carried out over countless cups of coffee: thanks to David Bader, Giuseppe Italiano, David S. Johnson, Richard Ladner, Peter Sanders, Matt Stallmann, and Cliff Stein. A huge thank you, especially, to Jon Bentley, whose comments, story ideas, and criticisms of draft versions of this book were immensely valuable. My editor Lauren Cowles also did a magnificent job of helping me to untangle knots in the draft manuscript.

Possibly more important to the final product than colleagues and readers are the family and friends who remind me that life is more than an endless bookwriting process: to Alex and Ian, Ruth and Stephen, Susan Landau, and Maia Ginsburg, thank you for keeping me sane.

And finally, very special thanks to the guy who fits all of the above categories and more: colleague, technical adviser, reader, supporter, husband, and friend. Thank you Lyle.

Catherine C. McGeoch
Amherst, Massachusetts
July 2011

# 1
# Introduction

The purpose of computing is insight, not numbers.
Richard Hamming, *Numerical*
*Methods for Scientists and Engineers*

Some questions:

- You are a working programmer given a week to reimplement a data structure that supports client transactions, so that it runs efficiently when scaled up to a much larger client base. Where do you start?
- You are an algorithm engineer, building a code repository to hold fast implementations of dynamic multigraphs. You read papers describing asymptotic bounds for several approaches. Which ones do you implement?
- You are an operations research consultant, hired to solve a highly constrained facility location problem. You could build the solver from scratch or buy optimization software and tune it for the application. How do you decide?
- You are a Ph.D. student who just discovered a new approximation algorithm for graph coloring that will make your career. But you're stuck on the average-case analysis. Is the theorem true? If so, how can you prove it?
- You are the adviser to that Ph.D. student, and you are skeptical that the new algorithm can compete with state-of-the-art graph coloring algorithms. How do you find out?

One good way to answer all these questions is: *run experiments to gain insight.*

This book is about *experimental algorithmics*, which is the study of algorithms and their performance by experimental means. We interpret the word *algorithm* very broadly, to include algorithms and data structures, as well as their implementations in source code and machine code. The two main challenges in algorithm studies addressed here are:

- *Analysis*, which aims to predict performance under given assumptions about inputs and machines. Performance may be a measure of time, solution quality, space usage, or some other metric.
- *Design*, which is concerned with building faster and better algorithms (and programs) to solve computational problems.

Very often these two activities alternate in an algorithmic research project – a new design strategy requires analysis, which in turn suggests new design improvements, and so forth.

A third important area of algorithm studies is *models of computation*, which considers how changes in the underlying machine (or machine model) affect design and analysis. Problems in this area are also considered in a few sections of the text.

The discussion is aimed at the newcomer to experiments who has some familiarity with algorithm design and analysis, at about the level of an undergraduate course. The presentation draws on knowledge from diverse areas, including theoretical algorithmics, code tuning, computer architectures, memory hierarchies, and topics in statistics and data analysis. Since "everybody is ignorant, only on different subjects" (Will Rogers), basic concepts and definitions in these areas are introduced as needed.

## 1.1  Why Do Experiments?

The foundational work in algorithm design and analysis has been carried out using a *theoretical* approach, which is based on abstraction, theorem, and proof. In this framework, algorithm design means creating an algorithm in pseudocode, and algorithm analysis means finding an asymptotic bound on the dominant operation under a worst-case or average-case model.

The main benefit of this abstract approach is universality of results – no matter how skilled the programmer, or how fast the platform, the asymptotic bound on performance is guaranteed to hold. Furthermore, the asymptotic bound is the most important property determining performance at large $n$, which is exactly when performance matters most. Here are two stories to illustrate this point.

- Jon Bentley [7] ran a race between two algorithms to solve the maximum-sum subarray problem. The $\Theta(n^3)$ algorithm was implemented in the fastest environment he could find (tuned C code on a 533MHz Alpha 21164), and the $\Theta(n)$ algorithm ran in the slowest environment available (interpreted Basic on a 2.03MHz Radio Shack TRS-80 Model II). Despite these extreme platform differences, the crossover point where the fast asymptotic algorithm started beating the slow algorithm occurred at only $n = 5,800$, when both programs took two minutes to run. At $n = 10,000$, the highly tuned cubic algorithm required seven days of computation while the poorly tuned linear algorithm required only 32 minutes.

- Steve Skiena [26] describes a project to test a conjecture about pyramid numbers, which are of the form $(m^3 - m)/6$, $m \geq 2$. An $O(n^{4/3} \log n)$ algorithm ran 30,000 times faster than an $O(n^2)$ algorithm at $n = 10^9$, finishing in 20 minutes instead of just over a year. Even tiny asymptotic differences become important when $n$ is large enough.

The main drawback of the theoretical approach is lack of specificity – a pencil-and-paper algorithm is a far cry from a working program, and considerable effort may be needed to fill in the details to get from one to the other. Furthermore, asymptotic analyses require greatly simplified models of computation, which can introduce significant inaccuracies in performance predictions.

Because of these gaps between theory and experience, some prefer to use an *empirical* approach to performance analysis: implement the algorithm and measure its runtime. This approach provides specificity but lacks generality – it is notoriously difficult to translate runtime measurements taken on one platform and one set of instances into accurate time predictions for other scenarios.

Experimental algorithmics represents a third approach that treats algorithms as laboratory subjects, emphasizing control of parameters, isolation of key components, model building, and statistical analysis. This is distinct from the purely empirical approach, which studies performance in "natural settings," in a manner akin to field experiments in the natural sciences.

Instead, experimental algorithmics combines the tools of the empiricist – code and measurement – with the abstraction-based approach of the theoretician. Insights from laboratory experiments can be more precise and realistic than pure theory provides, but also more general than field experiments can produce.

This approach complements but does not replace the other two approaches to understanding algorithm performance. It holds promise for bridging the long-standing communication gap between theory and practice, by providing a common ground for theoreticians and practitioners to exchange insights and discoveries about algorithm and program performance.

*Some Examples.* Here are some stories illustrating what has been accomplished by applying the experimental approach to problems in algorithm analysis.

- Theoretical analysis of Dijkstra's algorithm (on a graph of $n$ vertices and $m$ edges) concentrates on the cost of the decrease-key operation, which could be performed $m$ times, giving an $O(m \log n)$ or $O(m + n \log n)$ worst-case bound, depending on data structure. But experimental analysis has shown that the worst-case bound is overly pessimistic – the number of decrease-key operations is quite small for many types of graphs that arise in practical applications, such as network routing and roadmap navigation. In many real-world situations Dijkstra's algorithm exhibits $O(n + m)$ performance. See Cherkassky et al. [8] for experimental results and theorems.

- The history of average-case analysis of internal path length (IPL) in binary search trees, under a series of $t$ random insertions and deletions, also illustrates how experiments can guide theory. The expected IPL in a random binary tree is $O(n \log n)$. An early theorem showing that IPL does not change with $t$ was "disproved" by experiments (the theorem was correct but did not apply to the random model). Those experiments prompted a new conjecture that IPL decreases asymptotically with $t$. But later experiments showed that IPL initially decreases, then increases, then levels off to $\Theta(n \log^2 n)$. A more recent conjecture of $\Theta(n^{3/2})$ cost is well supported by experiments, but as yet unproved. See Panny [22] for details.
- LaMarca and Ladner performed a series of experiments to evaluate the cache performance of fundamental algorithms and data structures [15] [16]. On the basis of their results, they developed a new analytical model of computation that captures the two-tier nature of memory costs in real computers. Reanalysis of standard algorithms under this model produces much closer predictions of performance than the standard RAM model of computation used in classic analysis.

These examples show how experimental analysis can be used to:

1. Fill in the gaps between the simplifying assumptions necessary to theory and the realities of practical experience.
2. Characterize the differences among worst-case, average-case, and typical-case performance.
3. Suggest new theorems and guide proof strategies.
4. Extend theoretical analyses to more realistic inputs and models of computation.

Similarly, the experimental approach has made important contributions to problems in algorithm design and engineering. The term *algorithm engineering* has been coined to describe a systematic process for transforming abstract algorithms into production-quality software, with an emphasis on building fast, robust, and easy-to-use code. Algorithm design, which focuses on implementation and tuning strategies for specific algorithms and data structures (see Chapter 4 for details), is just one part of the larger algorithm engineering process, which is also concerned with requirements specification, interfaces, scalability, correctness, and so forth.

Here are a few examples showing how experiments have played a central role in both algorithm design and algorithm engineering.

- The 2006 *9th DIMACS Implementation Challenge–Shortest Paths* workshop contained presentations of several projects to speed up single-pair shortest-path (SPSP) algorithms. In one paper from the workshop, Sanders and Shultes [24] describe experiments to engineer an algorithm to run on roadmap graphs used in global positioning system (GPS) Routing applications: the Western Europe and the United States maps contain ($n = 18$ million, $m = 42.5$ million) and ($n = 23.9$ million, $m = 58.3$ million) nodes and edges, respectively. They estimate that their tuned implementation of Dijkstra's algorithm runs more than a million times faster on an average query than the best known implementation for general graphs.
- Bader et al. [?] describe efforts to speed up algorithms for computing optimal phylogenies, a problem in computational biology. The breakpoint phylogeny heuristic uses an exhaustive search approach to generate and evaluate candidate solutions. Exact evaluation of *each* candidate requires a solution to the traveling salesman problem, so that the worst-case cost is $O(2n!!)$ [*sic*–double factorial] to solve a problem with $n$ genomes. Their engineering efforts, which exploited parallel processing as well as algorithm and code tuning, led to speedups by factors as large as 1 million on problems containing 10 to 12 genomes.
- Speedups by much smaller factors than a million can of course be critically important on frequently used code. Yaroslavskiy et al. [27] describe a project to implement the Arrays.sort() method for JDK 7, to achieve fast performance when many duplicate array elements are present. (Duplicate array elements represent a worst-case scenario for many implementations of quicksort.) Their tests of variations on quicksort yielded performance differences ranging from 20 percent faster than a standard implementation (on arrays with no duplicates), to more than 15 times faster (on arrays containing identical elements).
- Sometimes the engineering challenge is simply to demonstrate a working implementation of a complex algorithm. Navarro [21] describes an effort to implement the LZ-Index, a data structure that supports indexing and fast lookup in compressed data. Navarro shows how experiments were used to guide choices made in the implementation process and to compare the finished product to competing strategies. This project is continued in [11], which describes several tuned implementations assembled in a repository that is available for public use.

These examples illustrate the ways in which experiments have played key roles in developing new insights about algorithm design and analysis. Many more examples can be found throughout this text and in references cited in the Chapter Notes.

## 1.2 Key Concepts

This section introduces some basic concepts that provide a framework for the larger discussion throughout the book.

### A Scale of Instantiation

We make no qualitative distinction here between "algorithms" and "programs." Rather, we consider algorithms and programs to represent two points on a *scale of instantiation*, according to how much specificity is in their descriptions. Here are some more recognizable points on this scale.

- At the most abstract end are *metaheuristics* and *algorithm paradigms*, which describe generic algorithmic structures that are not tied to particular problem domains. For example, Dijkstra's algorithm is a member of the greedy paradigm, and tabu search is a metaheuristic that can be applied to many problems.
- The *algorithm* is an abstract description of a process for solving an abstract problem. At this level we might see Dijkstra's algorithm written in pseudocode. The pseudocode description may be more or less instantiated according to how much detail is given about data structure implementation.
- The *source program* is a version of the algorithm implemented in a particular high-level language. Specificity is introduced by language and coding style, but the source code remains platform-independent. Here we might see Dijkstra's algorithm implemented in C++ using an STL priority queue.
- The *object code* is the result of compiling a source program. This version of the algorithm is written in machine code and specific to a family of architectures.
- The *process* is a program actively running on a particular machine at a particular moment in time. Performance at this level may be affected by properties such as system load, the size and shape of the memory hierarchy, and process scheduler policy.

Interesting algorithmic experiments can take place at any point on the instantiation scale. We make a conceptual distinction between the *experimental subject*, which is instantiated somewhere on the scale, and the *test program*, which is implemented to study the performance of the subject.

For example, what does it mean to measure an algorithm's time performance? Time performance could be defined as a count of the dominant cost, as identified by theory: this is an abstract property that is universal across programming languages, programmers, and platforms. It could be a count of instruction executions, which is a property of object code. Or it could be a measurement of elapsed time, which depends on the code as well as on the platform. There is one test program, but the experimenter can choose to measure any of these properties, according to the level of instantiation adopted in the experiment.

In many cases the test program may be exactly the subject of interest – but it need not be. By separating the two roles that a program may play, both as test subject and as testing apparatus, we gain clarity about experimental goals and procedures. Sometimes this conceptual separation leads to better experiments, in the sense that a test program can generate better-quality data more efficiently than a conventional implementation could produce (see Chapter 6 for details).

This observation prompts the first of many guidelines presented throughout the book. Guidelines are meant to serve as short reminders about best practice in experimental methodology. A list of guidelines appears in the Chapter Notes at the end of each chapter.

**Guideline 1.1** *The "algorithm" and the "program" are just two points on a scale between abstract and instantiated representations of a given computational process.*

### The Algorithm Design Hierarchy

Figure 1.1 shows the *algorithm design hierarchy*, which comprises six levels that represent broad strategies for improving algorithm performance. This hierarchical approach to algorithm design was first articulated by Reddy and Newell [23] and further developed by Bentley [6], [7]. The list in Figure 1.1 generally follows Bentley's development, except two layers–algorithm design and code tuning – are now split into three – algorithm design, algorithm tuning, and code tuning. The distinction is explained further in Chapter 4.

The levels in this hierarchy are organized roughly in the order in which decisions must be made in an algorithm engineering project. You have to design the algorithm before you implement it, and you cannot tune code before the implementation exists. On the other hand, algorithm engineering is not really a linear process – a new insight, or a roadblock, may be discovered at any level that makes it necessary to start over at a higher level.

Chapter 4 surveys tuning strategies that lie at the middle two levels of this hierarchy – algorithm tuning and code tuning. Although concerns at the other levels are outside the scope of this book, do not make the mistake of assuming that they are not important to performance. The stories in Section 1.1 about Bentley's race and Skiena's pyramid numbers show how important it is to get the asymptotics right in the first place.

In fact, the greatest feats of algorithm engineering result from combining design strategies from different levels: a 10-fold speedup from rearranging file structures at the system level, a 100-fold speedup from algorithm tuning, a 5-fold speedup from code tuning, and a 2-fold improvement from using an optimizing compiler, will combine *multiplicatively* to produce a 10,000-fold improvement in overall running time. Here are two stories that illustrate this effect.

- **System structure.** Decompose the software into modules that interact efficiently. Check whether the target runtime environment provides sufficient support for the modules. Decide whether the final product will run on a concurrent or sequential platform.
- **Algorithm and data structure design.** Specify the exact problem that is to be solved in each module. Choose appropriate problem representations. Select or design algorithms and data structures that are asymptotically efficient.
- **Implementation and algorithm tuning.** Implement the algorithm, or perhaps build a family of implementations. Tune the algorithm by considering high-level structures relating to the algorithm paradigm, input classes, and cost models.
- **Code tuning.** Consider low-level code-specific properties such as loops and procedure calls. Apply a systematic process to transform the program into a functionally equivalent program that runs faster.
- **System software.** Tune the runtime environment for best performance, for example by turning on compiler optimizers and adjusting memory allocations.
- **Platform and hardware.** Shift to a faster CPU and/or add coprocessors.

Figure 1.1. The algorithm design hierarchy. The levels in this hierarchy represent broad strategies for speeding up algorithms and programs.

*Cracking RSA-129.* Perhaps the most impressive algorithm engineering achievement on record is Atkins et al.'s [1] implementation of a program to factor a 129-digit number and solve an early RSA Encryption Challenge. Reasonable estimates at the time of the challenge were that the computation would take 4 quadrillion years. Instead, 17 years after the challenge was announced, the code was cracked in an eight-month computation: this represents a 6 quadrillion–fold speedup over the estimated computation time.

The authors' description of their algorithm design process gives the following insights about contributions at various levels of the algorithm design hierarchy.

- The task was carried out in three phases: an eight-month distributed computation (1600 platforms); then a 45-hour parallel computation (16,000 CPUs); then a few hours of computation on a sequential machine. Assuming optimal speedups due to concurrency, the first two phases would have required a total of 1149.2

years on a sequential machine. Thus *concurrency* contributed at most a 1150-fold speedup.

- Significant *system* design problems had to be solved before the computation could take place. For example, the distributed computation required task modules that could fit into main memory of all platforms offered by volunteers. Also, data compression was needed to overcome a critical memory shortage late in the computation.
- According to Moore's Law (which states that computer speeds typically double every 18 months), faster hardware alone could have contributed a 2000-fold speedup during the 17 years between challenge and solution. But in fact the original estimate took this effect into account. Thus no speedup over the estimate can be attributed to *hardware*.
- The authors describe *code tuning* improvements that contributed a factor of 2 speedup (there may be more that they did not report).
- Divide 6 quadrillion by $2300 = 1150 \times 2$: the remaining 2.6–trillion-fold speedup is due to improvements at the *algorithm design* level.

*Finding Phylogenies Faster.* In a similar vein, Bader et al. [2], [19] describe their engineering efforts to speed up the breakpoint phylogeny algorithm described briefly in Section 1.1.

- Since the generation of independent candidate solutions can easily be parallelized, the authors implemented their code for a 512-processor Alliance Cluster platform. This decision at the *systems* level to adopt a parallel solution produced an optimal 512-fold speedup over a comparable single-processor version.
- *Algorithm design* and *algorithm tuning* led to speedups by factors around 100; redesign of the data structures yielded another factor of 10. The cumulative speedup is 1000. The authors applied cache-aware tuning techniques to obtain a smaller memory footprint (from 60MB down to 1.8MB) and to improve cache locality. They remark that the new implementation runs almost entirely in cache for their test data sets.
- Using profiling to identify timing bottlenecks in a critical subroutine, they applied *code tuning* to obtain 6- to 10-fold speedups. The cumulative speedup from algorithm and code tuning was between 300 and 50,000, depending on inputs.

This combination of design improvements resulted in cumulative speedups by factors up to 1 million on some inputs.

**Guideline 1.2** *When the code needs to be faster, consider all levels of the algorithm design hierarchy.*

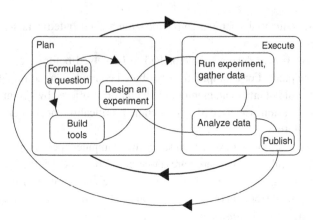

Figure 1.2. The experimental process. Experiments are carried out in cycles within cycles. Planning experiments alternates with executing them. In the planning stage, formulating questions alternates with building testing tools and designing experiments. In the execution stage, conducting experiments alternates with analyzing data. Individual steps may be carried out in different orders and are sometimes skipped.

### *The Experimental Process*

The major steps in the experimental process are defined in the following list and illustrated in Figure 1.2. Despite the numerical list structure, the process is not sequential, but rather loosely cyclical: planning experiments alternates with conducting experiments; the three steps in the planning stage may be carried out in any order; and steps may be skipped occasionally.

1.  Plan the experiment:
    a.  Formulate a question.
    b.  Assemble or build the test environment. The test environment comprises the test program, input instances and instance generators, measurement tools and packages, and data analysis software. These components might be readily available or might require considerable development time in their own right.
    c.  Design an experiment to address the question at hand. Specify, for example, what properties are to be measured, what input categories are applied, which input sizes are measured, how many random trials are run, and so forth.
2.  Execute the experiment:
    a.  Run the tests and collect the data.
    b.  Apply data analysis to glean information and insight. If the question was not answered, go back to the planning stage and try again.
    c.  (For academic experimenters.) Publish the results. Ideally, your publication prompts several new questions, which start the process over again.

A single round of planning and experimenting may be part of a larger process in a project developed for purposes of design or analysis, or both. The nature of the experiments tends to evolve as the project moves forward. For example, an algorithm engineering project may start with experiments to evaluate several abstract algorithms in order to select one or two for implementation, but later experiments may focus on code tuning and robustness tests. Similarly, an analysis project may start by looking at abstract performance properties and general input classes and may focus on more instantiated models and realistic inputs later on.

**Guideline 1.3** *The experimental path is not straight, but cyclical: planning alternates with execution; experimental design alternates with tool building; analysis alternates with data collection.*

### 1.3 What's in the Book?

This guidebook aims to assist theoreticians, practitioners, and algorithm engineers to carry out experiments to study algorithm performance, for purposes of design and/or analysis. Here are the major themes.

- Chapter 2 considers problems of designing experiments to study algorithmic questions. The chapter surveys common goals of experimental algorithmics and shows how to match tactics to goals. These concepts are illustrated with three algorithms for the graph coloring problem.
- Chapter 3 considers the question of which property to measure. A variety of time-measurement options are illustrated using the Markov Chain Monte Carlo algorithm for random text generation. The chapter also considers strategies for measuring solution quality when evaluating heuristics and approximation algorithms, illustrated with algorithms for bin packing. Measurement strategies for space usage and network communication costs are also surveyed.
- Chapter 4 considers the algorithm design problem: how to make it run fast. The discussion focuses on algorithm tuning and code tuning, which are the two middle layers of the algorithm design hierarchy. Several algorithms are used as illustrations in this chapter, including an exhaustive-search algorithm for bin packing and a greedy algorithm for a problem related to all pairs shortest paths in graphs.
- Chapter 5 presents practical tips for building the experimental environment, which comprises test programs, inputs and generators, measurement tools, and data analysis packages. The chapter ends with a cookbook of algorithms for generating random numbers, lists, permutations, and other combinatorial objects.
- Algorithm experimenters have unusual opportunities for building experiments that produce *analysis-friendly data*, which yield stronger results from data analysis. Chapter 6 discusses two strategies: variance reduction techniques (VRTs)

and simulation speedups. These ideas are illustrated using two algorithms for the self-organizing sequential search problem.

- Finally, Chapter 7 surveys data analysis and statistical techniques that are relevant to common scenarios arising in algorithmic experiments. Most of the data sets used as illustrations in this section come from the case study experiments described in previous chapters.

The case studies mentioned here play a central role in the presentation of concepts strategies, and techniques. All of the solver programs and input generators described in these case studies are available for downloading from the *Algorithmics Laboratory* (AlgLab), which is a companion Web site to this text. Visit `www.cs.amherst.edu/alglab` to learn more.

The reader is invited to download these materials and try out the ideas in this guidebook, or to extend these examples by developing new experiments. Suggestions for additional experiments appear in the Problems and Projects section at the end of each chapter.

## 1.4  Chapter Notes

The Chapter Notes section at the end of each chapter collects guidelines and gives references to further reading on selected topics. Here are the guidelines from this chapter.

*1.1 The "algorithm" and the "program" are just two points on a scale between abstract and instantiated representations of a given computational process.*

*1.2 When the code needs to be faster, consider all levels of the algorithm design hierarchy.*

*1.3 The experimental path is not straight, but cyclical: planning alternates with execution; experimental design alternates with tool building; analysis alternates with data collection.*

### *Readings in Methodology*

Here is a reading list of papers and books that address topics in experimental methodology for problems in algorithm design and analysis.

### Articles

"Designing and reporting on computational experiments with heuristic methods," by R. S. Barr et al. Guidelines on experimental design and reporting standards, emphasizing heuristics and optimization problems [3].

"Ten Commandments for Experiments on Algorithms," by J. L. Bentley. The title speaks for itself. [5]

"Algorithm Engineering," by C. Demetrescu, I. Finocchi, and G. F. Italiano. A survey of issues and problems in algorithm engineering. [10]

*How Not to Do It*, by I. P. Gent et al., Pitfalls of algorithmic experiments and how to avoid them. [12].

"Testing heuristics: We have it all wrong," by J. Hooker. A critique of experimental methodology in operations research. [13]

"A theoretician's guide to the experimental analysis of algorithms," by D. S. Johnson. Pet peeves and pitfalls of conducting and reporting experimental research on algorithms, aimed at the theoretician. [14]

"Toward an experimental method in algorithm analysis," by C. C. McGeoch. Early discussion of some of the ideas developed in this book. [17]

"How to present a paper on experimental work with algorithms," by C. McGeoch and B. M. E. Moret. Guidelines for presenting a research talk, aimed at the academic. [18]

"Algorithm Engineering – an attempt at a definition using sorting as an example," by Peter Sanders. A description of the field, including issues and open questions. [25]

*Books*

1. *Experimental Methods for the Analysis of Optimization Algorithms*, T. Bartz-Beielstein, et al., eds. Broad coverage of topics in experimental methodology, especially statistics and data analysis, emphasizing problems in optimization. [4]
2. *Programming Pearls*, by J. L. Bentley. Written for the practicing programmer, the book addresses topics at the interface between theory and practice and contains many tips on how to perform experiments. [7]
3. *Empirical Methods for Artificial Intelligence*, by P. Cohen. A textbook on statistics and data analysis, with many illustrations from experiments on heuristic algorithms. [9]
4. *Algorithm Engineering: Bridging the Gap between Algorithm Theory and Practice*, M. Müller-Hanneman and S. Schirra, eds. A collection of articles addressing topics in engineering and experimentation, aimed at graduate students and research scientists. [20]

*A timeline*

The discipline of experimental algorithmics has come of age in recent years, due to the efforts of a growing community of researchers. Members of this group have worked to organize workshops and publication venues, launch repositories and libraries for engineered products, and develop methodologies for this new approach to algorithm research.

Here is list of meetings and journals that provide publication venues for research in experimental algorithmics, in chronological order by date of launch. Consult these resources to find many examples of research contributions to algorithm design and analysis, as well as discussions of methodological issues.

1989   The *ORSA Journal on Computing* is launched to publish articles in the intersection of operations research and computer science. In 1996 the name of the sponsoring organization changed; the journal is now called the *INFORMS Journal on Computing*.

1990   The first ACM-SIAM Symposium on Data Structures and Algorithms (SODA) is organized by David Johnson. The call for papers explicitly invites "analytical or experimental" analyses, which may be "theoretical or based on real datasets."

1990   The first DIMACS Implementation Challenge is coorganized by David Johnson and Catherine McGeoch. The DIMACS Challenges are year-long, multiteam, cooperative research projects in experimental algorithmics.

1995   Inaugural issue of the ACM *Journal of Experimental Algorithmics*, Bernard Moret, editor in chief.

1997   The first Workshop on Algorithm Engineering (WAE) is organized by Giuseppe Italiano. In 2002 this workshop joins the European Symposium on Algorithms (ESA), as the "Engineering and Applications" track.

1999   The annual workshop on Algorithm Engineering and Experiments (ALENEX) is coorganized in 1999 by Mike Goodrich and Catherine McGeoch. It was inspired by the Workshop on Algorithms and Experiments (ALEX), organized in 1998 by Roberto Battiti.

2000   The first of several Dagstuhl Seminars on Experimental Algorithmics and Algorithm Engineering is organized by Rudolf Fleischer, Bernard Moret, and Erik Schmidt.

2001   The First International Workshop on Efficient Algorithms (WEA) is organized by Klaus Jansen and Evripidis Bampis. In 2003 it becomes the International Workshop on Experimental and Efficient Algorithms (WEA) coordinated by José Rolim. In 2009 it becomes the Symposium on Experimental Algorithms (SEA).

## 1.5  Problems and Projects

1. Find three experimental analysis papers from the publication venues described in the Chapter Notes. Where do the experiments fall on the scale of instantiation

described in Section 1.2. Why do you think the authors choose to focus on those instantiation points?

2. Read Hooker's [13] critique of current practice in experimental algorithmics and compare it to the three papers in the previous question. Is he right? How would you improve the experimental designs and/or reporting of results? Read Johnson's [14] advice on pitfalls of algorithmic experimentation. Did the authors manage to avoid most of them? What should they have done differently?

3. Find an algorithm engineering paper from one of the publication venues described in the Chapter Notes. Make a list of the design strategies described in the paper and assign them to levels of the algorithm design hierarchy described in Figure 1.1. How much did each level contribute to the speedup?

## Bibliography

[1] Atkins, Derek, Michael Graff, Aıjen K. Lenstra, and Paul C. Leyland, "The magic words are squeamish ossifrage" in Proceedings of *ASIACRYPT'94*, pp. 263–277, 1994.

[2] Bader, David A, Bernard M. E. Moret, Tandy Warnow, Stacia K. Wyman, and Mi Yan, "High-performance algorithm engineering for gene-order phylogenetics," Power Point talk. *DIMACS Workshop on Whole Genome Comparison*, DIMACS Center, Rutgers University, March 1 2001.

[3] Barr, R. S., B. L. Golden, J. P. Kelley, M. G. C. Resende, and W. R. Steward, "Designing and reporting on computational experiments with heuristic methods," *Journal of Heuristics* Vol 1, Issue 1, pp. 9–32, 1995.

[4] Bartz-Beielstein, Thomas, M. Chiarandini, Luis Paquette, and Mike Preuss, eds., *Experimental Methods for the Analysis of Optimization Algorithms*, Springer, 2010.

[5] Bentley, Jon Louis, "Ten Commandments for Experiments on Algorithms," in "Tools for Experiments on Algorithms," in R. F. Rashid, ed., *CMU Computer Science: A 25th Anniversary Commemorative*, ACM Press, 1991.

[6] Bentley, Jon Louis, *Writing Efficient Programs*, Prentice Hall, 1982.

[7] Bentley, Jon Louis, *Programming Pearls*, 2nd ed., ACM Press and Addison Wesley, 2000.

[8] Cherkassky, B. V., A. V. Goldberg, and T. Radzik, "Shortest paths algorithms: Theory and experimental evaluation," *Mathematical Programming* Vol 73, Issue 2, pp. 129–171, 1996.

[9] Cohen, Paul, *Empirical Methods for Artificial Intelligence*, MIT Press, 1995.

[10] Demetrescu, Camil, Irene Finocchi, and Giuseppe F. Italiano, "Algorithm Engineering," in the *Algorithms Column, EATCS Bulletin,* pp. 48–63, 2003.

[11] Ferragina, Paolo, Rodrigo González, Gonzalo Navarro, and Rosasno Venturini, "Compressed Text Indexes: From Theory to Practice," *ACM Journal of Experimental Algorithmics*, Vol 13, Article 1.12, December 2008.

[12] Gent, Ian P., S. A. Grant, E. MacIntyre, P. Prosser, P. Shaw, M. Smith, and T. Walsh, *How Not to Do It*, University of Leeds School of Computer Studies, Research Report Series, Report No. 97.27, May 1997.

[13] Hooker, John, "Testing heuristics: We have it all wrong," *Journal of Heuristics*, Vol 1, pp. 33–42, 1995.

[14] Johnson, David S., "A theoretician's guide to the experimental analysis of algorithms," in M. H. Goldwasser, D. S. Johnson, and C. C. McGeoch, eds., *Data Structures, Near Neighbor Searches, and Methodology: Fifth and Sixth Implementation Challenges*, AMS, pp. 215–50, 2002.

[15] LaMarca, Anthony, and Richard E. Ladner, "The influence of caches on the performance of heaps," *ACM Journal of Experimental Algorithmics*, Vol 1, 1996.

[16] LaMarca, Anthony, and Richard E. Ladner, "The influence of caches on the performance of sorting," *Journal of Algorithms*, Vol 31, Issue 1, pp. 66–104, April 1999.

[17] McGeoch, Catherine C., "Toward an experimental method in algorithm analysis," *INFORMS Journal on Computing*, Vol 8, No 1, pp. 1–15, Winter 1996.

[18] McGeoch, Catherine C., and Bernard M. E. Moret, "How to present a paper on experimental work with algorithms," *SIGACT News*, Vol 30, No 4, pp. 85–90, 1999.

[19] Moret, Bernard M. E., David A. Bader, and Tandy Warnow, "High-performance algorithm engineering for computational phylogenetics," *Journal of Supercomputing*, vol 22, pp. 99–111, 2002.

[20] Müller-Hanneman, Matthias, and Stefan Schirra, eds., *Algorithm Engineering: Bridging the Gap between Algorithm Theory and Practice, Lecture Notes in Computer Science*. Vol 5971, Springer, 2010.

[21] Navarro, Gonzalo, "Implementing the LZ-index: Theory versus Practice," *ACM Journal of Experimental Algorithmics*, Vol 13, Article 1.2, November 2008.

[22] Panny, Wolfgang, "Deletions in random binary search trees: A story of errors," *Journal of Statistical Planning and Inference*, Vol 140, Issue 9, pp. 2335–45, August 2010.

[23] Reddy, Raj, and Allen Newell, "Multiplicative speedup of systems," in A. K. Jones, ed., *Perspectives on Computer Science*, Academic Press, pp. 183–98, 1977.

[24] Sanders, Peter, and Dominik Schultes, "Robust, almost constant time shortest-path queries in road networks, " in C. Demetrescu, A. V. Goldberg, and D. S. Johnson, eds., *The Shortest Paths Problem: Ninth DIMACS Implementation Challenge*, AMS, 2009.

[25] Sanders, Peter, "Algorithm Engineering – an attempt at a definition," in *Efficient Algorithms*, Vol 5760 of *Lecture Notes in Computer Science*, pp. 321–430, Springer, 2009.

[26] Skiena, Steve, *The Algorithm Design Manual*, Springer, 1997. The companion Web site is *The Stony Brook Algorithm Repository*, Available From: www.cs.sunuysb.edu/~algorith/, 2008-07-10.

[27] Yaroslavskiy, Vladimir, Joshua Bloch, and Jon Bentley, "Quicksort 2010: Implementing and timing a family of functions." Power Point Slides. 2010.

# 2

# A Plan of Attack

Strategy without tactics is the slowest route to victory. Tactics without strategy is the noise before defeat.

Sun Tzu, *The Art of War*

W. I. B. Beveridge, in his classic guidebook for young scientists [7], likens scientific research "to warfare against the unknown":

> The procedure most likely to lead to an advance is to concentrate one's forces on a very restricted sector chosen because the enemy is believed to be weakest there. Weak spots in the defence may be found by preliminary scouting or by tentative attacks.

This chapter is about developing small- and large-scale plans of attack in algorithmic experiments.

To make the discussion concrete, we consider algorithms for the *graph coloring* (GC) problem. The input is a graph $G$ containing $n$ vertices and $m$ edges. A *coloring* of $G$ is an assignment of colors to vertices such that no two adjacent vertices have the same color. Figure 2.1 shows an example graph with eight vertices and 10 edges, colored with four colors. The problem is to find a coloring that uses a minimum number of colors – is 4 the minimum in this case?

When restricted to planar graphs, this is the famous map coloring problem, which is to color the regions of a map so that adjacent regions have different colors. Only four colors are needed for any map, but in the general graph problem, as many as $n$ colors may be required.

The general problem has many practical applications. For example, the vertices may represent cell phone towers in a given region, where an edge connects two towers within a small radius; the problem is to assign different broadcast frequencies (colors) to the towers so that nearby towers do not interfere with one another. Or the vertices may represent college courses, and the problem is to assign classrooms (colors) to courses so that no two courses meet at the same time in the same

17

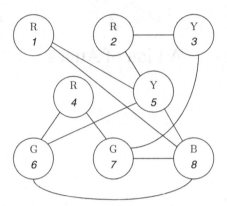

Figure 2.1. The graph coloring problem. The graph contains $n = 8$ nodes and $m = 11$ edges. The vertices are colored using 4 colors: red, yellow, green, blue (R,Y,G,B). No two adjacent vertices share the same color.

```
Greedy (G)
    for (v=1; v<=n; v++)
        for (c=1; c<=n; c++)
            if (G.checkColor(c, v)) {
                G.assignColor(c, v)
                break       // skip to next vertex
            }
    return G.colorCount()
```

Figure 2.2. Greedy. A sketch of the Greedy graph coloring algorithm.

room. Graph coloring is NP-hard, so we consider polynomial-time algorithms that do not guarantee to find optimal colorings.

The simple Greedy algorithm, sketched in Figure 2.2, iterates through the vertices and assigns to each the lowest-numbered color that does not conflict with previously colored neighbors. We assume the graph data structure G supports a function G.checkColor(c,v) that checks whether assigning c to v causes a conflict, and another function G.assignColor(c,v) that assigns c to v. The *color count* is the number of different colors in a coloring.

The coloring in Figure 2.1 results from applying Greedy to the vertices in order $1 \ldots 8$, using the color order $1 = $ red, $2 = $ yellow, $3 = $ green, $4 = $ blue. The full color assignment in Figure 2.1 can be written in a table as follows.

| 1 | 2 | 3 | 4 | 5 | 6 | 7 | 8 |
|---|---|---|---|---|---|---|---|
| Red | Red | Yellow | Red | Yellow | Green | Green | Blue |

```
Random (G, I)
    bestCount = Infinity
    bestColoring = null
    for (i=1; i<=I; i++){
        G.unColor()              //remove colors
        G.randomVertexOrder()
        count = Greedy(G)
        if (count < bestCount) {
            bestCount = count
            bestColoring = G.saveColoring()
        }
    }
    report (bestColor, bestCount)
```

Figure 2.3. The Random algorithm. Random applies Greedy repeatedly, using a random vertex order each time, and reports the best coloring found.

The color count achieved by Greedy depends on the order in which vertices are considered. For example, if vertices are colored in reverse order $8 \ldots 1$, the color count would be 3:

| 8 | 7 | 6 | 5 | 4 | 3 | 2 | 1 |
|---|---|---|---|---|---|---|---|
| Red | Yellow | Yellow | Green | Red | Red | Yellow | Green |

There must exist a vertex order for which Greedy finds an optimal coloring, but since there are $n!$ vertex orders, trying them all takes too much time. The Random algorithm in Figure 2.3 applies Greedy $I$ times, using a random vertex permutation each time, and remembers the best coloring it finds. The G.randomVertexOrder() function creates a random permutation of the vertices, and G.saveColoring() makes a copy of the current coloring.

Here are some questions we could ask about the performance of Greedy and Random.

1. How much time do they take on average, as a function of $n$ and $m$ (and $I$)?
2. Are they competitive with state-of-the-art GC algorithms?
3. On what types of inputs are they most and least effective?
4. How does $I$ affect the trade-off between time and color count in Random?
5. What is the best way to implement G.checkColor(c,v) and G.assign-Color(c,v)?

Each of these questions can be attacked via experiments – but each is best answered with a different experiment. For example, question 1 should be studied by measuring time performance on random graphs, with a wide range of $n, m$ values to evaluate function growth best. Question 2 should be attacked by measuring both time and solution quality, using a variety of graph classes and some state-of-the art algorithms for comparison, and problem sizes that are typical in practice.

An *experimental design* is a plan for an experiment that targets a specific question. The design specifies what properties to measure, what input classes to incorporate, what input sizes to use, and so forth. Like battle plans, experimental designs may be small and tactical, suitable for reconnaissance missions, or large and strategic, for full-scale invasions.

Experimental designs can be developed according to formal procedures from a subfield of statistics known as design of experiments (DOE). But the pure DOE framework is not always suitable for algorithmic questions – sometimes designs must be based upon problem-specific knowledge and common sense. The next section describes some basic goals of algorithmic experiments. Section 2.2 introduces concepts of DOE and shows how to apply them, formally and informally, to meet these goals.

### 2.1  Experimental Goals

The immediate goal of the experiment is to answer the particular question being posed. But no matter what the question, some goals are common to all experimental work:

1. Experiments must be *reproducible* – that is, anyone who performs the same experiment should get similar results. For an experiment to be reproducible, the results must be *correct*, in the sense that the data generated accurately reflect the property being studied, and *valid*, which means that the conclusions drawn are based on correct interpretations of the data.
2. An *efficient* experiment produces correct results without wasting time and resources. One aspect of efficiency is *generality*, which means that the conclusions drawn from one experiment apply broadly rather than narrowly, saving the cost of more experiments.

In academic research, a third goal is *newsworthiness*. A newsworthy experiment produces outcomes that are interesting and useful to the research community, and therefore publishable. Two prerequisites for newsworthy experiments are wise choice of experimental subject (so that interesting results can reasonably be expected) and familiarity with the current literature (so that new results can be recognized). David Johnson [16] also points out that newsworthiness depends on the "generality, relevance, and credibility of the results obtained and the conclusions drawn from them." Tips for increasing generality, relevance, and credibility of experimental results are presented throughout this section.

The rest of the section considers how to create experiments that meet these goals.

### The Pilot and the Workhorse

Experiments have two flavors: the less formal *pilot* or *exploratory* study, and the more carefully designed *workhorse* study. A pilot study is a scouting mission or skirmish in the war against the unknown. It typically occurs in the information-gathering stage of a research project, before much is known about the problem at hand. It may consist of several experiments aimed at various objectives:

1. To check whether basic assumptions are valid and whether the main ideas under consideration have merit.
2. To provide focus by identifying the most important relationships and properties and eliminating unpromising avenues of research.
3. To learn what to expect from the test environment. How long does a single trial take? How many samples are needed to obtain good views of the data? What is the largest input size that can feasibly be measured?

The pilot study may be motivated by fuzzy questions, like Which data structure is better? Which input parameters appear to be relevant to performance? The workhorse study comprises experiments built upon precisely stated problems: Estimate, to within 10 percent, the mean comparison costs for data structures A and B, on instances drawn randomly from input class C; bound the leading term of the (unknown) cost function $F(n)$.

Designs for workhorse experiments require some prior understanding of algorithm mechanisms and of the test environment. This understanding may be gleaned from pilot experiments; furthermore, a great deal of useful intelligence – which ideas work and do not work, which input classes are hard and easy, and what to expect from certain algorithms – may be found by consulting the experimental literature. See the resources listed in Section 1.4.

**Guideline 2.1** *Leverage the pilot study – and the literature – to create better workhorse experiments.*

How much reconnaissance is needed before the battle can begin? As a good rule of thumb, David Johnson [16] suggests planning to spend half your experimentation time in the pilot study and half running workhorse experiments. Of course it is not always easy to predict how things will turn out. Sometimes the pilot study is sufficient to answer the questions at hand; sometimes the formal experiments raise more questions than they answer. It is not unusual for these two modes of experimentation to alternate as new areas of inquiry emerge.

The pilot and workhorse studies play complementary roles in achieving the general goals of reproducibility and efficiency, as shown in the next two sections.

### Correct and Valid Results

A *spurious result* occurs when the experimenter mistakenly attributes some outcome to the wrong cause. Spurious results might seem unlikely in computational experiments, since the connection between cause and effect – between input and output – is about as clear as it gets. But the road to error is wide and well traveled. Here are some examples.

*Ceiling and floor effects* occur when a performance measurement is so close to its maximum (or minimum) value that the experiment cannot distinguish between effects and noneffects. For example, the following table shows solutions reported by three research groups (denoted GPR [15], CL [12], and LC [21] ), on 6 of the 32 benchmark graphs presented to participants in the DIMACS Graph Coloring Challenge [17]. The left column names the file containing the input graph, the next two columns show input sizes, and the three remaining columns show the color counts reported by each group on each input.

| File Name | $n$ | $m$ | GPR | CL | LC |
|---|---|---|---|---|---|
| R125.1.col | 125 | 209 | 5 | 5 | 5 |
| R125.5.col | 125 | 7501 | 46 | 46 | 46 |
| mulsol.i.1.col | 197 | 3925 | 49 | 49 | 49 |
| DSJ125.5.col | 125 | 7782 | 20 | 18 | 17 |
| DSJ250.5.col | 250 | 31336 | 35 | 32 | 29 |
| DSJ500.5.col | 500 | 125248 | 65 | 57 | 52 |

Looking at just the top three lines we might conclude that the algorithms perform equally well. But in fact these color counts are optimal and can be produced by just about any algorithm. It is spurious to conclude that the three algorithms are equivalent: instead we should conclude that the experiment leaves no room for one algorithm to be better than another. This is an example of a floor effect because color counts are the lowest possible for these instances. The bottom three lines do not exhibit floor or ceiling effects and are better suited for making comparisons – for example, that performance is ordered $LC < CL < GPR$ on these inputs.

In general, floor and ceiling effects should be suspected when all the measurements from a set of trials are the same, especially if they are all at the top or bottom of their range. This is a sign that the experiment is too easy (or too hard) to distinguish the algorithmic ideas being compared. A good time to identify and discard uninteresting inputs and poor designs is during the pilot study.

A second type of spurious reasoning results from *experimental artifacts*, which are properties of the test code or platform that affect measurements in some unexpected way – the danger is that the outcome will be mistakenly interpreted as a general property of the algorithm. Artifacts are ubiquitous: any experienced researcher can reel out cautionary tales of experiments gone awry. Here are some examples:

- Time measurements can depend on many factors unrelated to algorithm or program performance. For example, Van Wyk et al. [24] describe a set of tests to measure times of individual C instructions. They were surprised to find that the statement j -= 1; ran 20 percent faster than j--;, especially when further investigation showed that both instructions generated identical machine code! It turned out that the 20 percent difference was an artifact of instruction caching: the timing loop for the first instruction crossed a cache boundary while the second fit entirely within the cache.
- Bugs in test programs produce wrong answers. This phenomenon is pervasive but rarely mentioned in print, with the exception of Gent et al.'s [13] entertaining account of experimental mishaps:

  > We noticed this bug when we observed very different performance running the same code on two different continents (from this we learnt, Do USE DIFFERENT HARDWARE). All our experiments were flawed and had to be redone.
  >
  > All three implementations gave different behaviours .... Naturally our confidence went out the window. Enter the "paranoid flag." We now have two modes of running our experiments, one with the paranoid flag on. In this mode, we put efficiency aside and make sure that the algorithms and their heuristics do exactly the same thing, as far as we can tell.

- Pseudorandom number generators can produce patterns of nonrandomness that skew results. I once spent a week pursuing the theoretical explanation for an interesting property of the move-to-front algorithm described in Chapter 6: the interesting property disappeared when the random number generator was swapped out in a validation test. Gent et al. [13] also describe experiments that produced flawed results because "the combination of using a power of 2 and short streams of random numbers from random() had led to a significant bias in the way problems were generated."
- Floating point precision errors can creep into any calculation. My early experiments on bin packing algorithms (described in Section 3.2) were run on a VAX/750 and checked against a backup implementation on a Radio Shack TRS-80 Model III. At one point the two programs reported different answers when

run on identical instances: it turned out that the smaller precision on the TRS-80 was causing some input weights to round to zero.

Tips on avoiding and minimizing these types of artifacts appear in Sections 3.1.2 (timers), 5.1.1 (bugs and precision errors), and 5.2 (random number generators).

*Replication* is a general technique for avoiding artifactual results and boosting experimental validity. Replicate tests on different platforms to check for numerical precision errors; then swap out the random number generator and run the tests again. As a safeguard against spurious results, before concluding that "$A$ causes $B$," replicate the experiment with $A$ absent to check whether $B$ still occurs – and if it does, abandon the conclusion.

Ideally the pilot and workhorse programs should be implemented by two different people. The pilot code should represent a straightforward, no-frills version of the algorithm, while the workhorse may incorporate speedups (Chapter 4) and experimental tricks (Chapter 6) for fast turnaround. With two implementations of the algorithm it is possible to check for bugs by replicating key experiments: compare the codes on identical inputs, using the same random number generators and seeds, to check that they produce identical outputs.

The best protection against incorrect and invalid results is *attitude*. Be on the lookout for surprises and anomalies, and do not neglect to investigate their causes. These are indicators of great discoveries or nasty bugs: either way they should be dealt with early rather than late in the experimental process.

**Guideline 2.2** *Never assume. Create experiments with built-in safeguards against bugs and artifacts, and be sure you can replicate your own results.*

### Efficiency and Generality

*Efficiency* has many meanings in computational experiments. An efficient test program returns answers quickly, and an efficient test environment supports fast turnaround by being flexible and easy to use. In design of experiments (DOE), an efficient design maximizes the information gained per unit of experimental effort.

Exploratory pilot experiments may not be especially efficient – they may yield just a few nuggets of insight amid tons of uninteresting data, and pilot code is usually not fast, since simplicity and correctness should be the design priorities. But the one-two punch of pilot followed by workhorse can lead to more experimental efficiency. For example, one key insight from a pilot experiment might be that the test code needs to run faster – in which case pilot experiments can be used to locate code bottlenecks and guide tuning efforts. Also, by highlighting promising directions for inquiry and exposing bad and irrelevant ideas, pilot studies help the researcher to avoid wandering the dark alleys of failed and inconclusive experiments.

The *generality* of an experiment refers to how broadly the results can be applied. Like efficiency, generality can be considered from different points of view. First, as illustrated in Section 1.2, algorithmic experiments take place on a scale between abstraction and instantiation. Measuring a property of the abstract algorithm yields general results that hold for any implementation and platform. But if measurements at the abstract end are too coarse to meet experimental goals, generality must be traded for precision – move the experiment toward the instantiated end and measure properties tied to individual platforms and processes, such as CPU times.

Sometimes lost generality can be restored by greater *scope*, which means more variety in the experimental design. The drawback is that more scope means more time needed to carry out the experiments. Ultimately the scope of an experiment is constrained by available resources, in particular how much time you have to invest and how many minions (students) are available to implement your ideas. Section 3.1 illustrates how performance indicators can sometimes be combined to produce runtime predictions that are both precise and general.

Another component of generality is the level of ambition in data analysis. Some experiments are developed simply to compare performance across different scenarios. Others produce descriptive functions that capture the relationship between parameters and performance – functions are more general because interpolation yields predictions about scenarios that were not explicitly tested. The most ambitious goal is to develop a general functional model that goes beyond mere description, to explain and predict performance in situations outside the scope of the experiments.

**Guideline 2.3** *Experimental efficiency depends on the speed of the test program, the usability of the test environment, the quality of data returned, and the generality of conclusions drawn.*

Several aspects of efficiency and generality are discussed elsewhere in the text. Test program efficiency is considered in Chapter 4. Issues of environment design are surveyed in Chapter 5. Chapter 3 explains measurement options and their relation to the instantiation scale. The next section considers experimental efficiency as a problem in experimental design and surveys ideas for maximizing the quality of information gained from each experiment.

## 2.2 Experimental Design Basics

We start with a list of concepts from design of experiments, illustrated with the graph coloring algorithms sketched earlier. Statisticians will notice that some definitions are nonstandard: I chose alternative words to prevent confusion in cases where the DOE term – such as *variable*, *control variable*, or *parameter* – has quite strong connotations for programmers. A translation to standard DOE terminology appears in the Chapter Notes.

**Performance metric:** A dimension of algorithm performance that can be measured, such as time, solution quality (e.g. color count), or space usage.

**Performance indicator:** A quantity associated with a performance metric that can be measured in an experiment. For example, the time performance of Random might be measured as CPU time or as a count of the dominant operation. Performance indicators are discussed in Chapter 3 and not considered further here.

**Parameter:** Any property that affects the value of a performance indicator. Some parameters are *categorical*, which means not expressed on a numerical scale. We can recognize three kinds of parameters in algorithmic experiments:

- **Algorithm parameters** are associated with the algorithm or the test program. For example, Random takes parameter $I$, which specifies a number of iterations. Also, the `G.checkColor(c,v)` and `G.assignColor(c,v)` functions could be implemented in different ways: the source code found in each function is a categorical parameter.
- **Instance parameters** refer to properties of input instances. For example, *input size* is nearly always of interest – in graph coloring, input size is described by two parameters $n$ and $m$. Other graph parameters, such as maximum vertex degree, might also be identified. The (categorical) parameter *input class* refers to the source and general properties of a set of instances. For example, one collection of instances might come from a random generator, and another from a cell tower frequency assignment application.
- **Environment parameters** are associated with the compiler, operating system, and platform on which experiments are run.

**Factor:** A parameter that is explicitly manipulated in the experiment.

**Level:** A value assigned to a factor in an experiment. For example, an experiment to study Random might involve four factors set to the following levels: $class = (random, cell\ tower)$; $n = (100, 200, 300)$, $m = (sparse, complete)$, and $I = (10^2, 10^4, 10^6)$.

**Design point:** A particular combination of levels to be tested. If all combinations of levels in the preceding example are tested, the experiment contains $36 = 2 \times 3 \times 2 \times 3$ design points: one of them is $(class = random, n = 100, m = 4950, I = 100)$.

**Trial** or **test:** One run of the test program at a specific design point, which produces a measurement of the performance indicator. The design may specify some number of (possibly random) trials at each design point.

**Fixed parameter:** A parameter held constant through all trials.

**Noise parameter:** A parameter with levels that change from trial to trial in some uncontrolled or semicontrolled way. For example, the input class may contain random graphs $G(n, p)$, where $n$ is the number of vertices and $p$ is the probability that any given edge is present; the number of edges $m$ in a particular instance is a semicontrolled noise parameter that depends on factors $n$ and $p$. In a different experiment using instances from a real-world application, both $n$ and $m$ might be considered noise parameters (varying but not controlled) if, say, the design specifies that input graphs are to be sampled from an application within a given time frame.

Computational experiments are unusual from a DOE perspective because, unlike textbook examples involving crop rotations and medical trials, the experimenter has near-total control over the test environment. Also, very often the types of questions asked about algorithm performance do not exactly match the DOE framework. This creates new opportunities for developing high-yield designs, and for making mistakes. The next two sections survey two aspects of experimental design in this context. Section 2.2.1 surveys input classes and their properties, and Section 2.2.2 presents tips on choosing factors, levels, and parameters to address common categories of questions.

### *2.2.1 Selecting Input Classes*

Input instances may be collected from real-world application domains or constructed by generation programs. They can be incorporated in algorithmic experiments to meet a variety of objectives, listed in the following.

- *Stress-test inputs* are meant to invoke bugs and reveal artifacts by invoking boundary conditions and presenting easy-to check cases. An input generator for Greedy, for example, might build an empty graph (no edges), a complete graph (full edge sets), a variety of graphs with easy-to-check colorings (trees, rings, grids, etc.), and graphs that exercise the vertex permutation dependencies. Some generic stress-test resources are also available – for example, Paranoia [18] is a multilanguage package for testing correctness of floating point arithmetic.
- *Worst-case* and *bad-case instances* are hard (or expensive) for particular algorithms to solve. These instances are used to assess algorithm performance boundaries. For example, Greedy exhibits especially poor performance on

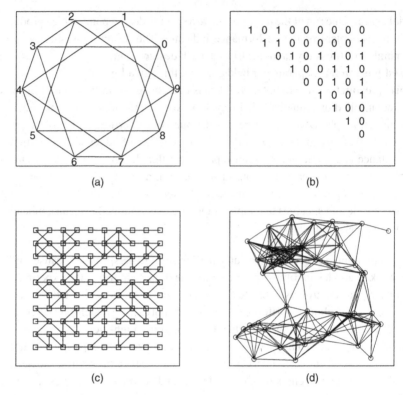

Figure 2.4. Input classes for graph coloring algorithms. Panel (a) shows a crown graph, which is known to be hard for Greedy to solve. Panel (b) shows the adjacency matrix for a random graph of $n = 10$ vertices, where each edge (labeled 1) is selected with probability $p = 0.5$. Panel (c) shows a semi-random grid graph. Panel (d) shows a proximity graph, which mimics a cell-phone tower application.

    *crown graphs* like the one shown in Figure 2.4 (a). In this graph each even-numbered vertex is connected to every odd-numbered vertex except the one directly across from it. Crown graphs can be colored by using just two colors, but Greedy may use up to $n/2$ colors.

- *Random inputs* are typically controlled by a small number of parameters and use random number generators to fill in the details. For example, Figure 2.4 (b) shows the upper diagonal of an adjacency matrix for a random graph $G(n, p)$: here $n = 10$ and each edge (denoted 1) is present with probability $p = 0.5$. Random inputs are useful for measuring average-case performance under some theoretically tractable model. Also, if every instance is generated with nonzero probability, experiments using random inputs can reveal the range of all possible outcomes.

- *Structured random inputs* come from generators built for two purposes:
  - *Algorithm-centered generators* are built with parameters that exercise algorithm mechanisms. For example, the performance of Greedy depends partly on the *regularity* of the input graph. In a perfectly regular graph all vertices have the same number of incident edges: an example of a regular graph of degree 8 is a grid-graph where each vertex has four neighbors at the N, S, E, W compass points and four neighbors on the NE, NW, SE, SW diagonals. Figure 2.4 (c) shows a semi-random grid graph – in this instance, each non boundary vertex is connected to its E, W neighbors with probability 1, and to each of its SW, S, SE neighbors with probability 1/3. A generator of these graphs can be used to focus on how Greedy responds to changes in graph regularity.
  - *Reality-centered generators* capture properties of real-world inputs. For example, the cell tower application described previously can be modeled by placing random points in the unit square, with edges connecting points that are within radius $r$ of one another. This type of graph is called a *proximity graph*. A proximity graph with $n = 50$ and $r = 0.25$ is shown in Figure 2.4 (d). These types of generators can often be improved with a little (Web) research into quantitative properties of reality: how many cell towers are typically found in different types of regions (urban, rural, mountainous, etc.)? What it the typical broadcast distance?
- *Real instances* are collected from real-world applications. A common obstacle to using these types of instances in algorithmic experiments is that they can be difficult to find in sufficient quantities for thorough testing.
- *Hybrid instances* combine real-world structures with generated components. This approach can be used to expand a small collection of real instances to create a larger testbed. Three strategies for generating hybrid graphs for graph coloring are as follows: (1) start with a real-world instance and then perturb it by randomly adding or subtracting edges and/or vertices; (2) create a suite of small instances from random sections of a large instance; or (3) build a large instance by combining (randomly perturbed) copies of small instances.
- Sometimes a *public testbed* is available for the algorithm being studied. In the case of graph coloring, testbed inputs are available at the DIMACS Challenge Web site [17], and Joseph Culberson's Graph Coloring Resources Page [11], among other sources. In academic circles, running experiments using testbed instances maximizes relevance and newsworthiness by producing results that are directly comparable to results of experiments carried out by others. But it is not necessary to restrict experiments to testbed instances; any of the categories in this list may be used to expand and improve on earlier work.

Each category has its merits and drawbacks. Input generators can produce large numbers of instances; they are more compact to store and share; and they can be tuned to provide broad coverage of an input space or to focus on properties that drive algorithm performance or mimic realistic situations. But they may fail to answer what may be the main question: how well does the algorithm perform in practice?

Inputs from real-world applications are ideal for answering that question, but, on the other hand, they can be hard to find in sufficient quantities for testing. Also they may contain highly problem-specific hidden structures that produce hard-to-explain and therefore hard-to-generalize results.

The choice of instance classes to test should reflect general experimental goals as well as the specific question at hand:

- To meet goals of correctness and validity, use stress-test inputs and check that random generators really do generate instances with the intended properties. Use pilot experiments to identify, and remove from consideration, instances that are too easy or too hard to be useful for distinguishing competing algorithmic ideas.
- For general results, incorporate good variety in the set of input classes tested. But avoid variety for variety's sake: consider how each class contributes new insights about performance. Worst-case instances provide general upper bounds; random generators that span the input space can reveal the range of possible outcomes. Real-world instances from application hot spots can highlight properties of particular interest to certain communities; algorithm-centered inputs reveal how the algorithm responds to specific input properties; and so forth.
- More ambitious analyses tend to require more general input classes and tight control of parameters. When the goal is to build a model of algorithm performance in terms of input parameters, success is more likely if the inputs obey simple random models or are produced by algorithm-centered generators that allow explicit control of relevant properties, so that experimental designs can focus on the question that prompts the experiment.

**Guideline 2.4** *Choose input classes to support goals of correctness and generality, and to target the question at hand.*

In addition to the preceding considerations, Dorothea Wagner [23] has proposed guidelines for developing and maintaining public instance testbeds to support algorithm research. One common complaint is that testbeds are often assembled without much of a screening process and may contain several uninteresting and/or unjustified instances. There is a need for more testbed instances that meet at least one of the following requirements.

- They have features that are relevant to algorithm performance.
- They have provable properties.
- They permit controlled experiments using parameterization.

- They are typical of real-world application domains.
- They display algorithm performance on a good variety of both applied and theoretical scenarios.
- They yield insights into underlying algorithm mechanisms.

Ideally, every instance should be accompanied by text explaining its provenance and properties and, when appropriate, a certificate showing a correct output (which can be used to validate new solvers). Generated instances should also be accompanied by their generators, so that researchers can extend testbed experiments to new design points.

The next section considers issues that arise when selecting factors, levels, and design points for the experiment.

### 2.2.2 Choosing Factors and Design Points

The motivating question in an algorithmic experiment typically falls into one of these four broad categories.

1. *Assessment.* These experiments look at general properties, relationships, and ranges of outcomes. Is there a performance bottleneck in Greedy? What are the range and distribution of color counts for a given input class? What input properties affect performance the most?
2. *The horse race.* This type of experiment looks for winners and losers in the space of implementation ideas. Which implementation of G.checkColor(c,v) and G.assignColor(c,v) is best? For which kinds of inputs is it best?
3. *Fitting functions.* This type of experiment starts with a functional model that describes some cost property and aims to fill in the details. For example, if a cost function is known to be of the form $f(n) = an^2 + bn + c$, experiments can be run to find the coefficients $a, b, c$.
4. *Modeling.* These experiments are concerned with finding the correct function family to describe a given cost – is it of the form $f(n) = an^2 + bn + c$, or $an^2 \log n + bn$, or something else? Very often the analysis focuses on bounding the first-order term, which is critical to asymptotic analysis, or it may try to fill in low-order terms as well.

Assessment experiments are typically performed at the very beginning of an experimental project and can even be used to identify good questions to ask.

For example, pilot experiments can help you decide which parameters should become factors. One general principle is that the factors should comprise those parameters having the greatest effect on performance. A pilot experiment might report a wide variety of algorithm, input, and environment parameter values (controlled or not) to identify the ones most strongly correlated with performance.

Decisions about what happens to nonfactors can be just as important as the choice of factors. Parameters that have no effect on performance (which can sometimes be identified by the pilot experiment mentioned earlier) can be fixed with no loss of generality.

For example, if the performance indicator does not depend on environment, then all the environmental parameters can be fixed by running experiments on one platform. This property often holds in the case of solution quality – the color count produced by Greedy is the same no matter what test platform is used – or when the performance indicator is an abstract cost (such as loop iteration counts).

Fixing a parameter that matters will narrow the scope of the experiment and may reduce the generality of results. This is especially true of categorical parameters – if you only measure option (a), you cannot comment on options (b) and (c). If the parameter is numeric, it may be possible to fix it at an extreme value to obtain upper or lower bounds on costs or to interpolate a line between measurements at extreme points.

Fixing a parameter sometimes has the salubrious effect of sharpening the relationship between factors and performance indicators, by removing a source of variation. For example, two algorithm properties $A$ and $B$ are easier to compare if tests are run using exactly the same set of instances on exactly the same platform, rather than allowing those parameters to vary among tests.

**Guideline 2.5** *Choose as factors those parameters that are most important to performance, fix the parameters that are least relevant to performance, and let the other parameters vary.*

The next few sections consider experimental designs to address questions in each of our four categories.

### General Assessment

Often the goal of the first experiment is to identify promising algorithm design options. Experimental designs for this question are fairly easy to develop – the main principle is, choose performance indicators and factors to highlight the differences between the options. For example, if the task is to compare data structures $A$, $B$, and $C$, choose a performance indicator that is common to all three and that changes the most when one data structure is substituted for another – this is likely to be a "narrow" cost associated with particular data structure operations, rather than a "broad" cost related to overall performance. Algorithm parameters other than this one should be fixed, or, if they are expected to affect performance of $A$, $B$, and $C$, choose a small number of parameters set to a small number of levels (low, medium, high).

**Guideline 2.6** *When comparing algorithm (or program) design options, choose performance indicators and factors to highlight the differences among the options being compared.*

Another early experimental goal is to get a rough idea of the functional relationship between key parameters (especially input size) and algorithm performance.

A good design strategy in this situation is to try a *doubling* experiment. Sedgewick [22] points that the growth rates of many common functions in algorithm analysis are easy to deduce if cost is measured as $n$ doubles. For example, suppose we measure cost $C(n)$ at problem sizes $n = 100, 200, 400, 800\ldots$. The results can be interpreted as follows:

1. If measurements do not change with $n$, $C(n)$ is constant.
2. If costs increment by a constant as $n$ doubles, for example, if $C(n) = 33, 37, 41, 45$, then $C(n) \in \Theta(\log n)$.
3. If costs double as $n$ doubles, $C(n)$ is linear.
4. To determine whether $C(n) \in \Theta(n \log n)$, divide each measurement by $n$ and check whether the result $C(n)/n$ increments by a constant.
5. If cost quadruples each time $n$ doubles, $C(n) \in \Theta(n^2)$.

Similar rules can be worked out for other common function classes; see Sedgewick [22] for details.

Doubling experiments are valuable for checking whether basic assumptions about performance are correct. For example, Bentley [5] describes a study of the `qsort` function implemented in the S statistical package. Although the function implements Quicksort, which is well known to be $O(n \log n)$ on average, his doubling experiment revealed the following runtimes (in units of seconds):

```
$ time a.out 2000
real   5.85s
$ time a.out 4000
real 21.65s
$ time a.out 8000
real 85.11s
```

This clearly quadratic behavior was caused by "organ-pipe" inputs of the form $123\ldots nn\ldots 321$ and was subsequently repaired.

An example of a doubling experiment that incorporates two parameters $n$ and $m$ appears in Section 3.1.1.

**Guideline 2.7** *Try a doubling experiment for a quick assessment of function growth.*

Another question that arises early in some experimental studies is to determine when the algorithm has converged. In the context of iterative-improvement heuristics, convergence means, informally, that the probability of finding further improvements is too small to be worth continuing. Another type of convergence arises in stochastic algorithms, which step through sequences of states according to certain probabilities that change over time: here convergence means that the transition probabilities have reached steady state, so that algorithm performance is no longer affected by initial conditions. In this context the problem of determining when steady state has occurred is sometimes called the *startup problem*.

A *stopping rule* is a condition that halts the algorithm (i.e., stops the the experiment) when some event has occurred. Experimental designs for incremental and stochastic algorithms require stopping rules that can terminate trials soon after – but no sooner than – convergence occurs.

A poorly chosen stopping rule either wastes time by letting the algorithm run longer than necessary or else stops the algorithm prematurely without giving it a chance to exhibit its best (or steady-state) performance. The latter type of error can create *censored data*, whereby a measurement of the (converged) cost of the algorithm is replaced by an estimate that depends on the stopping rule. See Section 7.1.1 for more about the problem of data censoring.

Good stopping rules are hard to find: here are some tips on identifying promising candidates.

- Avoid stopping rules based on strategies that cannot be formally stated, like "Stop when the cost doesn't appear to change for a while." A good stopping rule is precisely articulated and built into the algorithm, rather than based on hand tuning.
- To ensure replicability, do not use rules based on platform-specific properties, such as "Stop after 60 minutes have elapsed."
- If the total number of states in a stochastic process is small, or if a small number of states are known to appear frequently, consider implementing a rule based on state frequencies: for example, stop after every state has appeared at least $k$ times.
- A related idea is to assign a cost to every state and to compute running averages for batches of $b$ states in sequence – stop the algorithm once the difference in average cost $C(b_x..b_{x+i})$ and $C(b_y..b_{y+i})$ is below some threshold. A graphical display of batch measurements may show a "knee" in the data where the transition from initial states to steady state occurs.
- Sometimes it is possible to implement a test of some property that is a precondition for the steady state. For example, it may be known that a given stochastic graph coloring algorithm does not reach steady state until after every vertex has changed color at least once.

We next consider designs for fitting and modeling algorithmic cost functions.

*Analyzing Trends and Functions*

The central problem of algorithm analysis is to describe the functional relationship between input parameters and algorithm performance. A doubling experiment can give a general idea of this relationship but often we expect more precision and detail from the experiment.

Suppose we want to analyze time performance of two implementations of Random. This algorithm depends on how functions G.checkColor(c,v) and G.assignColor(c,v) are implemented. Let $k$ be the maximum color used by the algorithm in a given trial: checkColor is invoked at most $nk$ times, and assignColor is invoked $n$ times. Two implementation options are listed below.

*Option a.* Each vertex $v$ has a color field: check for a valid coloring by iterating through the neighbors of $v$. The total number of comparisons in checkColor is at most $mk$, once for each edge and each color considered; the cost per call to assignColor is constant. Therefore, total cost is $O(mk+n)$.

*Option b.* Each vertex has a color field and a "forbidden color" array that is updated when a neighbor is assigned a color. Each call to checkColor is constant time, and each call to assignColor is proportional to the number of neighbors of $v$. Total cost is $O(nk+m)$.

The experimental design includes factors *Option* = $(a,b)$, input sizes $n$, $m$, and iteration count $I$. The goal is to develop a function to describe the comparison cost of Random in terms of these four factors. Since *Option* is categorical, we use two functions $f_a(n,m,I)$ and $f_b(n,m,I)$. Since the algorithm iterates $I$ times, we know that $f(n,m,I)$ is proportional to $I$; let $g_a(n,m)$ and $g_b(n,m)$ equal the average cost per iteration of each option.

The experimental design problem boils down to how to choose levels for $n$ and $m$ to give the best views of function growth. One idea is to use a grid approach, with $n = 100, 200, \dots max\_n$, and $m = 100, 200, \dots max_m$, omitting infeasible and uninteresting combinations: for example, $m$ must be at most $n(n-1)/2$, and coloring is trivial when $m$ is small. Another idea is to select a few levels of $m$ that are scaled by $n$, for example, $m_1 = n(n-1)/2$ (complete graphs), $m_2 = m_1/2$ (half-full), and $\dots m_3 = m_1/4$ (quarter-full). Scaled design points are more informative than grid-based designs whenever the scaled functions are expected to have similar shapes – in this case, similar shapes would arise from a property that is invariant in the ratio $m/n$.

**Guideline 2.8** *The problem of analyzing a multidimensional function can be simplified by focusing on a small number of one-dimensional functions, ideally with similar shapes.*

Now the question is how to choose levels for $n$ to give best views of one-dimensional functions like $g_{a,m1}(n)$. Prior knowledge about the general shape of such a function, whether based on theory or on pilot experiments, can inform the experimental design.

Some tips are listed in the following. We assume here that the unknown function $f(n)$ has a random component, so that the problem is to model the average cost of $f(n)$ using several random trials at each level of $n$.

- In function-fitting problems, the general form of the function is either known or selected for descriptive convenience (with no claim of accuracy).

    For example, at level $m_1$ the graph is complete and we know $k = n$. Under Option $a$ the total cost of checking is described by $mk = n^3/2 - n^2/2$, and the cost of assigning is proportional to $m$. We may choose to ignore low-order terms that are also present and to assume that the costs of checking and assigning are fairly well described by $f(n) = an^3 + bn^2$ and $g(n) = cn$, respectively.

    If the function to be fitted is a polynomial, the design problem is easy: the number of levels of $n$ should be one more than the number of terms in the function. Take measurements at two endpoints to fit a line $ax + b$, take three evenly spaced levels to fit a quadratic function $ax^2 + bx + c$, and so forth. Note this rule depends on the number of *terms* in the function, not necessarily its degree: only two levels of $n$ are needed to fit a function like $an^3 + bn^2$.

- Many algorithmic structures (such as heaps) have cost functions with a stepped or sawtooth behavior that show discontinuities when $n$ is a power of 2. For example, the height of a heap of $n$ nodes is $h(n) = \lceil \log_2(n + 1) \rceil$. As Figure 2.5 illustrates, taking measurements at only the discontinuity points $n = 2^k$ and $n = 2^k - 1$ can simplify analysis by revealing the upper and lower envelopes of the cost function.

- If steady-state or asymptotic performance is dominated by startup costs, treat low and high levels of $n$ separately. Find a cutoff point $n_0$ where asymptotic costs dominate startup costs and use this as a break point for analyzing small-$n$ and large-$n$ performance. If costs at small $n$ are not important to the analysis, use $n_0$ as the smallest level in the design.

- When the goal is to model the cost function $f(n)$ – especially, to pin down the asymptotically leading term – start with a doubling experiment that includes the largest input size $n_m$ that can be feasibly tested. This might be called a halving experiment, with levels set at $n_m, n_m/2, n_m/4 \ldots$ Using large $n$ values reduces the effects of second-order terms, which can play havoc with data analysis; see Section 7.3 for details.

    If the leading term is hard to identify because of random noise in the data, refer to Chapter 6 for tips on improving the experiment. Another tactic is to

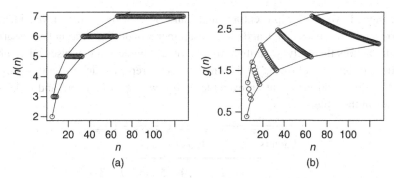

Figure 2.5. Choosing levels for discontinuous functions. In panel (a) the cost function is $h(n) = \lceil \log_2(n-1) \rceil$, which produces a step function with discontinuities at powers of 2. In panel (b) the cost $g(n) = h(n) - \log_2(n)$ shows a sawtooth behavior. Designs for these types of functions should choose levels at the discontinuity points. The lines show results of measuring costs at $n = 2^k$ and $n = 2^k + 1$.

increase the range between the minimum and maximum $n$ values in the design. That is, halving $n$ twice may be enough to distinguish between $\Theta(n)$ and $\Theta(n^2)$, but greater range may be needed to separate $\Theta(n)$ from $\Theta(n \log n)$.

- If very little is known about $f(n)$, try using many levels of $n$ within a large range. This allows a better view of how $f(n)$ may converge to its asymptotic behavior. Designs with scores of levels spaced evenly or randomly through their range can reveal unusual properties such as step functions, phase transitions, and cycles.
- When the smallest and largest values of $f(n)$ measured in the experiment span at least two orders of magnitude, analysis is likely to be performed on log-transformed data. In this case, it is better to increment $n$ using a constant multiplier, so that the transformed design points will evenly spaced in their range. The choice of multiplier depends on the range and number of levels desired: two common strategies are doubling $n = 20, 40, 80 \ldots$ and incrementing by powers of 10 $n = 10, 100, 1000, \ldots$.

**Guideline 2.9** *To study trends and functions, choose design points that exploit what you already know.*

### Making Comparisons with Factorial Designs

Another common goal of algorithm research is to compare performance across several algorithm and instance factors, to discover which implementation ideas work for which inputs. These types of questions arise in horse race experiments and assessment studies.

For this type of problem a *full factorial design*, a cornerstone of DOE, is simplest and often the best choice. In the classic $2^k$ factorial design, each of $k$ factors is assigned two levels representing "high" and "low" levels – these levels ideally correspond to expected high and low measurements of the *outcome*, not necessarily of the factors themselves. "Full factorial" means the design exercises all combinations of levels. Following DOE conventions we represent levels with $+$ (high) and $-$ (low) and write out an example design with $k = 3$ factors and 8 design points in the table.

| Factors |  | | Experiments | | | | | | |
|---|---|---|---|---|---|---|---|---|---|
|  | 1 | 2 | 3 | 4 | 5 | 6 | 7 | 8 |
| $F_1$ | - | + | - | + | - | + | - | + |
| $F_2$ | - | - | + | + | - | - | + | + |
| $F_3$ | - | - | - | - | + | + | + | + |

A full factorial design is the most efficient way to study *main effects* and *interaction effects* among factors. A main effect depends on one factor alone; interaction effect depends on combinations of factors.

Figure 2.6 illustrates the difference. The costs $C_1$ and $C_2$ are measured in a hypothetical experiment that incorporates a full factorial design with three factors $F_1, F_2, F_3$, each measured at two levels. For example, $F_1$ might represent graph density $d = m/n$, measured at two levels $d = (10, 20)$.

The eight points in panel (a) represent all measurements of $C_1$ in the full factorial design, plotted against factor $F_1$ (at levels 10, 20). The four lines are labeled according to their $F_2$ and $F_3$ levels; for example, the top line corresponds to $F_2 = +$, $F_3 = +$. From this graph we can observe the following:

- Factor $F_1$ has a positive main effect because every line has positive slope.
- Factor $F_2$ has a positive main effect since both solid lines are above both dotted lines.
- The main effect of $F_3$ is also positive, since in each pair the line marked (+) is above the line marked (−).
- Factor $F_2$ has the greatest main effect, since the distance between solid and dotted lines is greater than the distances that represent the effects of $F_1$ (left vs. right points) and $F_3$ (as labeled).

Panel (b) shows a different set of outcomes. Here the effect of $F_1$ on $C_2$ may be positive or negative, depending on whether the $F_2$ and $F_3$ match: the lines marked $++$ and $--$ have negative slope, and lines marked $-+$ and $+-$ have positive slope. This is an example of a three-way interaction effect, since $F_2$ and $F_3$ together modify the effect of $F_1$.

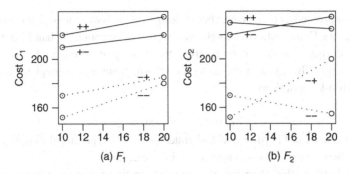

Figure 2.6. Main effects and interaction effects. Panel (a) shows three main effects from $F_1$, $F_2$ and $F_3$: $C_1$ increases by about the same amount when each factor changes from (-) to (+). Panel (b) shows an interaction effect: $C_2$ increases or decreases depending on whether $F_2$ matches $F_3$.

Full factorial designs maximize the information gained from an experiment because smaller designs must omit or combine some observations. The danger is that omissions lead to incorrect conclusions – for example, an experiment that fixes $F_2 = -$ will only report the dotted lines, giving a misleading view of the maximum cost. Allowing a factor like $F_3$ to take random values means that the averages of the solid endpoints (and separately of the dotted endpoints) would likely be reported. This is not a problem in panel (a), but in panel (b) the average of each pair is nearly horizontal, producing the misleading conclusion that $F_1$ has no effect on $C_2$.

**Guideline 2.10** *Full factorial designs maximize the information gained from one experiment.*

Although full factorial designs ensure that factor effects cannot be lost or obscured, they are not always the best designs for algorithmic problems:

- They are unnecessary when one factor is known to be independent of another. For example, in the Greedy algorithm we can be reasonably sure that doubling the number of iterations $I$ will double the mean number of comparisons during `assignColor`. It suffices to measure this cost at one level of $I$ and to calculate costs for design points with other levels of $I$.
- The assumptions underlying factorial designs do not always match algorithmic realities. For example, two levels are assigned to each factor because the outcome is presumed to have a linear dependency on the factor. This assumption may be adequate for rough assessments but not for more fine-tuned analyses. More sophisticated experimental design strategies can be applied when factorial designs fall short; some references appear in the Chapter Notes.

- A third problem is that the number of design points is exponential in the number of factors. Computational experiments are often fast enough to handle unusually large designs, but there is no escaping the tyranny of exponential growth. This problem is illustrated in the next section, which surveys strategies for coping with too-large designs.

### Factor-Reduction Strategies

Culberson and Luo [12] describe the Iterated Greedy (IG) graph coloring algorithm, a simplified version of which appears in Figure 2.7.

Like Random, this algorithm uses iteration to find better Greedy colorings of $G$. But instead of starting over with a new coloring at each iteration, IG permutes both the vertices and the colors and *recolors* $G$, respecting the old coloring when applying the new coloring. The permutations are selected so that the color count cannot increase at each iteration.

This algorithm was one of several evaluated in the DIMACS Challenge on Graph Coloring [17]. The original C implementation may be downloaded from Joseph Culberson's Web site [11]. C and Java implementations of the simplified version in Figure 2.7, called SIG, may be downloaded from AlgLab. Here's how it works:

SIG starts by reading an input graph $G$ and assigning it an initial coloring, according to a rule specified by the parameter INITIAL.

At each iteration, SIG groups the vertices by color according to the current coloring, reorders groups by a vertex rule $V$, and then reorders colors according to a color rule $C$. In Figure 2.8, Panel (a) shows an example coloring of $G$, with vertices grouped by colors in the order (1= red, 2= yellow, 3= green, 4= blue). In panel (b) the vertices are reordered using the `reverse` vertex rule, which reverses the color groups to become (1 = blue, 2 = green, 3 = yellow, 4 = red). Next the colors are reordered according to a color rule $C$: assume here the `random` rule is applied and the new color order is: green, blue, red, yellow. Panel (c) shows the graph after recoloring, respecting the original colors.

The order by which new colors are assigned to vertices is shown in the following table.

| 8 | 6 | 7 | 5 | 3 | 1 | 2 | 4 |
|------|-------|-------|-----|------|-------|-------|------|
| Blue | Green | Green | Red | Blue | Green | Green | Blue |

```
SIG ()    // Simplified Iterated Greedy
  G = inputGraph();
  current = G.initialColor(INITIAL);
  best = G.saveBest();

  t = 0;   //  iteration total count
  b = 0;   //  iterations since new best coloring
  r = 0;   //  iterations since last revert or save

  while ((b < MAXITER) && (best.color > TARGET)) {
      t++;  b++;  r++ ;

      C = RandomColorRule (CWEIGHTS);
      V = RandomVertexRule(VWEIGHTS);
      G.applyReorderRules(C, V);

      for (v : vertices in vertex order)
         for (c : colors in color order)
            if (G.checkColor (c,v)) {
                G.assignColor (c,v);
                break;       // skip to next vertex
            }
      if (G.colorcount < best.colorcount) {
        best = G.saveBest();
          b = 0; r=0;
      }
      else if (G.score < best.score) {
             best = G.saveBest();   // save if best
            b = 0; r = 0;
       }
      if (r > RLIMIT) {
         G.assignColors(best) ;
         r = 0;
      }
}
```

Figure 2.7. SIG. A simplified version of Culberson and Luo's Iterated Greedy algorithm.

In this case the recoloring operation reduces the total number of colors from four to three. More generally, the reorder – recolor step can never increase the total number of colors used: repeated application of this operation should tend to shrink the color count over time.

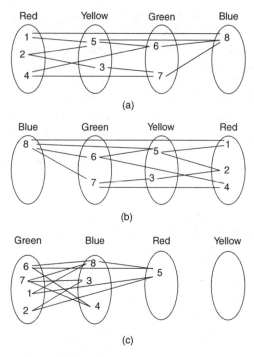

Figure 2.8.  Greedy recoloring. SIG reorders vertices at each iteration according to a color rule. Panel (a) shows the original coloring. Panel (b) shows the vertices reordered by the `reverse` rule, which reverses the color groups. Panel (c) shows a recoloring with vertices, considered by color group (blue, green, yellow, red) and colors considered in a new order: green, blue, red, yellow.

This implementation of SIG employs four vertex rules and six color rules, which are selected randomly at each iteration according to probabilities specified by vectors VWEIGHTS and CWEIGHTS.

In addition to the color count, the algorithm keeps track of a "color score" that incorporates more details about the coloring. If RLIMIT iterations occur with no improvement in color count or color score, the algorithm reverts to a previous-best coloring. If MAXITER iterations occur with no improvements, the algorithm halts. The algorithm also halts if it achieves a TARGET color count specified by the user.

SIG fairly bristles with algorithm parameters: six are shown capitalized in Figure 2.7: INITIAL specifies the initial coloring assigned to graph $G$; VWEIGHTS and CWEIGHTS are probability vectors of size 4 and 6, respectively; MAXITER and TARGET control total iterations; and RLIMIT controls when to revert to an earlier solution. This is not unusual for heuristic algorithms – Culberson and Lou's original version has at least 12 parameters, and heuristics with scores of parameters are fairly common.

The design approach suggested by Guideline 2.5 is to include as factors all algorithm parameters that are important to performance. Suppose all six parameters are important and consider creating a full factorial design for SIG.

The first problem is that some factors cannot be limited to just two levels. For example, CWEIGHTS is a vector of six integers that assigns weights to six rules (named reverse, random, largest, smallest, increase, and decrease). A factorial design for this vector alone needs six levels (000001, 000010, 000100, etc.) to ensure that each rule is used at least once. It needs at least $64 = 2^6$ levels to ensure that all combinations of rules are considered in the experiment. And it needs at least $720 = 6!$ levels to measure the effects of relative weight orders (because there are 6! permutations of $1 \ldots 6$). A full factorial design for CWEIGHTS alone is simply impossible to implement.

Suppose we scale down the scope of the experiment and use a pilot study to find, say, 10 promising levels for each vector (VWEIGHTS and CWEIGHTS), and 2 levels each for the other four factors. Since solution quality is platform-independent, we fix all environmental parameters. We use the input testbed of 31 instances from the DIMACS Graph Coloring Challenge [17], and take 10 random trials per design point per instance.

This design would require $49,600 = 2^4 \times 10 \times 10 \times 31$ design points, totaling 496,000 random trials. Assuming average runtimes around 100 seconds per trial (as reported by Culberson and Luo [12]) the experiment should finish in 574 days, or just more than 18 months. This design is still too big. Additional *factor-reduction strategies* are needed to get this experiment down to reasonable size.

Here are some general tactics for shrinking experimental designs, illustrated with SIG. As always, pilot experiments can provide the information needed to exploit these ideas.

- *Merge similar factors:* If two factors have a similar effect on performance, treat them as one, by restricting the experiment to just the design points $++$ and $--$ (omitting $+-$ and $-+$). For example, TARGET and MAXITER represent stopping rules that control the number of main loop iterations. These factors can be merged into a single factor ITERATIONS that specifies total iteration count.
- *Use trace data to infer effects of omitted factors:* After replacing TARGET and MAXITER with ITERATIONS, modify the test code to report a trace of the color count at every iteration t where color count decreases. With those trace data is it possible to trace which values would have stopped the algorithm had they been used.

- *Trial overloading:* If the program reports *t* and color count in this way, there is no need to set ITERATIONS to a low level because it can be inferred from the trace data what would have happened at low values of this factor – thus one trial is used to report outcomes for several levels of ITERATIONS. This trick is discussed further in Section 6.2.
- *Convert factors to noise parameters:* Instead of explicitly setting levels for a factor, let the levels vary according to a simple probability distribution and report their values in random trials. This creates a pool of levels and performance measurements that can be examined for correlations. For example, instead of using a design that selects 10 specific vectors for CWEIGHTS, a tool could be built to generate random weight vectors for each random trial – report both the vector and the performance indicator in each trial and look for correlations during data analysis.
- *Limit the scope of the experiment* by fixing some factors or reducing the number of levels, because of time constraints. For example, if the pilot study (or published work) shows that some testbed instances produce similar performance profiles, reduce from 31 to, say, 10 instances (five small and five large) that represent distinct classes. For another example, Culberson and Luo [12] identify two VWEIGHT vectors (rather than 10) that worked especially well in their pilot experiments on random graphs.
- The preceeding factor-reduction strategies exploit problem-specific knowledge about SIG. A *fractional factorial design* is a problem-generic strategy from DOE that concentrates on main effects and two-way interactions, fixing some factors so that higher-degree interactions are omitted from analysis. A $2^{k-p}$ fractional design is $2^p$ times smaller than the full design – designs for given $k$ and $p$ can be looked up in published tables. Reference sources on fractional designs appear in the Chapter Notes.
- *Factor-screening* strategies of DOE can also be applied to eliminate factors that appear to have little effect on performance. See the Chapter Notes.

Suppose we apply these ideas to merge TARGET and MAXITER into ITERATIONS, which is fixed at one high value. Next, change CWEIGHTS to a randomly generated noise parameter and use the two levels for VWEIGHTS that were identified by Culberson and Luo [12]. With four levels representing combinations of INITIAL and RLIMIT, this reduces to eight design points per input instance. Shrink the testbed scope from 31 to 10 instances (five large and five small from a variety of input classes). Increase the number of random trials to 25, so that more samples of the randomized parameter (CWEIGHTS) and of the iteration counts *t* can be reported in each trial. At 100 seconds per trial, this new design takes a little more than 2.6 days to complete, which may be within the realm of feasibility. Further design adjustments may be guided by additional pilot experiments.

**Guideline 2.11** *When the experimental design is too big, apply factor-reduction strategies to reduce the size of the design with least damage to generality of results.*

## 2.3 Chapter Notes

This chapter has considered the planning stage of the experimental process: how to identify goals and how to develop experimental designs to meet those goals. Two key components of a well-planned experimental project are the pilot study and the workhorse study.

As mentioned in Section 2.2.2, the terminology of factors and parameters used here is not standard in the design of experiments field. Here is a table of standard statistical terminology.

- A **factor** is any property that influences or is associated with the outcome of an experiment, including the outcome itself. In some texts, the term is used in a narrow sense to refer to properties that are explicitly manipulated in the experiment.
- A **variable** is a *numerical* quantity associated with a factor (in the broad sense) – for example, the factor "time performance" might be associated with variables such as CPU time or main-loop iteration counts, or the factor "input size" might be measured in terms of number of vertices or of byte counts. **Independent variables** correspond to factors that are explicitly manipulated, and **dependent variables** to outcomes.

  A **control variable** is constant (fixed) in an experiment. An **extraneous variable** is not independent but has an effect on outcomes. A **confounding variable** is an extraneous variable that is correlated with both a dependent variable and an independent variable. Confounding variables are considered threats to experimental validity, because outcomes may be wrongly attributed to the independent variable rather than the confounding variable. A **random variable** is a variable (usually an outcome) that can be described by a probability function.
- The experiment is described by a **model**, which is a numerical function that describes the relationship between independent variables and dependent variables. The function belongs to a family, such as the quadratic family $f(x) = ax^2 + bx + c$. Often the model is a probability density function, such as the uniform distribution $u_{a,b}(x) = 1/(b-a)$ for $a \le x \le b$. The unknown constants $a, b, c$ in these function families are called **parameters**.
- In DOE it is usually assumed that the goal of the experiment is either to *estimate* (find experimentally supported values for) the parameters of the model or else

to test some hypothesis about the parameters (for example, that the distributions means $\mu_x$ and $\mu_y$ are different for two levels $x$ and $y$.

The standard meanings of other terms (*level, design point*) are as used in this chapter.

The main goal in this chapter was to avoid use of the word *variable* because it has strong connotations for programmers: control variables, for example, are found in `for` loops. Also, in programming a *parameter* is a special type of input variable that is never considered unknown (in the DOE sense). Adopting substitute definitions for concepts related to "variables" seemed the best way to prevent confusion.

To learn more about concepts of DOE, see textbooks on simulation and on experimental design, for example, by Baron [1], Bartz-Beielstein et al [2], Bratley, Fox, and Schrage [8], or Cohen [9]. Design strategies like *response surface methodology* and *sequential designs* can be used to tackle more complex situations than simple factorial designs can. Kleijnen [20] describes *factor screening* strategies with applications to optimization algorithms; see also [6].

*Guidelines in This Chapter.*  Here is a list of the experimental guidelines developed in this chapter.

2.1 *Leverage the pilot study – and the literature – to create better workhorse experiments.*

2.2 *Never assume. Design experiments with built-in safeguards against bugs and artifacts, and be sure you can replicate your own results.*

2.3 *Experimental efficiency depends on the speed of the test program, the usability of the test environment, the quality of data returned, and the generality of conclusions drawn.*

2.4 *Choose input classes to support goals of correctness and generality, and to target the question at hand.*

2.5 *Choose as factors those parameters that are most important to performance, fix the parameters that are least relevant to performance, and let the other parameters vary.*

2.6 *When comparing algorithm (or program) design options, choose performance indicators and factors to highlight the differences among the options being compared.*

2.7 *Try a doubling experiment for a quick assessment of function growth.*

2.8 *The problem of analyzing a multidimensional function can be simplified by focusing on a small number of one-dimensional functions, ideally with similar shapes.*

2.9 *To study trends and functions, choose design points that exploit what you already know.*

Question: *(Random) How does average color count in random graphs depend on number of iterations I?*
Performance indicators: *Color count.*
Factors: *Random graphs $(n, p)$, algorithm parameter $I$.*
Levels: *$n = 200 \ldots 800$, increment by 100. $p = 0.25 \ldots 1$ by 0.25. $I = n^2$.*
Trials: *25 per design point.*
Design points: *Full factorial.*
Outputs: *All factors, color count every 100 iterations, number of nodes per color at beginning and end of each trial, full coloring at end of each trial (for validation tests).*

Figure 2.9. Experimental design template. An example experimental design.

2.10 *Full factorial designs maximize the information gained from one experiment.*

2.11 *When the experimental design is too big, apply factor-reduction strategies to reduce the size of the design with least damage to generality.*

## 2.4 Problems and Projects

1. A good habit when planning an experiment is to try writing out the design on paper. Here are four questions about algorithms familiar to most undergraduate computer science students (see any algorithms textbook, such as [10] or [14], for definitions). Write out an experimental design to address each question, following the template in Figure 2.9.

   a. Strassen's matrix multiplication algorithm is asymptotically faster than the conventional matrix multiplication algorithm. Where is the cutoff, when you measure scalar arithmetic operations? Where is the cutoff when you measure CPU time? How much overhead is required to adapt the algorithm to general matrix sizes?

   b. Dijkstra's shortest paths algorithm can be adapted to solve all pairs shortest paths (APSP) and is recommended for sparse graphs; Floyd's algorithm is recommended for dense graphs. Where is the cutoff? How does the cutoff depend on $n$ and $m$?

   c. Many schemes have been proposed for maintaining balance in binary search trees (including red-black trees and splay trees). A certain amount of "natural" balance occurs in many real-world applications such as counting the

number of words or characters in English text. Are these schemes necessary in real-world applications? Is the extra cost due to balancing worth the
savings in average path length?

2. Download implementations of Greedy, Random, and SIG from AlgLab and run
pilot experiments to become familiar with their general properties. What is the
largest problem size that each implementation can handle? How much variation
in solution quality is there as a function of algorithm parameters?

3. Write out an experimental design for an experiment to address one of questions
asked about Greedy and Random at the beginning of this chapter.

4. Run experiments to test whether the CPU time of Random scales proportionally
to the iteration count $I$. Run this test at a range of $n$ and $m$ values.

5. Apply your own factor reduction ideas to the experimental design SIG,
described in Figure 2.7.

## Bibliography

[1] Baron, Michael, *Probability and Statistics for Computer Scientists*, Chapman & Hall/CRC, 2007.

[2] Bartz-Beielstein, Thomas, M. Chiarandini, Luis Paquette, and Mike Preuss, eds., *Experimental Methods for the Analysis of Optimization Algorithms*, Springer, 2010.

[3] Bentley, Jon Louis, "Experiments on Traveling Salesman heuristics," in *Proceedings of the First Symposium on Data Structures and Algorithms (SODA)*, ACM-SIAM, 1990, pp. 91–99.

[4] Bentley, Jon Louis, "Tools for experiments on algorithms," in *CMU Computer Science: A 25th Anniversary Commemorative*, Richard F. Rashid, ed. Anthology Series, ACM Press, 1991.

[5] Bentley, Jon Louis, "Software exploratorium: The trouble with Qsort," *Unix Review*, Vol 10, No 2, pp. 85–93, February 1992.

[6] Bettonvil, B., and J. P. C. Kleijnen, "Searching for important factors in simulation models with many factors: Sequential bifurcation," *European Journal of Operations Research*, Vol 96, Issue 1, pp. 180–184, 1997.

[7] Beveridge, W. I. B., *The Art of Scientific Investigation*, Vintage Books, 1950.

[8] Bratley, Paul, Bennet L. Fox, and Linus E. Schrage, *A Guide to Simulation*, Springer-Verlag, 1983.

[9] Cohen, Paul R., *Empirical Methods for Artificial Intelligence*, MIT Press, 1995.

[10] Cormen, Tom, Charles E. Leiserson, Ronald L. Rivest, and Clifford Stein, *Introduction to Algorithms*, 2nd ed., MIT Press and McGraw-Hill, 2002.

[11] Culberson, Joseph, *Joseph Culberson's Graph Coloring Resources Page*. Available from: www.cs.ualberta.ca/~joe/Coloring, dated March 31, 2004, accessed 11/2009.

[12] Culberson, Joseph, and Feng Luo, "Exploring the k-colorable landscape with Iterated Greedy," in *Cliques, Coloring and Satisfiability: Second DIMACS Implementation Challenge,* AMS 1991, pp. 245–284.

[13] Gent, Ian P., Stuart A. Grant, Ewen MacIntyre, Patrick Prosser, Paul Shaw, Barbara M. Smith, and Toby Walsh, *How Not to Do It*, Research Report 97.27,

School of Computer Studies, University of Leeds, May 1997. Available from: www.cs.st-andrews.ac.uk/~ipg/pubs.html.

[14] Goodrich, Michael T., and Roberto Tamassia, *Algorithm Design: Foundations, Analysis, and Internet Examples*, John Wiley & Sons, 2002.

[15] Glover, Fred, Mark Parker, and Jennifer Ryan, "Coloring by Tabu Branch and Bound," in *Cliques, Coloring and Satisfiability: Second DIMACS Implementation Challenge*, AMS 1991. pp. 285–307.

[16] Johnson, David S., "A Theoretician's Guide to the Experimental Analysis of Algorithms," in Michael H. Goldwasser, David S. Johnson, and Catherine C. McGeoch, eds., *Data Structures, Near Neighbor Searches, and Methodology: Fifth and Sixth DIMACS Implementation Challenges*, DIMACS Series in Discrete Mathematics and Computer Science, Vol 59, American Mathematical Society, 2002, pp. 215–250.

[17] Johnson, David S., and Michael A. Trick, eds., *Cliques, Coloring, and Satisfiability: Second DIMACS Implementation Challenge*, AMS, 1991. See www.dimacs.rutgers.edu/Challenges for more information.

[18] Kahan, William, *Paranoia*, Available from: www.netlib.org (keyword search 'paranoia') Basic implementation 1983; implementations in other languages by several authors. For a description, see Richard Karpinski, "Paranoia: A floating-point benchmark," *Byte Magazine*, Vol 10, No 2, pp. 223–235, February 1985.

[19] Kleijnen, Jack P. C., *Design and Analysis of Simulation Experiments*, International Series in Operations Research and Management Science, Springer, 2008.

[20] Kleijnen, Jack P. C., "Design and Analysis of Computational Experiments: Overview," in T. Bartz-Beielstein, M. Chiarandini, L. Paquette, and M. Preuss, eds., *Experimental Methods for the Analysis of Optimization Algorithms*, Springer, 2010.

[21] Lewandowski, Gary, and Anne Condon, "Experiments with Parallel Graph Coloring Heuristics and Applications of Graph Coloring," in *Cliques, Coloring, and Satisfiability: Second DIMACS Implementation Challenge*, AMS, 1991, pp. 309–34.

[22] Sedgewick, Robert, *Algorithms in Java, 3rd ed.*, Addison-Wesley, 2003. The doubling principle is discussed in chapter 2.

[23] Wagner, Dorothea, "Benchmark instances, testbeds, and code repositories" *Dagstuhl Workshop on Algorithm Engineering 6325,* June 30, 2010.

[24] Van Wyk, Christopher J., Jon L. Bentley, and Peter J. Weinberger, *Efficiency Considerations for C Programs on a VAX 11/780*, Carnegie-Mellon University Department of Computer Science, TR CMU-CS-82-134, 1982.

# 3

# What to Measure

One accurate measurement is worth a thousand expert opinions.
                                  Rear Admiral Grace Murray Hopper, USNR

The performance metric of interest in most algorithm research projects is that old devil, *time* – how long must I wait for my output to appear? Running a close second is *solution quality* – how close to optimal is the answer produced by my algorithm? Other important performance metrics include space usage and network communication cost.

Whatever the metric, the choice of *performance indicator*, the quantity actually measured in the experiment, plays a big role in the quality of information gained about performance. This chapter surveys a variety of performance indicators and presents guidelines for choosing among them. Section 3.1 considers options for measuring time performance. Section 3.2 surveys strategies for measuring solution quality.

## 3.1 Time Performance

Which is better: accuracy or precision? The following table illustrates the difference. Each row shows an experimental measurement of the speed of light in kilometers per second, published by the Nobel physicist Albert Michelson in different years.

| Year | Result |
|------|--------|
| 1879 | $299,910 \pm 50$km/s |
| 1926 | $299,796 \pm 4$km/s |
| 1935 | $299,774 \pm 11$km/s |

The *precision* of an experimental result corresponds to how much variation is seen in repeated measurements: Michelson's results ranged in precision from a low of ±50km/s to a high of ±4km/s, depending on his instruments. The *accuracy* of a result is how close it is to the truth: since none of these results overlap, at most one can be accurate. (The 1926 result turns out to be compatible with modern measurements. In 1980 the length of a meter was redefined by international agreement so that the speed of light is now exactly 299,792.458km/s.)

In algorithm analysis the two most common time performance indicators are *dominant costs* and *CPU times*. A dominant operation, such as a comparison, has the property that no other operation in the algorithm is performed more frequently. An asymptotic bound on the dominant cost, like *"The algorithm performs $O(n^2)$ comparisons in the worst case,"* is perfectly accurate. Furthermore, the bound is universal, since it holds no matter what input, platform, or implementation is used. But it lacks precision: will the program take seconds or hours to run?

A CPU time measurement (explained in Section 3.1.2) is precise down to fractions of seconds. But as we shall see, precision guarantees neither accuracy nor generality. System timing tools can return non-replicable results, and runtimes measured on one platform and input instance are notoriously difficult to translate to other scenarios.

To illustrate this point, Figure 3.1 shows results of time measurements carried out by participants in the 2000 DIMACS TSP Challenge [14]. CPU times of one TSP program on a suite of nine input instances were recorded on 11 different platforms – runtimes varied between six seconds and 1.75 hours in these tests. Each line corresponds to a platform; the nine measurements for each are divided by times on a common benchmark platform $P$. Times are ordered by input size (ranging from $10^3$ to $10^7$ cities) on the $x$-axis. The dotted top line shows, for

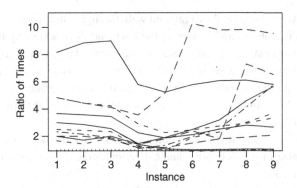

Figure 3.1. Relative CPU times. CPU times for a single program were recorded on 11 platforms and 9 inputs. The inputs are ordered by size on the $x$-axis. Each line shows the ratio of times on one platform to times on a common benchmark platform. Time ratios vary from 0.91 to 10, and there is no obvious pattern in these variations.

example, that on this platform the program ran about 4 times slower than on $P$ with small inputs, and about 10 times slower with large inputs.

In an ideal world, each line would be horizontal, and mapping CPU times from one platform to another would be a simple matter of finding the right scaling coefficient. If the lines had the same general shape, we could build an empirical model that predicts times on the basis of input sizes. Instead there is no common pattern: it is like weighing an object on Earth and trying to predict its weight on the Moon, except there is no known function that describes the relationship between gravitational forces and object weights. Millisecond-scale measurement precision is useless if predictions based on CPU times can be wrong by seconds or hours.

Fortunately, the experimenter has more choices than just these two performance indicators. The fundamental trade-off between precision and universality cannot be eliminated, but it can be controlled to obtain time measurements that are more precise than asymptotic bounds and more general than CPU times. The following section introduces a case study problem to illustrate various time performance indicators and their merits.

### Case Study: Random Text Generation

The *text generation problem* is to generate a random text that looks as if it was written by a human being. The problem arises in diverse applications including generating parodies and circumventing spam filters. One well-known approach is to set a hundred monkeys working at typewriters until a good-looking text appears. But we can get faster results using a *Markov Chain Monte Carlo* (MCMC) approach. The algorithm described here (called MC) has been employed by Bentley [4] and by Kernighan and Pike [16] to illustrate principles of algorithm design and of code tuning.

An MCMC algorithm makes a random walk through a state space. At time $t$, the algorithm is in state $S_t$, and it steps to the next state $S_{t+1}$ according to *transition probabilities* that map from states to states. The output of the algorithm corresponds to a trace of the states it passes through during its random walk. The MC text generation algorithm creates a state space and transition probabilities based on a sample of real text and then generates a random text by stepping through the states according to those probabilities.

MC starts by reading text $T$ containing $n$ words, together with two parameters: $m$ is the number of words to print, and $k$ determines the size of the state space and the transition table.

Every sequence of $k$ words is a *key*, and every key is followed by a one-word *suffix*. For example, Figure 3.2 shows all keys and suffixes for $k = 2$ and $T = $ **this is a test this is only a test this is a test of the emergency broadcasting system**. The algorithm builds a dictionary $D$ containing all $k$-word keys and their suffixes.

| 2-Word Key | Suffix | 2-Word Key | Suffix |
|---:|---|---:|---|
| this is | a | this is | a |
| is a | test | is a | test |
| a test | this | a test | of |
| test this | is | test of | the |
| this is | only | of the | emergency |
| is only | a | the emergency | broadcasting |
| only a | test | emergency broadcasting | system |
| a test | this | broadcasting system | this |
| test this | is | system this | is |

Figure 3.2. Keys and suffixes. From the text *T = this is a test this is only a test this is a test of the emergency broadcasting system*, with $k = 2$. Notice the suffixes for the last two keys wrap around to the beginning.

Once the dictionary is built, the string `phrase` is initialized to contain the first $k$ words of $T$, and those words are printed. The remaining $m - k$ words are generated by iterating this process:

1. **Lookup.** Find all keys in $D$ that match `phrase`. Return a set $S$ of suffixes of the matching keys.
2. **Random Selection.** Choose a suffix uniformly at random from $S$. Print it, append it to `phrase`, and drop the first word from the phrase.

For example, suppose `phrase` contains **this is**. The lookup step returns three suffixes: **a**, **only**, and **a**. With probability 2/3, the random selection step picks **a** and the new phrase is **is a**; with probability 1/3, **only** is selected and the new phrase is **is only**.

Not surprisingly, larger values of $k$ yield better-looking results. The two examples that follow were generated from a text containing the nine comedies by William Shakespeare. The first sample was generated by MC with $k = 1$:

ALL'S WELL THAT ENDS WELL ACT II Troy. DON JOHN And he, If I heard of all the giddiness of the pairs of Beatrice between her song and till they've swallowed me are in sin in jest. I his characters; He'd Lay on't. Perdita I think you beat thee. Fie on him: 'Tis false. Soft, swain, Pompey surnamed the PRINCESS, KATHARINE, ROSALINE, MARIA, KATHARINE, BOYET, ROSALINE, MARIA, and let him keep not o'erthrown by mis-dread.

The following sample, generated with $k = 3$, shows much better grammar and punctuation, although meaning remains elusive.

ALL'S WELL THAT ENDS WELL ACT III SCENE III A church. [Enter DON PEDRO, CLAUDIO, and LEONATO] BENEDICK Will your grace command me any service to the world's end will have bald followers. ANTIPHOLUS OF SYRACUSE Thy sister's sister. LUCIANA That's my sister. ANTIPHOLUS OF SYRACUSE There's none but asses will be bridled so.

The next few sections describe experiments using several performance indicators to evaluate the time performance of this algorithm. Note that these small experiments are developed for demonstration purposes only – a full-scale experimental study of MC would incorporate a much larger range of text files and design points than are presented here.

The markov.c program described in this section was written by Jon Bentley [4]. It is available for downloading from *AlgLab*, together with an alternative hash-table implementation.

### 3.1.1  Adding Counters to Source Code

The first option we consider is to insert *code counters* into the source code, which are integer variables that increment each time some interesting operation – such as a dominant operation – is performed. So far our description of the algorithm is too abstract for the dominant cost to be identified. Therefore, we select an implementation strategy for the dictionary data structure $D$.

The markov.c implementation of MC stores the text $T$ in an array of characters. The dictionary $D$ is implemented using a sorted array called word that contains indices to all words in $T$. The indices are sorted according to the $k$-word keys they reference.

For example, Figure 3.3 shows an input text with indices, together with a table sorted by two-word keys, showing their suffixes. The indices in the last column are stored in word.

### *Modeling Word Comparisons*

The cost of initialization is dominated by the number of key-to-key comparisons needed to sort word. Comparisons are performed by a function called wordcmp, which is invoked by the C qsort library function.

The text generation loop is shown in Figure 3.4. The lookup step performs a binary search in word to find the beginning of the subarray of keys that match the current phrase. The dominant cost is the number of calls to wordcmp during the binary search.

The random selection loop iterates over the subarray of matching keys and selects each with appropriate probability, assigning the corresponding suffix to p (this *reservoir sampling* technique is explained in Section 5.2.3.) The dominant cost is the number of comparisons performed by wordcmp, which equals the number of keys matching the current phrase.

```
Text:        this is a test this is only a test
Indices:     0123456789012345678901234567890123
             0         1         2         3
```

| Key | Suffix | Index |
|----:|:-------|:-----:|
| a test | this | 8 |
| a test | this | 28 |
| is a | test | 5 |
| is only | a | 20 |
| only a | test | 23 |
| test this | is | 10 |
| test this | is | 30 |
| this is | a | 0 |
| this is | only | 15 |

Figure 3.3. Words sorted by key. After sorting, the word array contains the indices on the right.

Our goal is to understand how the dominant cost of MC – that is, the number of calls to wordcmp – depends on parameters $n$, $m$, and $k$.

It is straightforward to insert a counter inside wordcmp to tally the number of times it is invoked and to run experiments to tease out the shape of this cost function. This "black box" approach is sometimes necessary, but it is usually more productive to adopt a "glass box" approach that exploits what is already known about the algorithm. Here, for example, we know that the three cost components are independent.

**Guideline 3.1** *It is easier to measure components separately and analyze their combined cost than to measure an aggregate cost and try to break it into components during analysis.*

For simplicity we start with the assumption that MC is run using one-word keys, so $k = 1$. We insert three counters into the code, as specified in the following; refer to Figure 3.4.

- To measure initialization cost, put the statement qcount++ inside the key comparison function called by the C library qsort, which calls wordcmp. Assuming qsort contains a reasonably efficient implementation of quicksort, we expect this cost to be proportional to $qn \log_2 n$, for some constant $q$ yet to be determined.
- To measure the cost of binary search, place bcount++ inside the binary search loop, just above the call to wordcmp. Binary search is performed once per output

```
// Text Generation Loop
// phrase = initialize to first k words of T

print (phrase);
for (wordsleft = m-k ;  wordsleft > 0;  wordsleft--) {
    // Lookup with binary search
    lo = -1;
    hi = nword;
    while (lo+1 != hi) {
        mid = lo+(hi-lo)/2;
        if (wordcmp(word[mid], phrase) < 0)  lo=mid;
        else hi = mid;
    }
    // hi = index of leftmost key that matches phrase

    // Random Select
    for (i = 0; wordcmp(phrase, word[hi+i]) == 0; i++)
        if (rand() % (i+1) == 0)
            p = skip(word[hi+i],k);  // get next suffix
    print (p);
    phrase = updatePhrase(phrase,  p) ;
}
```

Figure 3.4.  Text generation. This is the text generation loop of the MC algorithm. The dictionary $D$ is implemented with a sorted array called word.

word and requires $O(\log n)$ comparisons on average. Therefore, this cost should be proportional to $bm \log_2 n$, for some constant $b$.

- Random selection is also performed once per output word. The cost of this step is equal to the number of calls to wordcmp in the header of the for loop. Place rcount++ in two spots: inside the loop for tests that evaluate to true and once outside the loop for the test that evaluates to false.

```
for (i=0; wordcmp(phrase, word[hi+i])==0; i++) {
    rcount++;                              //true
    if (rand() % (i+1) == 0) p=skip(word[hi+i],k);
}
rcount++;                                  //false
```

This cost depends on $m$ and on the average number of duplicate keys in a text of size $n$. This number probably increases with $n$, but it is not clear exactly how. We start with the tentative cost model $rmn$ for some constant $r$.

This rough analysis, which ignores low-order terms and relies on some untested assumptions, yields the following preliminary cost formula:

$$W(n,m) = qn\log_2 n + bm\log_2 n + rmn. \qquad (3.1)$$

To check the validity of this model we use a simple doubling experiment as described in Section 2.2.2. Since this is a randomized algorithm running on real-world inputs, we expect a reasonably close correspondence, but not a perfect match between the model and the data.

**Guideline 3.2** *Use a doubling experiment to perform a quick validation check of your cost model.*

The validation experiment runs MC on a file called total that contains three volumes of English text described in the table that follows. All text files mentioned in this section were downloaded from Project Gutenberg [20].

| File | Text | $n$ |
|------|------|-----|
| huckleberry | *Huckleberry Finn*, by Mark Twain | 112,493 |
| voyage | *The Voyage of the Beagle*, by Charles Darwin | 207,423 |
| comedies | Nine comedies by William Shakespeare | 337,452 |
| total | Combined comedies, huckleberry, voyage | 697,368 |

The experiment reads the first $n$ words of total and measures qcount, bcount, and rcount in one trial each at design points with $k = 1$, $n = (10^5, 2 \times 10^5, 4 \times 10^5)$, and $m = (10^5, 2 \times 10^5, 4 \times 10^5)$.

First we check whether qcount is proportional to $n\log_2 n$. Since doubling $n$ increases $\log_2 n$ by 1, we expect qcount/$n$ to increment by a constant at each level. The following table shows the results.

| | $n = 10^5$ | $2 \times 10^5$ | $4 \times 10^5$ |
|------|------|------|------|
| qcount/$n$ | 12.039 | 13.043 | 14.041 |

The data behave as expected, so we accept $qn\log_2 n$ to model the cost of initialization. Next we consider bcount, which should grow as $m\log_2 n$.

| | $n = 10^5$ | $n = 2 \times 10^5$ | $n = 4 \times 10^5$ |
|------|------|------|------|
| $m = 10^5$ | 133,606 | 143,452 | 153,334 |
| $m = 2 \times 10^5$ | 267,325 | 287,154 | 306,553 |
| $m = 4 \times 10^5$ | 534,664 | 574,104 | 613,193 |

If bcount is proportional to $m \log_2 n$, the data should double going down each column (with fixed $n$). The data should increment by a constant across each row, and the constant should be proportional to $m$. This also looks good: costs in the first row increase by about 10,000, in the second row by about 20,000, and in the third row by about 40,000.

Finally we check whether rcount is proportional to $nm$. Again, the data in the table match the model reasonably well, since the numbers approximately double across each row and down each column.

|                    | $n = 10^5$ | $n = 2 \times 10^5$ | $n = 4 \times 10^5$ |
|--------------------|------------|---------------------|---------------------|
| $m = 10^5$         | 1,234,334  | 2,298,021           | 4,500,283           |
| $m = 2 \times 10^5$ | 2,367,523  | 4,617,355           | 9,009,292           |
| $m = 4 \times 10^5$ | 4,933,294  | 9,394,869           | 18,284,907          |

On the basis of this quick test we adopt formula (3.1) to model the cost of MC as a function of $n$ and $m$ when $k = 1$.

The second experiment is designed to find values for the coefficients $q$ (quicksort), $b$ (binary search), and $r$ (random selection). Figure 3.5 shows results of tests using three separate text files, comedies, huckleberry, and voyage, with $n$ equal to file size in each case. Each line corresponds to one file. Panels (a), (b), and (c) show measurements of

$$q = \text{qcount}/n \log_2 n$$
$$b = \text{bcount}/m \log_2 n$$
$$r = \text{rcount}/nm$$

for our three terms. The ratios are plotted as a function of $m$, which increases from 1000 to 12,800, doubling each time; note the logarithmic scale on the $x$-axes. We expect these ratios to be constant, that is, approximately horizontal, in each panel.

In panel (a) the perfectly horizontal lines confirm that $q$ does not depend on $m$. The results for three files differ by less than 0.6 percent, indicating good agreement. The three lines are ordered by $n$, which may indicate a lurking second-order term, but the effect is small and is ignored here. The average over all three files is $q = 0.9286$.

The coefficients in panels (b) and (c) are reasonably horizontal, allowing for some variation due to randomization in the algorithm. These measurements show less variation as $m$ increases because more numbers are averaged together. In panel (b) the three costs differ by no more than 0.03 percent at large $m$; their average at the top five $m$ values (ignoring the relatively large variation at small $m$) is $b = 1.0045$.

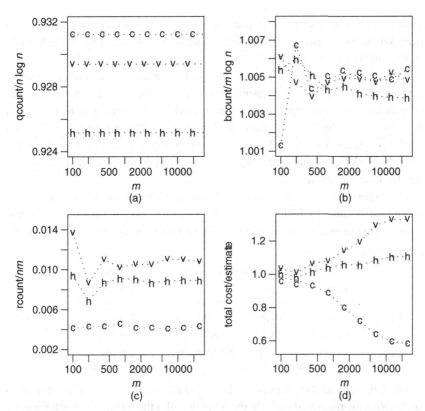

Figure 3.5. Word comparison costs. Panels (a) Quicksort, (b) binarysearch, and (c) random selection show estimates of coefficients $q$, $b$, and $r$. The $x$ axis corresponds to output size $m$, shown on a log scale. The $y$ axis shows ratios obtained by dividing operation counts by the corresponding terms in formula (3.1). Results are shown for three input files c (Shakespeare's comedies), h (*Huckleberry Finn*), and v (*Voyage of the Beagle*). Panel (d) shows the ratio of total measured cost to total predicted cost.

In panel (c) the ratio rcount/$nm$ shows considerable variation among the three files: the coefficient for voyage is almost twice that for comedies. The average at the top five $m$ levels is $r = 0.0079$.

These results yield the following formula, which describes word comparison cost for the MC algorithm.

$$W(n,m) = 0.9286n \log_2 n + 1.0045m \log_2 n + 0.0079nm \qquad (3.2)$$

Panel (d) shows measured comparisons divided by the estimates produced by formula (3.2). The formula underestimates total cost for voyages by about 25 percent and overestimates cost for comedies by about 40 percent. A little arithmetic shows that the random selection term dominates total cost at these design points, and the large variation in panel (c) is the source of the discrepancies seen here. When coefficients for individual text files are substituted for $r$, the formula is accurate to within 3 percent.

The main benefit of a cost formula like (3.2) is that it can be extended to predict performance of MC at other design points. To test the accuracy of the formula on general inputs, the third experiment runs MC using three new text files: (1) *Persuasion* and *Pride and Prejudice* by Jane Austen, (2) ten tragedies by William Shakespeare, and (3) *The Adventures of Tom Sawyer, A Connecticut Yankee in King Author's Court*, and *Following the Equator*, by Mark Twain and *The Gilded Age* by Twain and Warner.

This experiment sets $k = 1$ and $m = 256,000$, which is twice the largest $m$ in the previous experiment. The following table shows file sizes $n$, measured total cost (rounded to the nearest hundred thousand), and ratios of measured costs to those predicted by formula (3.2).

| File | $n$ | Cost | Cost / $W(n,m)$ |
|------|-----|------|-----------------|
| austen | 204,839 | $372.0 \times 10^6$ | 0.881 |
| tragedies | 251,181 | $253.8 \times 10^6$ | 0.491 |
| twain | 532,895 | $835.8 \times 10^6$ | 1.057 |

The largest prediction gap is on the `tragedies` file, where the estimate is about twice the measured cost. On the other two files the formula overestimates by about 12 percent and underestimates by about 6 percent. This cost formula could be improved by expanding the input file testbed and refining the random selection term with better model of key duplications in general texts. The reader is invited to download `markov.c` from *AlgLab* and pursue this interesting project.

Now we consider how to modify formula (3.2) to reflect changes in parameter $k$. A quick experiment (not shown here) reveals that the quicksort and binary search terms do not vary much with $k$. But inspection of the code tells us that coefficient $r$ should decrease as $k$ grows, since the number of iterations in the random selection loop depends on the number of key duplicates. We can expect many duplicates of one-word keys like **we**, but few duplicates of three-word keys like **we catched fish**.

The next experiment looks at dependence of the cost of random selection on $k$, using our original text files, with $m = 800\ldots1200$ incrementing by 100, and $k = 1\ldots5$. Each entry in the table that follows shows `rcount/m`, which corresponds to $rn$ in our model. This is the number of key comparisons per output word performed during random selection. The column means (denoted $\overline{rn}$) appear in the bottom row.

| File | $n$ | $k=1$ | $k=2$ | $k=3$ | $k=4$ | $k=5$ |
|------|-----|-------|-------|-------|-------|-------|
| huckleberry | 112,492 | 1002.4 | 19.9 | 2.8 | 2.1 | 2.0 |
| voyage | 207,423 | 2063.3 | 69.1 | 2.8 | 2.2 | 2.0 |
| comedies | 377,452 | 1649.0 | 19.2 | 3.5 | 2.1 | 2.1 |
| $\overline{rn}$ | | 1571.6 | 36.1 | 3.0 | 2.1 | 2.0 |

The minimum possible value in this table is 2. This corresponds to one `true` and one `false` evaluation in the `for` loop header (in the selection step), which occurs when the current phrase has no duplicates. The rightmost column indicates that nearly every five-word phrase in these texts is unique; that means that MC will simply reproduce the original input.

As expected, the number of calls to `wordcmp` during random selection decreases with $k$, quite sharply from $k = 1$, but then tapering off. We also note that this cost depends more on $k$ than on $n$. Although the model $rnm$ worked well in the original validation experiment, in this experiment with $k \geq 1$, we get a better fit to the data using the model $r_k m$ instead of $rnm$, with mean coefficients $r_k$ summarized as follows.

$$r_1 = 1571.6$$

$$r_2 = 36.1$$

$$r_{k \geq 3} = 2.5$$

The new cost formula is

$$W_k(n,m) = 0.9286n \log_2 n + 1.0045m \log_2 n + r_k m. \tag{3.3}$$

Parameter $k$ has different status in this formula because it ranges over a few integers rather than growing to asymptopia.

Additional experiments show that this formula is accurate within a factor of 2 when applied to the same range of problem sizes. More work is needed to extend this formula, especially the third term, to problems with much larger or smaller $n$ values.

The next section considers an alternative cost model that is more closely tied to computation time.

### Counting Character Comparisons

The `wordcmp` function implemented in `markov.c` is shown in the following. This function takes two pointers p and q that reference words in the text; words are stored sequentially, and each word is terminated by the null character 0. It

returns a negative integer if key *p is lexicographically less than *q, zero if the
two keys are equal, and a positive integer if *p > *q.

```
int wordcmp(char *p, char* q) {
    int n=k;
    chcomps=0;
    for (; *p == *q; p++, q++){
        chcomps++;
        if (*p == 0 && --n == 0) return 0;
    }
    return *p - *q;
}
```

The for loop compares keys character-by-character and stops when a non-
matching pair is found. The if statement returns 0 if no differences are found
after k words have been checked – note that the C && operator does not evaluate
the right side of the expression when the left side is false, so n decrements only
when *p is the null character (0). When the keys match, the cost of this loop is
equal to total key length; otherwise it equals the number of matching characters
in the prefixes of the two keys. This cost increases with $k$, since total key length
grows with $k$.

We can measure the number of character comparisons performed for each program component (initialization, binary search, random selection) by introducing
a global counter chcomps that is initialized to 0 at the beginning of wordcmp
and incremented inside the loop. The resulting value of chcomps is added to a
running total in the respective program components after each function call.

Why might we choose to measure character comparisons instead of word comparisons? The merits of these alternative performance indicators are considered in
Section 3.1.4. Briefly, word comparisons are associated with a more abstract view
of the algorithm because they do not depend on how exactly wordcmp is implemented. Character comparisons reflect the dominant cost of this implementation
of MC and are more closely tied to the real time taken by the program.

The following table shows the number of character comparisons per call to
wordcmp, averaged over tests on our original three text files. In this experiment
$n$ equals file size, $m = 800 \ldots 1200$, and $k = 1 \ldots 5$.

|                  | $k = 1$ | $k = 2$ | $k = 3$ | $k = 4$ | $k = 5$ | $k \geq 3$ |
|------------------|---------|---------|---------|---------|---------|------------|
| quicksort        | 3.24    | 4.02    | 4.17    | 4.20    | 4.20    | 4.19       |
| binary search    | 3.26    | 4.52    | 5.02    | 5.35    | 5.78    | 5.38       |
| random selection | 4.56    | 9.43    | 13.75   | 16.23   | 19.35   | 16.44      |

Notice that the cost for random selection is much higher than the costs of the other two program components. Character comparisons are maximized in this step since the selection loop iterates through equal-valued keys. Binary search has slightly higher cost than quicksort because a higher proportion of near-equal keys are compared during the search; therefore matching prefixes are longer.

We can develop a new formula $C_k(n,m)$ for character comparisons, with the same general shape as formula (3.3) except for new coefficients that depend on $k$. Plugging in the data from the preceding experiment we obtain:

$$C_1(n,m) = 3.01n\log_2 n + 3.27m\log_2 n + 7166.5m \qquad (3.4)$$

$$C_2(n,m) = 3.44n\log_2 n + 3.73m\log_2 n + 340.4m$$

$$C_{k\geq 3}(n,m) = 3.89n\log_2 n + 5.41m\log_2 n + 32.89m$$

Further experiments (not shown here) indicate that this formula is accurate to within 20 percent when predicting character comparisons on our three files, comedies, huckleberry, and voyage. The formula is less successful when applied to other inputs, because the coefficients depend more on individual properties of each text.

The next section considers a very different definition of time performance and surveys tools and techniques for measuring it.

### 3.1.2 Clocks and Timers

It is easy enough to run the markov program while keeping an eye on the clock. For example, a test run with comedies, $k = 1$, and $m = 1200$ on the computer in my office takes less than a second. This stopwatch technique is suitable when measurement precision within a couple of seconds is needed, but internal computer clocks can achieve much greater precision when necessary.

We start with a tutorial on time measurement techniques in the Unix family of operating systems (including Linux, Unix, and Mac OS X). These tools are illustrated with a small experiment to measure markov.c. A discussion of timing on Windows systems and a list of timing utilities for Windows and Unix systems appear at the end of Section 3.1.4.

### CPU Time and Real Time

A *process* is an actively running program. A given process may contain one or more *threads*, which are separate instruction streams that can run concurrently with one another. To simplify the discussion, for now we refer to both threads and processes as processes.

Most modern computers have *multicore* processors containing a small number (say, 2 to 16) of independent processing units, called cores. The operating system can run processes concurrently by scheduling them to execute on different cores. At any moment, the CPU on each core is running a process, and the other processes are waiting their turns.

The *process scheduler* runs multiple processes on a single CPU by interleaving them in time. When a CPU *interrupt* occurs, the active process pauses and the scheduler takes over; after handling the interrupt, the scheduler may decide to let the paused process resume or to swap it out and start up a new one. Interrupts can occur for many reasons; in particular, a timer interrupt is emitted at regular intervals by a timer circuit.

Figure 3.6 shows how a white process and a gray process might alternate use of one CPU, sharing time with the scheduler shown in black. The active process may be running in *user mode*, which means it is executing instructions from the program, or in *system mode*, which means executing operating system instructions on behalf of the program. Time spent in system mode is shown with hash marks. Seven timer interrupts are marked by arrows at the bottom of the time band, and four miscellaneous interrupts appear above it.

In this example, instructions execute at a rate of one per nanosecond and timer interrupts occur every 10 milliseconds. The scheduler takes a few microseconds (a few thousand instruction cycles) to handle an interrupt and several more to perform a process swap: these times are depicted by narrow and wide black bands in the figure.

Apart from all this, the *system clock*, also called the *time-of-day clock*, increments a clock register at regular intervals. The numbers at the top of Figure 3.6 show the low-order digits of the system clock over this period. The time interval used by the system clock is called the *timestamp resolution*. Here the resolution is five

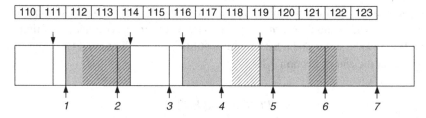

Figure 3.6. CPU time. The white and gray processes alternate in the CPU, together with the process scheduler shown in black; time spent in system mode is depicted with hashmarks. The arrows at the top and bottom of the the CPU band denote interrupts. The numbers at the top show elapsed time according to the system clock.

milliseconds; in real computers timestamp resolution can vary from nanoseconds to milliseconds.

There are two basic approaches to measuring process time. The first is to calculate *real time*, also called *wall clock time* or *elapsed time*, by comparing two timestamps of the clock register taken at the start and end of the process. For example, a wall clock measurement for the gray process in Figure 3.6 would report $12 = 123 - 112 + 1$ time units.

*Cycle counting* is a variation on elapsed time measurement. Recent Intel platforms have a Time Stamp Counter Register (TSCR) that increments once per instruction cycle, and a Read Time Stamp Counter (RDTSC) instruction to access it. Counting nanosecond-scale instruction cycles instead of millisecond-scale clock ticks represents a million-fold improvement in clock resolution.

The main problem with elapsed-time measurements, whether done by cycle counts or by clocks, is that they include a great deal of noise in the form of time used by competing processes, which have nothing to do with the process being measured. The *system load* refers to the number of processes being run in a given period: higher system loads mean lower timer accuracy because the process being measured gets a smaller slice of elapsed time.

The second approach is to use *interval timing* to report what is commonly called CPU time. Unix systems have a device that checks which process is active in the CPU during each timer interrupt and assigns one time credit for the interval to that process. Thus in Figure 3.6 the white process is assigned two units of user time (intervals 1 and 3), and the gray process is assigned five units of CPU time, three in user mode (intervals 4 ,5, 7) and two in system mode (intervals 2, 6). (Scheduler time is always assigned to an adjacent process.) This approach is designed to be less sensitive to system load, but obviously some amount of sampling error must occur.

Modern computing platforms add several complications to this basic scenario. For example, some Intel processors feature *hyperthreading*, by which two threads (perhaps from different processes) can be interleaved to run like one thread on a core. Both processes are considered to be active in the CPU, so the interval timer allocates 50 percent of the interval to each. This can cause significant timing discrepancies, since hyperthreading can appear to halve CPU time and double wall clock time. For best results, turn off the hyperthreading feature when conducting timing experiments on these systems.

Furthermore, interactions with the memory hierarchy can skew time measurements in significant ways, and time measurements can show huge variations when a process containing multiple threads is executed on multiple cores. These types of timing difficulties, together with some coping strategies, are discussed further in Section 3.1.4.

So which timing strategy is best? As a general rule, when measuring a single process, algorithm researchers prefer to use interval timers, because CPU times ignore time taken by extraneous processes, are more stable from run to run, and are easier to translate from one platform to another.

As process time increases, CPU timers become more accurate because interval sampling errors average out, while elapsed times become less accurate as a result of interrupts, background system activity, and other processes. A good rule of thumb is to design each experimental trial so that the process runs for at least 0.1 second, which is 10 times longer than the standard 10ms timer interval. Bryant and O'Hallaron [7] report that once total process time exceeds this threshold, CPU times are typically accurate to within 10 percent.

**Guideline 3.3** *For best timer accuracy, use an interval timer and design tests so that the process being measured runs for at least 100 milliseconds; a second or more is better.*

Interval timers are less reliable on shorter-lived processes because the number of samples is too small. High-resolution wall clocks and cycle counts may be adequate in these cases, but note that *timer latency* – the amount of time needed during a system call to obtain a timestamp value – can be surprisingly large. Bryant and O'Halloran [7] report, for example, that the Java `System.currentTime-Millis()` method may have latency as high as half a millisecond. This means that the time-in, time-out operations themselves contribute measurement errors as large as a millisecond.

Cycle counters are recommended for measuring elapsed times shorter than the timer interrupt interval. Note that if time is stored as a 32-bit number, a nanosecond-scale counter can only measure intervals up to 1.43 seconds because of overflow; with 64 bits, intervals up to 194 years can be measured. Also, it is sometimes difficult to translate cycle counts to time units because cycle times can change dynamically depending on factors such as battery power and network activity. Bryant and O'Hallaron [7] (section 9.4) point out that since noise from competing processes can only increase cycle counts, the *smallest* cycle counts recorded over several runs of a process must be the most accurate.

**Guideline 3.4** *If short-lived processes must be measured, use cycle counts or elapsed time, but check that the measured time interval is greater than both timer resolution and timer latency. When using a cycle counter, take several measurements and record the smallest cycle count observed.*

See Bryant and O'Hallaron [7] for more information about clocks and timers.

## Timing markov.c

Let us perform a small experiment to learn how much variation to expect from CPU and elapsed-time measurements. We run the `markov` program on the `comedies` file, with $m = 1,000,000$ and $k = 1$. The random number generator seed was fixed throughout so that the same instruction sequence is executed in every trial. Therefore, all time variations reported here are due to environmental factors.

Program runtime is measured using the Unix `time` command as follows:

```
time markov 1 1000000 <comedies.txt
```

The `time` command reports both wall clock time and CPU time, with user time and system time reported separately.

The first experiment was performed on an HP ProLiant DL160 G5 server, with two Intel Xeon E5472 processors each containing four cores (totaling eight cores), instruction cycle time 3GHz, running Ubuntu Server Linux 8.04, no hyperthreading. The system has 12MB of L2 cache (6MB per processor) and 32GB of RAM memory) On this platform the interval timer has 10ms resolution.

The results of three tests under different system conditions are shown in the table that follows. The CPU column shows user time plus system time, and the Wall column shows elapsed time, as reported by the `time` command. All times are in units of seconds.

|   | Platform | Test | CPU | Wall |
|---|----------|------|-----|------|
| 1 | HP | Unoptimized, light | 43.02 | 43.02 |
| 2 | HP | Optimized, light | 27.96 | 28.19 |
| 3 | HP | Optimized, heavy 1 | 36.02 | 43.63 |
| 4 | HP | Optimized, heavy 9 | 37.64 | 43.41 |

Row 1 shows times for unoptimized code run on a lightly loaded system (with no other user processes running). Row 2 shows times for optimized code (compiled with the GNU C compiler using `gcc -o3`), also run on a lightly loaded system. The third test increased the system load by running nine copies of the program simultaneously. Rows 3 and 4 show the processes with the fastest and slowest user times among these nine. Here are some observations about the data in this table.

1. Comparing rows 1 and 2, we see that the optimized code runs about 35 percent faster than the unoptimized code.
2. Rows 1 and 2 show that CPU times are quite close to elapsed times on the lightly loaded system.
3. Running nine processes on eight cores should increase elapsed time for each process by about 12.5 percent (9/8). We expect no increase in CPU times

because interval timing is considered to be unaffected by system load. But comparing rows 2 and 3 we see that elapsed times are at least 50 percent higher and CPU times are at least 28 percent higher.

4. The process with the fastest CPU time had one of the slowest elapsed times, and in general there was no relationship between CPU time and elapsed time for the nine processes.

The following table shows results of running the same tests on an Apple MacBook Pro2.2 laptop containing two cores (an Intel Core 2 Duo processor with 2.16GHz instruction cycle time, running Mac OSX 10.5.8. The platform has a 4MB L2 cache and 1GB of RAM). The interval timer has 10 ms resolution.

|   | Platform | Test | CPU | Wall |
|---|----------|------|-----|------|
| 1 | Mac | Unoptimized, light | 108.15 | 115.18 |
| 2 | Mac | Optimized, light | 67.33 | 79.08 |
| 3 | Mac | Optimized, heavy 1 | 96.97 | 630.06 |
| 4 | Mac | Optimized, heavy 9 | 100.38 | 649.48 |

Here are some observations.

1. Given their clock speeds we might predict the ratio of times on the two platforms to be near 1.4 (3GHz/2.16GHz), but in fact the ratios of CPU times in the first two rows of the tables are 2.5 and 2.4.
2. Moving from unoptimized to optimized code yields about the same speedup on both platforms.
3. We expect elapsed times in rows 3 and 4 to be about 4.5 times those in row 2 (9/2), but instead elapsed times for the nine processes are eight times slower. CPU times are 1.44 times higher on the loaded system than on the unloaded system.

The effect of system load on measured runtimes is much larger than predicted by conventional wisdom. Elapsed times were much higher than simple process-per-core arithmetic would indicate, increasing by 55 percent instead of 25 percent on the HP and slowing down by a factor of 8 instead of 4.5 on the Mac. CPU times, which are supposed to be oblivious to system loads, increased by more than 28 percent on the 8-core HP and 44 percent on the 2-core Mac.

The lesson is clear: timing experiments should be run on lightly loaded systems whenever possible. For best results, kill all competing applications and background processes and avoid generating keystroke interrupts and screen update events on personal computers and laptops. Good results can be obtained if the scheduler can find an empty core to assign to the process.

**Guideline 3.5** *Whenever possible, measure time on lightly loaded systems; in any case, find out how much timing variation to expect from your test environment.*

The next experiment measures instruction cycle times on lightly loaded systems. In this experiment the RDTSC (Read Time Stamp Counter) instruction was invoked from inside markov.c at the beginning and end of the program. Following Guideline 3.4, table entries show the smallest cycle counts observed over three trials for each row.

The first three columns show times reported by the time command. The fourth column shows instruction counts rounded to the nearest 0.1 billion. The last column shows the result of multiplying instruction counts by advertised instruction frequencies, 3GHz for the HP and 2.16GHz for the Mac. (A small validation experiment showed that actual instruction frequencies were within 2 percent of advertised rates.) All times are in units of seconds.

| System | CPU user | CPU sys | Wall | Instr Count | Cycle Time |
|---|---|---|---|---|---|
| HP Unopt | 27.61 | 0.35 | 28.19 | $84.8 \times 10^9$ | 28.27 |
| HP Opt | 43.96 | 0.40 | 43.35 | $128.7 \times 10^9$ | 42.93 |
| Mac Unopt | 55.53 | 1.22 | 59.79 | $115.9 \times 10^9$ | 53.66 |
| Mac Opt | 92.41 | 1.22 | 95.55 | $237.9 \times 10^9$ | 110.16 |

Cycle times are reasonably consistent with wall clock times on the HP platform. However, these times are quite difficult to reconcile on the Mac: in row 3, cycle time is six seconds less than wall clock time and more than a second less than CPU time, and in row 4, cycle time is about 15 seconds more than wall clock time. Repeated measurements on this platform give similarly inconsistent results, showing variations of as much as 30 percent from elapsed times. *Caveat timer.*

### 3.1.3 Code Profilers

Sometimes a computational experiment is developed to study a section of code rather than the whole process. Code counters are ideal for this purpose, since they can be inserted with surgical precision exactly where needed. An alternative approach is to surround the section of interest with timein/timeout instructions; Section 3.1.4 contains a list of suitable timing tools. A third option is to use a *code profiler*, which is a software tool that reports counts and runtime statistics for program components.

```
$ gcc -pg markov.c -o markov
$ markov 1 1000000 <comedies.txt
$gprof
```

```
Flat profile:
Each sample counts as 0.01 seconds.
   %    cumulative   self              self     total
  time    seconds   seconds    calls  ns/call  ns/call  name
 64.98     13.31     13.31 1628788583   8.17     8.17   wordcmp
 34.38     20.36      7.04                              main
  1.08     20.58      0.22                              frame_dummy
  0.20     20.62      0.04                              sortcmp
  0.00     20.62      0.00  3000000    0.00     0.00    skip
  0.00     20.62      0.00  1000000    0.00     0.00    writeword
```

Figure 3.7.  Sample gprof output. See the Unix manual page for gprof to learn about additional statistics that can be reported beyond the defaults shown here.

A variety of commercial and open source profilers are available; two are illustrated here. First is the Unix gprof utility, which is available for many languages including C, C++, Pascal, and Fortran. The second is *Cachegrind*, which is part of the Valgrind [21] suite of program instrumentation tools. Valgrind is also compatible with many languages including C, C++, Java, Perl, Python, Fortran, and Ada.

## gprof

The gprof profiler reports invocation counts and CPU times for individual functions (procedures) in a program. Using gprof is a three step process:

1. Compile the source code using the -pg option. This causes profiling instructions to be inserted into the object code.
2. Run the program. This produces a file of statistics named gmon.out.
3. Run gprof to see a human-readable version of gmon.out.

The command sequence and output for one test of markov are shown in Figure 3.7. The profiler report lists functions in order by CPU times: the wordcmp function used 13.31 seconds, which was almost 65 percent of total CPU time for the program. It was invoked almost 1.63 billion times and took 8.17 nanoseconds per call on average. The second most time-consuming function was main, and the combined time for wordcmp and main was 20.36 seconds. The remaining functions had negligible impact on total cost, even though two were invoked millions of times. Invocation counts are not recorded for sortcmp because it is called from the system qsort function, which could not be annotated.

The gprof profiler makes a direct connection between function invocation counts and function CPU times, this can be a valuable analysis tool. This profiler is also handy for identifying code *hot-spots* that consume the most computation time – in this case, any project to speed up markov.c should clearly focus on the wordcmp function. Profiling and code tuning are discussed further in Chapter 4.

CPU times in gprof are recorded by an interval timer that assigns time units to individual functions in the program. The remarks in Section 3.1.2 (in CPU Time and Real Time) about interval timer inaccuracies for short-lived code blocks apply, although, in this case, the sampling errors are smoothed out by averaging over 1.68 billion invocations.

Compiler-based profilers like gprof that insert profiling instructions into object code should not be used in combination with compiler optimization, because the optimizer moves code blocks around in ways that confuse the profiling code and create reporting errors. For example, compiling with gcc -pg -O3 and running the same trial produce the following nonsense report shown in its entirety:

```
 %     cumulative   self              self    total
time    seconds    seconds   calls  Ts/call  Ts/call  name
100.21    7.72      7.72                                main
  0.46    7.75      0.04                                writeword
```

**Guideline 3.6** *Do not use compiler-based code profilers in combination with compiler optimization.*

### Cachegrind

The Cachegrind profiler simulates the execution of a program on a specified platform and records statistics about individual instructions, including execution counts and memory references. Here is the command sequence to profile markov.c:

```
gcc  -g  markov.c -o markov
valgrind  --tool=cachegrind  markov 1 100000 <comedies.txt
cg_annotate  cachegrind.out.1234   --auto=yes
```

The gcc -g compiler option causes the compiler to insert trace instructions into the object code in markov. Then Valgrind runs markov with the Cachegrind option, to produce a data file tagged with a process number (cachegrind.out.1234 in this example). The cg_annotate command creates a human-readable report, and the auto option specifies a format that includes counts of instruction executions per line of source code.

A small excerpt of the report, showing instruction execution counts for wordcmp, is presented here. The counts on lines 2 and 9 correspond to instructions for function calls and returns.

```
1                        int wordcmp (char *p, char* q)
2    32,668,088          {
3    16,334,044            int n = k;
4   196,291,370            for ( ; *p == *q; p++, q++){
5    91,500,879              if (*p == 0 && --n == 0)
6     6,268,506                return 0;
7                          }
8    53,461,943            return  *p - *q;
9    16,334,044          }
```

This type of report is not restricted to function-level statistics (like gprof) and can be used to study code sections large and small. For example the for loop header on line 4 contains the dominant instruction in markov.c – the character comparison – which is executed more times than any other instruction in the program. Running Cachegrind at several design points reveals that the loop header performs 7.1 instructions per iteration on average; note that the first iteration costs less than later iterations because there is no increment step. This observation can be combined with instruction cycle times to yield an estimate of 2.37 nanoseconds per iteration on the 3GHz HP platform.

Cachegrind counts do not include instructions inside system functions like qsort and printf, which cannot be annotated. Like gprof, Cachegrind should not be used in combination with compiler optimization.

### *3.1.4  The Right Tool for the Job*

Which type of performance indicator is the right choice for your next experimental project? This section surveys some points to consider. A list of timing tools and utilities for Unix and Windows platforms appears at the end of this section, in the subsection Tools and Utilities.

#### *Instantiation*

The performance indicators discussed in preceding sections can be matched to points on the instantiation scale that was described in Section 1.2, as follows:

- Word comparison count is a property of the abstract algorithm, instantiated with a sorted array data structure. This performance indicator is invariant with respect to choice of programming language, coding strategy, and runtime environments. In the case study, analysis of word comparison cost yielded formulas (3.2) and (3.3), which predicted the cost of MC to within a factor of 2 on general text files.
- The character comparison cost is instantiated with the implementation of the wordcmp function. A different implementation, strategy, for example, might be to calculate numerical signatures for each word during initialization and use the signatures to compare words in constant time. Measurement of character

comparisons produced formula (3.4), which was able to predict character comparisons to within 20 percent on the files used to build the formula. Because character comparisons are more dependent on individual file properties, formula (3.4) is less accurate than formula (3.3) when extended to a wider range of texts.

- The gprof profiler returned an exact count of invocations of wordcmp (equal to word comparisons) and a measurement of 8.17 nanoseconds per call. Function structures and their counts are instantiated at the source code level. Both character comparison counts and function invocation counts are platform independent.

- The instruction execution counts reported by Cachegrind are instantiated with the object code, which is a product of the source code, the compiler, and the target platform. Assuming a fixed random number seed, the instruction execution sequence does not vary from run to run.

- The Unix time command reports real time and CPU time measurements for the process, and gprof reports CPU times for individual functions. The RDTSC instruction can be invoked to produce cycle counts for a process or a code section. Wall clock times and cycle counts depend on the instruction sequence as well as external factors such as system load and scheduler decisions. CPU times lie somewhere between Cachegrind-style instruction counts and elapsed time measurements on this instantiation scale, since they are more robust than wall clock times with respect to external factors.

As discussed in Section 1.2, interesting experiments may be found at any point on the instantiation scale. Experiments to study abstract algorithm properties produce general results that are platform- and implementation-independent; experiments on source code give more precise measurements that remain platform independent; and highly instantiated performance indicators can reveal how processes interact with runtime environments.

The point is that the performance indicator should match the instantiation level set for the experiment. Do not measure CPU times if you want to understand how the abstract algorithm works; do not count dominant operations if you want to evaluate design alternatives on the scale of seconds.

**Guideline 3.7** *Performance indicators can be aimed at different points on the scale between abstract algorithms and instantiated code. Match your choice to the larger goals of the experiment.*

One advantage of using abstract performance indicators is that they are easier to model and show less variation from trial to trial because there are fewer moving parts. An advantage of instantiated performance indicators like CPU times is that they give more realistic views of time performance. Sometimes good results accrue from combining the best of both worlds.

For example, suppose we want to estimate the CPU time needed for markov.c to generate $m = 100,000$ words with $k = 1$, based on the works of Jane Austen ($n = 204,893$), running optimized code on the HP platform described in the first timing experiment of Section 3.1.2: call this the *target experiment*. We can reason as follows:

1. Using formula (3.2) we can predict that the target experiment will perform around 166,994,970 calls to wordcmp.
2. The gprof profile in Figure 3.7 reports that each function call takes 8.17 nanoseconds, which yields an estimate of 1.36 seconds. The profile also shows that the function represents about 64.98 percent of total computation time, which gives an estimate of 2.10 seconds for the whole program.
3. Profiling was performed on unoptimized code, but the time trials in Section 3.1.2 show that the time ratio of optimized to unoptimized code is near 0.65. This works out to an estimate of 1.36 seconds for the target experiment.
4. Recalling that formula (3.2) is only accurate to a factor of 2, we can predict that the target experiment might run between 0.68 and 2.72 seconds. Additional estimation errors might have crept in from generalizing function times and speedups from optimization to this new scenario, but their impact should be in the 20 percent range or less.

In fact, the target experiment take 2.50 seconds of CPU (user) time, which is within range of the prediction. One of the central open problems in experimental algorithmics is to find the right general procedure for making accurate and precise predictions of the time required by program A when run on platform B using input class C. The procedure outlined here shows that good results can be obtained using a combination of abstract cost models and instantiated time measurements.

**Guideline 3.8** *Build runtime predictions by combining platform-independent models of dominant costs with platform-specific measurements of those costs.*

Ahuja, Magnanti, and Orlin [2] propose a similar procedure that starts by identifying *representative operation counts* tied to code blocks that dominate computation time in practice, rather than in theory. These counts are used to identify bottleneck operations that use the largest proportion of computation time, and then profiling is used to attach CPU times to the bottleneck operations. This approach is also promising. More work is needed to address this important methodological question.

### Narrow and Wide Apertures

A second consideration in selecting a performance indicator is whether to focus narrowly on a key section (or sections) of code or more widely on the total cost.

Suppose we want to compare the sorted array implementation of dictionary *D* in `markov.c` to an alternative hash table implementation (a version of `markov.c` with a hash table can be downloaded from *AlgLab*). A narrow performance indicator would focus only on the differences between the two design alternatives:

1. **Initialization.** The cost of reading the input text is identical in both implementations, so ignore it. Compare the cost of building a sorted array of *n* words to the cost of building a hash table of *n* words.
2. **Lookup.** Compare the cost of finding all matching keys using binary search to the cost of finding all matching keys using hash table lookups.
3. **Random selection.** The cost of selecting a suffix at random is identical in both programs.

A performance indicator that focuses narrowly on cost differences in the initialization and lookup steps sharpens our view of the relative performance of these two design alternatives.

The performance indicator should also provide a common basis for comparison. In this case, word-level operations have fundamentally different base costs: in the sorted array, keys are compared using `wordcmp`, while in the hash table, the cost per word involves a hash function calculation and some number of probes in the table. If these two costs cannot be calibrated, it is necessary to find a more instantiated performance indicator that does permit direct comparisons. Character-level operations could work if the per-character costs of comparison, hashing, and probing are about equal. If not, measurements of machine instructions or clock ticks may provide common ground.

While narrow performance indicators isolate and highlight these differences, it is also important to understand differences in context: does switching to a hash table affect total runtimes by 9 percent or 90 percent?

**Guideline 3.9** *Choose narrow performance indicators to highlight differences between design strategies. Choose wide performance indicators to understand those differences in context.*

### Relevance

Another consideration for academic researchers is that performance indicators should be selected to allow direct comparison to work by other researchers. This means, first, that performance indicators should match those reported in the previous literature. Second, to ensure wide applicability of your results, always include platform-independent measurements in your paper (perhaps together with platform-specific measurements). If readers have no way of comparing your findings to old and new results, all your hard work will be ignored.

When reporting timing experiments in published work, your goal is to give the reader the best possible information about what to expect, under the assumption that your test conditions cannot be exactly replicated. Here are some guidelines:

1. **Full disclosure.** Report all properties of the test environment that might affect time measurements. These include the instruction cycle rate, the compiler and compiler optimization level, cache and main memory sizes, the system load during measurement, and which timing tool was used.
2. **Platform variety.** Runtime measurements taken on several platforms are more informative than measurements on one platform. At least report runtimes on the fastest and the slowest environments available to you.
3. **Tuned environments.** Run your tests in an environment tuned for speed: set compiler optimization switches to maximum levels and test on lightly loaded systems. This produces less variation in your data and gives lower bounds on times that are easier for readers to apply to their own circumstances.

While the code counters and timing tools discussed so far in this chapter are adequate for most types of algorithmic experiments, they do not solve every measurement problem that can arise. Two scenarios are especially problematic. First, the cost of memory access can skew runtimes in unpredictable ways; and second, time measurements on multicore, parallel, or distributed systems can be especially difficult to interpret and generalize. The next two sections discuss these special hazards and suggest some remedies.

*Time and Memory*

Algorithms and programs that make heavy use of memory can exhibit significant timing anomalies, as illustrated in Figure 3.8.

The figure shows CPU (user) and elapsed (real) times for two C programs that perform matrix addition. Runtimes were measured on the HP platform described in the timing experiments of Section 3.1.2, using the `time` command. The two programs are identical, except the one with times marked "row" performs addition by traversing the matrices in row-major order as follows:

```
for (r=0; r<n; r++)
    for (c=0; c<n; c++)
        C[r][c] = A[r][c] + B[r][c];
```

and the program times marked "col" traverse the matrices in column-major order like this:

```
for (c=0; c<n; c++)
    for (r=0; r<n; r++)
        C[r][c] = A[r][c] + B[r][c];
```

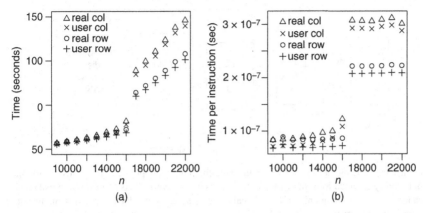

Figure 3.8. Runtimes and memory. These graphs show measurements of CPU and wall clock times for two matrix addition programs. Panel (a) shows that runtimes are different depending on whether the matrices are scanned in row-major or column-major order; also, both programs experience significant jumps in running time when their memory footprints cross a boundary. Panel (b) shows times normalized by dividing by $n^2$.

The total instruction count, proportional to $n^2$, is identical in both programs. But panel (a) shows a growing gap between the two, in both CPU (user) times and elapsed (real) times: the `col` program is almost 50 percent slower at $n = 22000$. Furthermore, both programs experience a big jump in runtimes between $n = 16000$ and $n = 17000$. Panel (b) shows normalized CPU times obtained by dividing total cost by $n^2$, the number of loop iterations. The number of instructions per iteration is constant throughout this range, but time per iteration clearly is not. The culprit is the *memory hierarchy*; here is how it works.

Recall that the CPU on each (core) processor executes a sequence of instructions (called a thread). A given instruction may use one or two data values, called *words*, which are typically four or eight bytes long. The words are located in nearby registers or else in memory. If the data are in a register, the instruction executes without delay, but if not, the CPU sends a request to the memory unit, specifying a *virtual address* for each word it needs. The instruction cannot proceed until the data arrive from memory.

As Figure 3.9 illustrates, the virtual address space is supported by a hierarchy of physical memories arranged by distance from the CPU. The memories closer to the CPU, called *caches*, are fast and small, and the memories farther from the CPU are slow and large. Memories are labeled in the figure with access times in units of instruction cycles and capacities in units of bytes. For example, an instruction must wait two to four cycles if the word it needs is in the L1 cache, but it must wait 100 cycles or more if the data must be fetched from main memory. These numbers

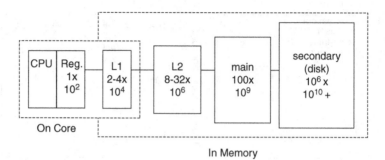

Figure 3.9. The memory hierarchy. In this simplified diagram, physical memories are arranged in order by distance from the CPU. Access times are shown in units of instruction cycles, and capacities are shown in units of bytes. Real memory systems may have capacities and response times that vary considerably from the numbers shown here and may contain additional memories not shown in the diagram.

should be considered rough approximations only, since memories in real systems vary considerably in size, speed, and configuration.

The implication for time measurement is that the time needed for any particular instruction to execute can vary by several orders of magnitude depending on where its data are located in the memory hierarchy. Time depends on memory access in several ways.

First, the memory system tries to be proactive in keeping data that will be needed soon closest to the CPU. This means it tries to predict which words will be requested next, or, conversely, which words will not be needed and so can be evicted from fast memories to make room for new requests.

Therefore, instruction times depend on whether virtual address requests are emitted by the CPU in patterns that the memory system expects to see. This accounts for the time differences recorded for row-major versus column-major matrix addition. Matrices in C programs are stored in row-major order: in the row-major computation the CPU emits virtual addresses in strict sequential order, a pattern that enjoys fast response from the memory system. The column-major computation generates addresses that step from row to row in increments by row size, a pattern that suffers slower response from the memory system. Section 4.2.1 contains more discussion of how memory access patterns affect computation time.

Second, the average time per instruction depends on the total size of the virtual address space – called the *memory footprint* – used by a given program. The large jumps in runtimes between $n = 16000$ and $n = 17000$ in Figure 3.8 occur because the program footprints cross a boundary of main memory space allocated by the operating system. When $n$ is below the boundary, the matrix data are held entirely

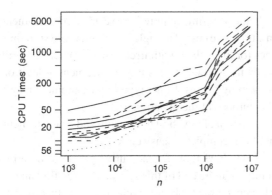

Figure 3.10. CPU times. The graph shows CPU times reported by participants in the DIMACS TSP Challenge. The x-axis (logarithmic scale) shows problem size $n$, and the $y$-axis (logarithmic scale) shows user time in seconds. Each curve shows "knees" corresponding to memory limits on the platform.

in main memory; when $n$ is above the boundary, an increasing proportion of the data are stored in secondary memory.

Similar jumps may be found when the memory footprint outgrows the capacity of any of the physical memories in the hierarchy. As a result, rather than growing smoothly as $cn^2$, runtimes for matrix addition programs are piecewise-quadratic, with different coefficients at different ranges of $n$.

This phenomenon also explains the complex arrangement of CPU time ratios shown in Figure 3.1 at the beginning of this chapter. Figure 3.10 shows the unnormalized CPU times reported by DIMACS TSP Challenge participants in that experiment. The $x$-axis shows input size $n$, and the $y$-axis shows user time in seconds (both have logarithmic scales). Each curve corresponds to a different test environment and shows a "knee" where the program footprint crosses a physical memory capacity or limit.

Finally, in Figure 3.8 we can observe a gap between CPU and elapsed times that increases with $n$. Although elapsed time measurements include all time spent waiting on the memory system, CPU times include some types of memory waits but not others. Details vary from platform to platform, but very roughly, if the data are in a nearby cache, the CPU will stall and the wait is recorded as CPU time; if the data are lower in memory, an interrupt is generated that causes the process to be swapped out of the CPU, so waiting time is not recorded.

Another memory-based timing anomaly not illustrated here arises in connection with caches. If the same code segment runs several times in a loop, the address sequence emitted by the CPU contains repetitions. Later iterations of the loop may receive faster response than early iterations because the data are still available in caches. As a result, the total time required to execute a code segment in $k$ iterations may be less than $k$ times the cost of a single iteration. A *cold start* time measurement empties all caches (or loads them with irrelevant data) before starting a time trial, while a *warm start* measurement runs the test segment at least once to "prime" the caches before timing begins. Either type of measurement may be appropriate, depending on the purpose of the experiment.

In general, the question of how best to measure and evaluate memory-expensive programs has not been completely answered.

Some Unix and Windows tools for measuring program footprints and memory usage appear in the list at the end of this section (Under Tool and Utilities). Many commercial and open-source tools are available for evaluating the way a process interacts with a memory system. These tools fall into two categories: a *trace driven simulator* runs the program and makes a record of all memory references, producing a trace file for subsequent analysis (Cachegrind is an example), and a *memory monitor* periodically checks the memory state by a method similar to interval sampling.

One property of the trace-driven approach is that processes are measured in isolation rather than in competition with other processes: this may be a flaw or a feature depending on the experiment. One problem with memory monitors is that their own use of memory interferes with process measurement.

Knuth [17] proposes an interesting approach that uses code counters to tally *mems*, which correspond to instructions likely to cause main memory requests. He argues that mem counts are more portable than runtime measurements, and provide more accurate predictions of real computation time on programs that make heavy use of memory.

### Coping with Concurrency

New measurement challenges arise when the goal of the experiment is to study time performance on multicore systems. The CPU time of a multithreaded process running on several cores is typically reported as the sum of times for all threads on all cores, while elapsed time is the interval between the start of the first thread and the end of the last thread. As a result, CPU times can be significantly higher or lower than elapsed times for a given process, depending on system loads and scheduler policies.

Elapsed time measurements depend on the whims of the scheduler. Furthermore, cycle counters and high-resolution clocks introduce timing errors because they are not perfectly synchronized among cores. A process that starts on one core and finishes on another can sometimes be observed to run backward in time!

Nevertheless, since CPU times do not reflect speedups due to concurrency, most researchers prefer to measure elapsed time using the following procedure:

1. Start the program on a single core and obtain a timestamp using a cycle counter or time-of-day clock.
2. Run the process concurrently, creating new threads as needed.
3. When all threads have finished, obtain a second timestamp from the "parent" process on the original core.

Interactions between individual cores and the memory hierarchy create more measurement problems. Suppose each core has its own set of registers and an L1 cache, but two cores share an L2 cache, and four cores share the main memory. When two threads on separate cores access (and possibly change) data values at the same virtual address, the local values in their separate caches may not agree: this is called the *cache coherence problem*. If the operating system does not guarantee cache coherence, the application programmer must write it into the program. Either way, extra time may be needed to *synchronize* the caches.

As a result, the time for one thread on one core is affected by how much its address space overlaps those of other threads. Huge swings in runtimes can occur because of complex interactions among the scheduler, the memory hierarchy, and cache synchronization mechanisms. Processor and memory configurations vary widely on modern systems, making time measurements extremely difficult to translate from one system to another.

Programs running concurrently on parallel and distributed systems are equally hard to measure. The main difference is that, unlike threads, programs typically do not share an address space. But two processes can experience *synchronization* problems when, for example, both need to access the same file or database or when one sends messages to another. Unpredictable schedulers and a wide range of platform configurations make time measurements difficult to replicate and generalize.

The usual goal in a concurrency experiment is to measure not just total time, but also the *parallel speedup*, which captures the relationship between time and the number of processors. Speedup can be defined in several ways; here are some common metrics and their meanings.

- The *absolute speedup* $A_p$ is the ratio of elapsed time $T_s$ of the fastest known sequential algorithm running on a sequential platform to the elapsed time $T_p'$ of a given parallel algorithm running on $p$ processors: that is, $A_p = T_s/T_p'$. The sequential and parallel algorithms need not be similar. It is possible to observe an absolute slowdown with this metric, when $A_p \leq 1$.
- If an algorithm is parameterized to run on $p$ processors, the *relative speedup* $R_P$ is the ratio of time on a one-processor implementation of the algorithm, to time on a $p$-processor implementation. That is, relative speedup is $R_p = T_1'/T_p'$ on a specified concurrent platform.

- The *efficiency* $E_p$ of a concurrent algorithm is the ratio of the (absolute or relative) speedup to the number of processors it uses. That is, $E_p = A_p/p$ or $E_p = R_p/p$, depending on context. While it seems reasonable to assume that $E_p$ can never be greater than 1 – doubling $p$ should not make the program more than twice as fast – such surprising behavior is not unknown to practice. Superlinear speedups may occur because of cache effects or dependencies between processor count and input size.

See Bader, Moret, and Sanders [3] for an overview of timing issues for concurrent systems.

Similar difficulties arise when the goal is to study time performance in algorithms and programs that are dominated by input/output costs and/or network communication overhead. From the point of view of a process, these systems work like (very slow) memory systems that run concurrently, can be accessed explicitly via I/O or network functions, and move data in units of blocks instead of words. Clock discrepancies can be much larger, data latency (the time between a request and the arrival of the first word of data) both larger and more variable, data transfer time is larger, and synchronization more complicated.

### Tools and Utilities

Here is a short list of tools and utilities for measuring time performance on Unix and Windows platforms.

- On Unix systems the C `sysconf()` and `clock_getres()` functions can be invoked to learn the interrupt timer interval and the clock resolution. Also see the `time(7)` manual page.
- The Unix/C `profil()` function works as `gprof` does but allows the programmer to specify which code blocks (not just functions) should be measured by the interval timer.
- The C `gettimeofday()` function returns wall clock time with resolution 0.01 second; times are reported in units of milliseconds. The `getrusage()` function reports CPU user and system times and other statistics about time, memory, and messaging.
- Code to access the time stamp counter via the RDTSC instruction and to call most of the C functions listed previously from other languages is published widely on the Internet.
- Timing of Java programs is complicated by garbage collection and the virtual machine. The JDK application launcher's `-Xprof` and `-Xrunhprof` profilers work the way `gprof` does. The `-verboseusage` flag can be used to separate out time spent during garbage collection. The `java.lang.System` package provides methods for accessing the time of day clock. Version 5 provides the

java.lang.management package with methods that report CPU times per thread.

- Different versions of Windows provide different timing tools. The GetTickCount and GetTickCount64 time-of-day counters are available on all Windows platforms, with resolutions of 10 to 16 milliseconds. On some versions timeGetTime or timeGetSystemTime provides higher resolution and/or lower latency. Windows Multimedia supports time-of-day clocks at the highest resolution permitted by the hardware. Use the C timeGet-DevCaps() function to learn the minimum and maximum timer resolutions available; use timeBeginPeriod and timeEndPeriod to increase the default timer precision temporarily; and use QueryPerformanceCounter and QueryPerformanceFrequency for high-resolution measurements.
- Windows NT and some later systems provide GetThreadTimes and Get-ProcessTimes, which work as interval timers.
- In some situations a measurement of *CPU usage* – what percentage of the CPU's cycle capacity is in use during a given period – can be more important than elapsed or CPU times. Unusually high percentages are associated with bottleneck processes that can lock up the system; on some processors, a long period of 100 percent CPU usage will overheat the core and trigger a slowdown of the instruction cycle rate. Unusually low CPU usage may indicate that the process is spending too much time waiting, say, for I/O. The Windows Usage tool reports the CPU time usage in a given time interval. In Unix, similar information can be obtained from the top and ps commands.
- Use the Unix top, free, and vmstat utilities to look at memory usage by a process or group of processes. Use iostat in Unix to measure use of the I/O system.

More information about Unix tools may be found in the manual pages. See the Intel documentation [24] for more information about processor-specific timing tools. See Wilson [23] for a survey of Windows timing functions and their merits.

## 3.2 Solution Quality

The second most commonly studied algorithm performance metric, after time, is *solution quality*. This metric is of interest for evaluating algorithms for combinatorial optimization problems, which ask for the minimum cost (or sometimes maximum cost) solution from a set of all feasible solutions for the given input instance; feasible means the solution must obey certain structural properties.

The graph coloring problem discussed in Chapter 2 is an example of an optimization (minimization) problem: given an input graph $G$, a feasible solution is defined as a coloring of the vertices such that no two adjacent vertices share the same color, and an optimal solution is a coloring that uses a minimum number of distinct colors. The related clique problem, which asks for the largest complete subgraph of $G$, is an example of a maximization problem.

An algorithm that guarantees to find the optimal solution to a problem is called an *exact* or *optimal* algorithm. Many important optimization problems are NP-hard; therefore all known exact algorithms run in exponential time. A large number of heuristic algorithms that run in polynomial time but do not guarantee to find optimal solutions have been proposed.

Let $A(I)$ denote the cost of the best solution that algorithm $A$ can find when run on instance $I$, and let $O(I)$ denote the cost of the optimal solution. If $A$ has a theoretical guarantee that $A(I)/O(I) \leq r$ for all instances in a given class, we call $A$ an *approximation algorithm* with a *performance guarantee* (or *performance ratio*) of $r$. In the case of maximization problems, the performance guarantee is usually defined by $O(I)/A(I) \leq r$ so that $r$ is always at least 1.

Heuristics and approximation algorithms are also of interest in cases where polynomial-time exact algorithms are known but are too slow to be run in a given application or context. Examples include Williamson and Goemans's study of an algorithm that computes an almost-minimum weight perfect matching in a graph [22], and Liu et al.'s algorithm for finding $k$ almost-nearest neighbors of a query point in Euclidean space [18]. Section 4.1.1 under Iterative Paradigms describes an example where approximate distance calculations are used to speed up an exact algorithm for a problem similar to all pairs shortest paths.

Solution quality can also be an important metric for problem areas besides optimization, including geometric problems involving points, lines, and objects in a D-dimensional space, and numerical problems involving mathematical analysis. Algorithms for these problems are evaluated according to a different type of "solution quality" that refers to the amount of numerical approximation error that may arise as a result of finite-precision arithmetic. Geometric algorithms are often vulnerable to *degenerate* inputs that, because of approximation errors, create impossible structures: for example, a line may be tangent to a circle but have no computable point of intersection with the circle. This section does not address solution quality in the numerical sense; some techniques described here may be applicable to the "structural" component of geometric algorithms.

The performance indicator for an experiment to evaluate a solution to an optimization problem is directly suggested by the definition of cost in the problem statement, and there may be relatively few options to consider. Nevertheless, solution quality presents particular measurement challenges, outlined in this

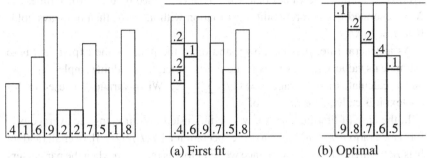

(a) First fit (b) Optimal

Figure 3.11. Bin packing. A list of 10 weights in the range [0,1]. In (a) the weights are packed by the first fit algorithm, which uses 6 bins. In (b) the weights are packed optimally in 5 bins.

section. When choices are available, thoughtful selection of performance indicators can boost the quality of information gained from the experiment. This point is illustrated in the following case study.

### Case Study: Bin Packing

To illustrate these ideas, we consider an algorithm for the NP-hard *one-dimensional bin packing problem*: given an input list $L$ of $n$ weights in the range [0,1], pack the weights into bins of capacity 1, so as to minimize the total number of bins used.

Figure 3.11 shows a list of 10 weights packed two different ways. Packing (a) is the result of the first fit (FF) approximation algorithm, which works through the weight list from left to right: for each weight, it scans the packing, looking for the first (leftmost) bin that can contain it, and if there are no such bins, it starts a new one on the right. Here first fit packs the weights into six bins, while the optimal packing (b) uses only five bins. First fit has a worst-case performance guarantee of $r = \lceil 17/10 \rceil$ and runs in $O(n \log n)$ time [11]. A C implementation of first fit, and an exponential-time exact algorithm described in Section 4.1.1 under Recursion-Heavy Paradigms can be downloaded from *AlgLab*. See [8] for a good survey of the problem and its algorithms.

The *average case* performance of first fit has been well studied both theoretically and experimentally. In the standard average-case model, the input $L \in \mathcal{L}(n, \ell, u)$ is a list of $n$ real weights drawn uniformly and independently at random from the range $[l, u]$, where $0 \leq \ell < u \leq 1$. Let $F(L)$ denote the number of bins used by first fit to pack $L$, and let $O(L)$ be the optimal number of bins needed to pack $L$.

Suppose an experiment is developed to study average case performance of an algorithm like first fit. Let $X$ be a random variate, presumably a performance indicator, generated in one trial. The *expectation* of $X$, denoted $E[X]$, is the weighted average of all possible values that $X$ can take (weighted by their probabilities). If $X$ is generated from a probability distribution with mean $\mu$, then it always holds that $\mu = E[X]$.

As a general rule, $\mu$ is unknown, and often the point of the experiment is to estimate its value. One way to estimate $\mu$ is to generate $t$ random samples $X_1 \ldots X_t$ and to calculate their average $\overline{X} = (1/t) \sum_{i=1}^{t} X_i$. When variate $X$ is used in this context it is called an *estimator* of $\mu$.

In the case of first fit, suppose we are interested in estimating the average performance ratio $\rho(n, \ell, u)$ equal to the expectation $E[F(L)/O(L)]$, over all random lists $L \in \mathcal{L}(n, \ell, u)$. For convenience we refer to this ratio as $\rho$ when the parameters are understood.

An experiment to estimate $\rho$ would generate a sample of $t$ random lists $L_1 \ldots L_t$ from $\mathcal{L}(n, \ell, u)$ and run first fit on each. The estimate can be calculated by

$$\overline{R} = \frac{1}{t} \sum_{i=1}^{t} \frac{F(L_i)}{O(L_i)},$$

but since bin packing is NP-hard, the value of $O(L_i)$ is not available.

The next few sections consider alternative strategies for finding estimates and bounds on $\rho$, as well as alternatives to $\rho$. Although first fit is used for illustration purposes, these strategies can be considered in any experiment where solution quality is to be evaluated.

### 3.2.1  Bounding the Optimal Solution

For some minimization problems it is possible to identify a lower bound on the cost of the optimal solution that is easy to compute for each input instance. Such a lower bound provides a convenient and reliable way to estimate an upper bound on $\rho$. For maximization problems an upper bound on optimal cost would be needed.

In bin packing, the sum of the weights in list $L_i$ is such a lower bound: for example, if the weights sum to 123.4, the optimal packing must use at least 124 bins. Let $S(L_i)$ denote the sum of the weights in list $L_i$ and consider the empirical ratio $R_1(L_i)$ defined as follows.

$$R_1(L_i) = \frac{F(L_i)}{S(L_i)}$$

A statistician would call $R_1$ a *biased estimator* of $\rho$, since $R_1(L_i) \geq R(L_i)$ for any list. This implies that the mean

$$\overline{R_1} = \frac{1}{t} \sum_{i=1}^{t} \frac{F(L_i)}{S(L_i)}$$

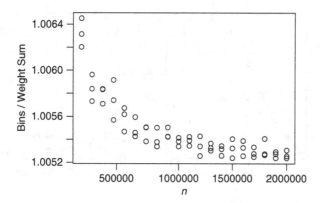

Figure 3.12. First fit. Measurements of $R_1(L_i)$ for parameters $l = 0$, $u = 0.5$, three random trials at each design point.

is an upper bound estimate on $\rho$.

Bias can be a powerful ally whenever the experiment involves estimating some quantity $q$: if direct measurement of the estimator is difficult or expensive, consider measuring quantity $q'$ that is a known upper or lower bound on $q$.

**Guideline 3.10** *To find a bound on quantity x, look for a biased estimator that is experimentally more tractable than an unbiased estimator of x.*

Figure 3.12 shows measurements of $R_1(L_i)$ for FF in three random trials at design points $\ell = 0$, $u = 0.5$, and $n = (1 \times 10^5 \ldots 2 \times 10^6)$. The ratio $R_1(L_i)$ tends to decrease toward 1 as $n$ increases; overall the highest ratio observed in these tests is 1.0065. Since we know that $\rho \geq 1$, this provides an upper bound estimate of $\rho$ that is within .065 percent of its true value.

Experimental measurements of this type are easy to misinterpret if the lower bound is not very close to the optimal cost or if the gap between the two varies with problem parameters. For example, an alternative lower bound on $O(L_i)$ is the number of weights in the list that are larger than 0.5 (half a bin), since no two such weights can share a bin. Let $H(L_i)$ denote the number of weights in $L_i$ that occupy more than half a bin.

When weights are drawn uniformly at random from $(0, 1)$, the expected value of $H(L_i)$ is identical to the expected value of the weight sum $S(L_i)$. But when $\ell > 0$, it is possible that $H(L_i) \geq S(L_i)$.

Figure 3.13 illustrates the difference. Panel (a) shows how $S(L_i)$ and $H(L_i)$ vary with $\ell$ when $u$ is fixed at 1 and $n$ is fixed at 100,000. Panel (b) shows how the two ratios $\overline{R_1}$ and $\overline{R_2}$ (defined analogously to $R_1$ with $H(L_i)$ in the denominator) create different views of first fit. The performance ratio $\overline{R_1}$, based on weight sums, can be as large as 1.35 when $\ell = 0.5$, but the performance ratio $\overline{R_2}$ is never more

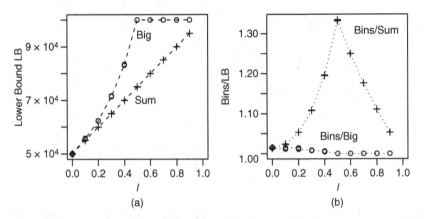

Figure 3.13.   Lower bounds on packings. Panel (a) compares weight sums $S(L_i)$ to the number of large weights $H(L_i)$ in three trials at each design point $n = 100000$, $u = 1.0$, and $\ell$, as shown on the x-axis. Panel (b) compares the ratios $R_1(L_i)$ and $R_2(L_i)$ from these lower bounds.

than 1.016. The difference is not in how well the first fit algorithm performs, but rather how our perception of performance is shaped by these two performance indicators.

**Guideline 3.11** *When evaluating solution quality, use tight bounds on optimal solutions to obtain tight bounds on performance ratios. Do not assume that trends observed experimentally imply similar trends in performance guarantees.*

This technique can be applied to any optimization problem where a suitable bound on optimal cost can be found. For example, the traveling salesman problem (TSP) is, given a set of $n$ points with distances defined among them, to find a minimum-length tour through all the points. Several easy-to-compute lower bounds on optimal tour lengths are known, including the costs of the minimum spanning tree and of the minimum-weight perfect matching. Johnson et al. [13] have shown empirically that the Held-Karp lower bound on tour cost is within 0.8 percent of optimal tour length for many categories of random graphs.

A general technique for finding lower (and upper) bounds in this context – which in fact produced the Held-Karp lower bound – is to cast the problem into linear programming form. Every minimization problem $A$ expressed as a linear program has a maximization counterpart $B$ (and vice versa). The weak duality theorem implies that the cost of any feasible solution to $A$ is a lower bound on the optimal solution to $B$. Therefore, any heuristic algorithm for $B$ produces a solution that can be translated into a lower bound on the optimal solution to $A$. See [15] or [19] for more about linear programming problems and their properties.

### 3.2.2  Linearity of Expectation

Our second strategy for measuring solution quality looks at sums and differences in costs rather than ratios like $\rho$.

In statistics, a property known as *linearity of expectation* assures that the following identities hold for any random variates $X$ and $Y$ and constants $a$ and $b$.

$$E[X \pm a] = E[X] \pm a$$

$$E[X \pm Y] = E[X] \pm E[Y]$$

$$E[aX \pm bY] = aE[X] \pm bE[Y]$$

It does not matter whether $X$ and $Y$ are independent or correlated with one another. In contrast, it cannot be assumed in general that $E[X/Y] = E[X]/E[Y]$.

Linearity of expectation can be exploited in several ways. For example, suppose the goal of the experiment is to estimate the expected number of bins used by first fit. Let $f = E[F(L_i)]$ denote this expectation for a given design point $(n, \ell, u)$. The straightforward way to estimate $f$ is to calculate the mean of $F(L_i)$ measured over several random trials. However, an alternative strategy might yield better estimates, as follows.

First, note that the expected value of the sum of $n$ weights drawn uniformly from $[\ell, u]$ can be calculated by

$$E[S(L_i)] = \frac{n(\ell + u)}{2}.$$

Define the *empty space* in a first fit packing as the difference between the number of bins used and the sum of weight in the packing, and let $G(L_i) = F(L_i) - S(L_i)$ denote this "gap" between total weight and total capacity. We have

$$E[F(L_i)] = E[G(L_i) + S(L_i)]$$
$$= E[G(L_i)] + E[S(L_i)]$$
$$= E[G(L_i)] + \frac{n(\ell + u)}{2}.$$

Instead of measuring $F(L_i)$ directly, we could instead measure $G(L_i)$ and use it as shown in the bottom formula to estimate $f$.

Figure 3.14 shows results of 15 trials at the design points $n = 100000$, $\ell = 0$, and $u = (0.5 \ldots 1.0)$; all measurements are divided by $u$ for easier comparison on this scale. The circles show (scaled) measurements of $F(L_i)$, and the plusses show $G(L_i) + n(\ell + u)/2$ in the same trials. Both samples have the same expectation at each design point, but the much smaller range in the latter set yields tighter estimates of $f(n, \ell, u)$. This is an example of a *variance reduction technique* described more fully in Section 6.1.

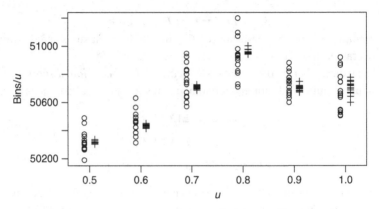

Figure 3.14. Two estimators. The graph shows two ways to estimate the mean $f(100000,0,u)$ for $u = (0.5, \ldots 1.0)$. Circles show direct measurements of $F(L_i)$ in 15 random trials, scaled by $u$ for easy comparison. The crosses show measurements of $G(L_i) + n(\ell + u)/2$, also scaled. Both data samples have the same expectations, but variance is much smaller in the second set.

Next, linearity of expectation can sometimes be applied to yield better insights about asymptotic performance. The asymptotic performance ratio of first fit is defined as $\rho(\ell, u) = \lim_{n \to \infty} \rho(n, \ell, u)$. We know that $\rho(\ell, u) \leq R_1$ (the estimator based on weight sums); assuming that $R_1$ approaches its asymptote from above, we could run tests at very large $n$ to get an upper bound on the asymptotic ratio. But no test at finite $n$ can be used to evaluate whether that ratio equals 1 (its lower bound) or is strictly greater than 1. (A result of $\rho(\ell, u) = 1$ would imply that first fit is asymptotically optimal in the average-case model.)

We can approach the question from a different direction, however. Since $F(L_i) = G(L_i) + S(L_i)$ we know that

$$\rho(\ell, u) = \lim_{n \to \infty} E\left[ \frac{F(L_i)}{O(L_i)} \right]$$

$$= \lim_{n \to \infty} E\left[ \frac{G(L_i) + S(L_i)}{O(L_i)} \right]$$

$$= \lim_{n \to \infty} E\left[ \frac{G(L_i)}{O(L_i)} \right] + E\left[ \frac{S(L_i)}{O(L_i)} \right]$$

$$\leq \lim_{n \to \infty} E\left[ \frac{G(L_i)}{S(L_i)} \right] + 1$$

The constant 1 can be substituted on the bottom line because weight sum is a lower bound on the optimal number of bins. If the ratio on the bottom line is asymptotically 0, we know that $\rho(\ell, u) = 1$ and that first fit is asymptotically optimal. Since $E[S(L_i)] = n(\ell + u)/2$, this condition is met whenever $G(L_i)$ is sublinear in $n$.

From a data analysis point of view, we have converted the problem of trying to determine whether the ratio $E[F(L_i)/S(L_i)]$ converges to 1 or to a constant $1 + \epsilon$ – which is impossible using data at finite $n$ – to the problem of trying to determine whether $E[G(L_i)]$ is a sublinear function of $n$.

The latter problem turns out to be more amenable to data analysis. Figure 7.14 shows that $G(L_i)$ gives strong evidence of growing no faster than $n^{0.69}$ when weights are drawn uniformly from $[0, 1]$. Bentley et al. [5] first reported this experimental result; subsequent theoretical analysis has produced an $O(n^{2/3})$ bound on empty space, which implies that FF is asymptotically optimal. See [8] for details.

In general, there is no guarantee that one formulation of a question about an asymptotic property will be easier than another to study experimentally. But since ratios and differences have distinct convergence rates and variance properties, it never hurts to check.

Linearity of expectation can also be applied in cases where the expected value of the optimal solution is known for a class of inputs. In bin packing average case analysis, the expected optimal number of bins, $\omega(n, \ell, u) = E[O(L_i)]$, can be calculated for specific combinations of $\ell$ and $u$. For example, when the list is symmetric around 0.5 (i.e., when $\ell = 1 - u$), the list allows a *perfect packing*, which means that the optimal bin count is asymptotically equal to the weight sum. That is, $\lim_{n\to\infty} \omega(n, \ell, u) = n(\ell + u)/2$.

This fact does not help with estimating the asymptotic performance ratio $\rho(n, \ell, u) = E[F(L_i)/O(L_i)]$, since it cannot be assumed that $E[F(L_i)/O(L_i)] = E[F(L_i)]/E[O(L_i)]$. But it can be used to estimate the expected performance difference $\delta(n, \ell, u) = E[F(L_i) - O(L_i)]$, which is equal to $E[F(L_i)] - \omega(n, \ell, u)$.

**Guideline 3.12** *Exploit linearity of expectation to reformulate the experimental problem, and substitute calculated expectations for empirical averages when possible.*

This idea can be applied more generally whenever optimal expected costs are known or can be closely estimated. For example:

- In the geometric TSP the asymptotic expected optimal tour cost on $n$ points drawn uniformly from the unit square is of the form $\alpha\sqrt{n}$. Experiments have bounded the asymptotic constant $\alpha$ by $.7124 \pm .0002$. Similar bounds are known for geometric point sets in higher dimensions, under different distance metrics, and for random graphs with uniform edge weights. See [13] for details.
- The expected optimal graph coloring cost – called the chromatic number – is known for some random graph classes. Let $G(n, p)$ be a random graph on $n$ vertices such that each edge appears with probability $p$. The expected chromatic number of $G(n, 1/2)$ is asymptotically $n/2\log_2 n$; bounds are also known for

graphs parameterized by $G(n, d/n)$ for given values of $d$. See Bollobás [6] or Achlioptas and Naor [1] for more.

- Input to the 3CNF satisfiability problem is a Boolean formula $B$ in a special format, containing $m$ clauses and $n$ variables. Suppose a random Boolean formula is constructed of $m$ clauses drawn uniformly from the set of all clauses on $n$ variables. Let $k = m/n$. Some exact formulas and experimental bounds are known on the expected proportion of satisfiable Boolean formulas drawn at random according to $k$. (For details see the survey by Dubois [10].) Since satisfiability is not an optimization problem, our standard definition of performance ratio $r$ does not apply: to evaluate a satisfiability algorithm, generate pools of random instances according to $k$ and compare the proportion of instances satisfied by the algorithm to the expected proportion of satisfiable instances in the pool.

### 3.2.3   Known Optimal Solutions

Our next strategy for evaluating solution quality is to restrict the experiment to instances for which optimal solutions are known or can be easily calculated. This approach may be used in two scenarios: when optimal solutions are known by construction and when optimal solutions have been reported in the research literature.

In the first scenario, inputs are built in such a way that the optimal cost (or a bound on it) can be inferred from the construction method. For example, we could build a random list of $n$ weights from $[0, 1]$ by repeating the following process $n/2$ times: generate a random uniform $x$ from $(0, 1)$ and create a pair of weights $x, 1 - x$. Since each weight can be matched perfectly with its mate, the optimal packing uses exactly as many bins as the weight sum $n/2$. With this class of random instances $O(L_i)$ is known exactly, so it is possible to measure $\overline{R} = E[F(L_i)/O(L_i)]$ directly. More list-generation ideas could be developed along these lines by using random numbers to "break" up a block of completely filled bins. The weight lists could then be randomly scrambled to "hide" the optimal packing from the first fit algorithm.

One drawback to this idea is that these generation schemes do not meet our original definition of the random input space $\mathcal{L}(n, \ell, u)$ because weights are not drawn *independently* at random: instead, the value of one weight depends on the value of another. Experimental results using these inputs cannot be applied to the original question about average-case performance. More generally, it may be hard to justify the relevance of such an input class to standard questions about performance.

Another objection is that the optimal solution may not be very well hidden from the algorithm: first fit can pack these lists very well, and so can most other approximation algorithms. Experiments on contrived easy-to-solve instances do not, as a general rule, shed new light on algorithm performance. A few promising exceptions to this objection have appeared, for example:

- A generator of k-colorable graphs that avoids some known pitfalls, is available at Joseph Culberson's graph coloring resources, Page [9]. The generator can produce six different types of graphs with known (but hidden) k-colorings. A generator of graphs with hidden maximal independent sets, suitable for studying algorithms for the clique problem, is also available.
- The BHOSLIB site, maintained by Ke Xu [25], contains benchmark instances for several optimization problems, including clique, independent set, vertex cover, and vertex coloring. Most graphs are produced by generating hard random satisfiability instances and then using standard transformations to create instances for the target problems, on the theory that hard Satisfiability instances remain hard under these transformations.

The second scenario involves using testbed and benchmark instances for which optimal solutions have been reported in the scientific literature. A simple Web search will reveal many online repositories containing instances for bin packing, several accompanied by announced optimal solutions.

Two pitfalls arise when using this approach. First, as is often the case with constructed inputs, testbed instances may not be hard enough to challenge the algorithm. Long-standing testbeds often contain instances that become obsolete over time – too small, or too well-understood – because of improvements in algorithms and computing technologies. Such inputs may not be relevant to modern computational problems. There is always a danger that good results on easy test sets lead to misplaced optimism: your algorithm may perform brilliantly on those instances, but so might a much simpler and faster algorithm.

A second pitfall occurs when a "best known solution" becomes confused with an "optimal solution" for a given instance. Even experienced researchers have been caught in this trap. Gent [12] mentions one published benchmark set for bin packing in which all but one of the announced optimal solutions are now known to be incorrect.

### 3.2.4 *The Right Tool for the Job*

A key lesson from this discussion of performance indicators for solution quality is that it is not necessary to limit the experiment to measuring "solution cost" as defined by the problem. The fundamental difficulty of computing optimal solutions to NP-hard problems is an obstacle to experimental analysis, but not an insurmountable one. A little maneuvering may turn up alternative performance indicators that are better suited to experimental analysis.

In particular, since algorithm analysis is often concerned with finding bounds on theoretical quantities, biased estimators can be more tractable and more useful than straightforward estimators in many cases.

As a general rule, the most reliable and useful experimental (upper) bounds on performance ratios are likely to come from tight (lower) bounds on solution quality. Unfortunately, suitable bounds are not always known, and if too far from optimal, they can give misleading and overpessimistic views of performance.

As the examples using linearity of expectation illustrate, it is sometimes possible to apply arithmetic manipulations to find alternative performance indicators that are equally informative from an algorithm analysis point of view but have better properties from a data analysis point of view.

Another good strategy is to replace an experimental measurement of some quantity with an exact calculation of that quantity, when possible. This principle can be applied to computing the expected optimal solution cost for random classes of inputs and, in some cases, computing exact optimal costs for specific instances.

Finally, in any experiment it is usually a worthwhile exercise to look at the data set from many angles – ratios, differences, proportions, inverses, et cetera – to compare convergence rates and variance properties and find the best "view" of performance. Several more tips and guidelines for choosing performance indicators to maximize the quality of data analysis may be found in Chapter 6.

### 3.3  Chapter Notes

This chapter has surveyed a large assortment of performance indicators to be used in experiments on algorithms. Here are the guidelines presented in this chapter.

3.1 *It is easier to measure components separately and analyze their combined cost than to measure an aggregate cost and try to break it into components during analysis.*

3.2 *Use a doubling experiment to perform a quick validation check of your cost model.*

3.3 *For best timer accuracy, use an interval timer and design tests so that the process being measured runs for at least 100 milliseconds; a second or more is better.*

3.4 *If short-lived processes must be measured, use cycle counts or elapsed time, but check that the measured time interval is greater than both timer resolution and timer latency. When using a cycle counter, take several measurements and record the smallest cycle count observed.*

3.5 *Whenever possible, measure time on lightly loaded systems; in any case, find out how much timing variation to expect from your test environment.*

3.6 *Do not use compiler-based code profilers in combination with compiler optimization.*

3.7 *Performance indicators can be aimed at different points on the scale between abstract algorithms and instantiated code. Match your choice to the larger goals of the experiment.*

3.8 *Build runtime predictions by combining platform-independent models of dominant costs with platform-specific measurements of those costs.*

3.9 *Choose narrow performance indicators to highlight differences between design strategies. Choose wide performance indicators to understand those differences in context.*

3.10 *To find a bound on quantity $x$, look for a biased estimator that is experimentally more tractable than an unbiased estimator of $x$.*

3.11 *When evaluating solution quality, use tight bounds on optimal solutions to obtain tight bounds on performance ratios. Do not assume that trends observed experimentally imply similar trends in performance guarantees.*

3.12 *Exploit linearity of expectation to reformulate the experimental problem, and substitute calculated expectations for empirical averages when possible.*

## 3.4 Problems and Projects

The C program `markov.c` discussed in Section 3.1, as well as an alternative version that uses a hash table instead of a sorted array to implement data structure $D$, may be downloaded from *AlgLab*. A C implementation of the first fit algorithm discussed in Section 3.2, called `ff.c`, is also available together with implementations of other bin packing algorithms. Here are some suggestions for experimental projects using these and other test programs that might be at hand.

1. Modify the word and character cost formulas (3.2) and (3.3), by adding terms and/or finding better coefficients, to increase their accuracy and range of applicability. Do different languages (English, German, Spanish) require substantially different cost models? What about files containing poetry or computer programs?

2. Suppose character cost is adopted as the performance indicator. Would it be better to specify the input parameters $n, m, k$ in units of characters rather than words? Why or why not? How would this change the analysis? How would this change the experiment?

3. Replicate the timing experiments using `markov.c` in your home environment, on different platforms if possible. How much variation in runtimes do you observe? How much do environmental factors such as system load affect your measurements? Where are the "knees" due to physical memory boundaries located?

4. Can you combine abstract cost models and platform-specific time measurements to predict computation time on your own system? What is the maximum

range (in terms of algorithm parameters $n, m, k$) for which your predictions are
accurate? How accurate are they?

5. Compare the sorted array and the hash table implementations of markov.c.
What performance indicator is best for this comparison? How do different
performance indicators give different views of comparative performance?

6. Jon Bentley points out that the elapsed time of the random generation step
in markov.c is probably improved because it immediately follows a binary
search, which warms up the caches with the same memory addresses. How large
is this effect? Compare the runtimes of the random selection code using warm
and cold starts for the cache. Read about cache-efficient versions of binary
search and evaluate their effectiveness in this context.

7. Implement an approximation algorithm for your favorite NP-hard problem and
apply the techniques of Section 3.2 to find alternative performance indicators for measuring solution quality. Which ones give the best insights about
performance?

8. Develop an instance generator for which optimal costs are known but hidden
from your approximation algorithm. How well do your algorithm and simpler
algorithms perform on these instances?

9. Visit several input repositories for bin packing on the Web and run ff.c on
their contents. Does your choice of performance indicator change depending
on whether the instances are from generators or real applications?

## Bibliography

[1] Achlioptas, Dimitris, and Assaf Naor, "The two possible values of the Chromatic
Number of a random graph," *Annals of Mathematics* Vol 162, Issue 3, pp. 1333–49,
2005.

[2] Ahuja, Ravindra K., Thomas L. Magnanti, and James B. Orlin, Chapter 18 in *Network
Flows: Theory, Algorithms, and Applications*, Prentice Hall, 1993.

[3] Bader, David A., Bernard M. E. Moret, and Peter Sanders, "Algorithm Engineering for
Parallel Computation," in R. Fleischer, B. Moret, and E.K. Schmidt, eds., *Experimental
Algorithmics: From Algorithm Design to Robust and Efficient Software*, Dagstuhl
Seminar 00371, Springer LNCS 2547, 2002.

[4] Bentley, Jon L., Section 15.3, "Generating Text", in *Programming Pearls*, 2nd ed.,
Addison-Wesley, 2000. See also the companion Web site www.cs.bell-labs.
com/csm/cs/pearls.

[5] Bentley, Jon L., David S. Johnson, F. Tom Leighton, Catherine C. McGeoch, and Lyle
A. McGeoch, "An experimental study of bin packing" *Proceedings of the 21st Annual
Allerton Conference on Computing, Control, and Communication*, 1983.

[6] Bollobás, Bélla, *Random Graphs*, 2nd ed., Cambridge University Press, 2001.

[7] Bryant, Randal E., and David R. O'Hallaron, Chapter 9 in *Computer Systems: A
Programmer's Perspective*, Prentice-Hall, 2003.

[8] Coffman, E. G., Jr., M. R. Garey, and D. S. Johnson, "Approximation Algorithms for Bin Packing: A Survey," in D. Hochbaum, ed., *Approximation Algorithms for NP-Hard Problems*, PWS Publishing Boston, pp. 46–93, 1997.

[9] Culberson, Joseph, "Joseph Culberson's Graph Coloring Resources Page" Available from: webdocs.cs.ualberta.ca/~joe/Coloring.

[10] Dubois, Olivier, "Upper bounds on the Satisfiability threshold," *Theoretical Computer Science*, Elsevier Science Publishers, Vol 265, pp. 187–97, August 2001.

[11] Garey, M. R., R. L. Graham, D. S. Johnson, and A. C. Yao, "Resource constrained scheduling as generalized bin packing," *Journal of Combinatorial Theory Series A*, Vol 21, pp. 257–298, 1976.

[12] Gent, Ian, "Heuristic solution of open bin packing problems," *Journal of Heuristics*, Vol 3, Issue 4, pp. 299–304, March 1998.

[13] Johnson, D. S., L. A. McGeoch, and E. E. Rothberg, "Asymptotic experimental analysis for the Held-Karp traveling salesman bound." in *Proceedings of the Seventh Annual ACM-SIAM Symposium on Discrete Algorithms*, pp. 341–50, January 1996.

[14] Johnson, D. S., and L. A. McGeoch, "Experimental Analysis of Heuristics for the STSP," in G. Gutin and A. P. Punnen, eds., *The Traveling Salesman Problem and Its Variations*, Kluwer, Boston, 369–443. 2002. See also the Results Page at www.research.att.com/~dsj/chtsp.

[15] Karloff, Howard, *Linear Programming*, Birkhäuser, 1991.

[16] Kernighan, B. W., and R. Pike, Chapter 3, "Design and Implementation", in *The Practice of Programming*, Addison-Wesley, 1999.

[17] Knuth, Donald E., in *The Stanford GraphBase: A Platform for Combinatorial Computing*, ACM Press and Addison-Wesley, 464–467 1993. For an example of mem counting, see the MILES_SPAN program at the companion Web site www-cs-faculty.stanford.edu/~knuth/sgb.html

[18] Liu, Ting, Andrew W. Moore, Alex Gray, and Ke Yang, "An investigation of practical approximate nearest neighbor algorithms," Proceedings of *Neural Information Processing Systems (NIPS 2004)*, Vancouver, BC, Canada, 2004.

[19] Papadimitriou, Christos H., and Kenneth Steiglitz, *Combinatorial Optimization: Algorithms and Complexity*, Dover Publications, 1998.

[20] *Project Gutenberg*, Availabel from: www.gutenberg.org.

[21] *Valgrind Home*, Availabel from: valgrind.org.

[22] Williamson, David P., and Michel X. Goemans, "Computational experience with an approximation algorithm on large-scale Euclidean matching instances," *INFORMS Journal on Computing*, Vol 8, No 1, pp. 28–40, Winter 1996.

[23] Wilson, Matthew, "Win32 performance measurement options," *Dr. Dobbs Journal*, May 1, 2003. Available from: www.ddj.com/windows/184416651.

[24] Work, Paul, and Khang Nguyen, "Measure code sections using the Enhanced Timer," January 13, 2009. Availabel from: software.intel.com/en-us/intel-sdp-home/, accessed 1/2011, keyword search on RDTSC.

[25] Xu, Ke, "BHOSLIB: Benchmarks with hidden optimum solutions for graph problems," *The Math Forum @ Drexel*, Drexel University, 1994–2010. Available from: mathforum.org/library/view/65366.html, accessed 10/7/2010.

# 4

# Tuning Algorithms, Tuning Code

In almost every computation a great variety of arrangements for the succession of the processes is possible, and various considerations must influence the selection amongst them for the purposes of a Calculating Engine. One essential object is to choose that arrangement which shall tend to reduce to a minimum the time necessary for completing the calculation.

Ada Byron, *Memoir on the Analytic Engine*, 1843

This chapter considers an essential question raised by Lady Byron in her famous memoir: How to make it run faster?

This question can be addressed at all levels of the algorithm design hierarchy sketched in Figure 1.1 of Chapter 1, including systems, algorithms, code, and hardware. Here we focus on tuning techniques that lie between the algorithm design and hardware levels. We start with the assumption that the system analysis and abstract algorithm design work has already taken place, and that a basic implementation of an algorithm with good asymptotic performance is in hand. The tuning techniques in this chapter are meant to improve upon the abstract design work, not replace it.

Tuning exploits the gaps between practical experience and the simplifying assumptions necessary to theory, by focusing on constant factors instead of asymptotics, secondary instead of dominant costs, and performance on "typical" inputs rather than theoretical classes. Many of the ideas presented here are known in the folklore under the general rubric of "code tuning." But in this chapter we distinguish between *algorithm tuning*, which considers higher-level constructs like data structures and algorithm paradigms, and *code tuning*, which looks at low-level structures like loops and procedure calls.

As was pointed out in Section 1.1, best performance is achieved by combining speedups at all layers of the algorithm design hierarchy. Bentley [4] illustrates this point with an engineering project to speed up an exact algorithm for TSP.

He implemented eight versions of the algorithm, each incorporating either an "algorithm tuning" or "code tuning" technique. The table that follows shows the running times (in seconds) on problem sizes $N = 10\ldots30$; each version is marked (a) or (c), denoting an algorithmic or code-tuning speedup, respectively.

| | $N = 10$ | 13 | 14 | 20 | 27 | 30 |
|---|---|---|---|---|---|---|
| V1 | 69.68 | | | | | |
| V2 (a) | 6.97 | | | | | |
| V3 (c) | 2.81 | | | | | |
| V4 (c) | .57 | 13.71 | 74.86 | | | |
| V5 (a) | .10 | .08 | .43 | 49.52 | | |
| V6 (a) | | .02 | .07 | 2.61 | 92.85 | |
| V8 (a) | | .01 | .04 | 1.09 | 60.42 | 137.92 |

While Version 8 requires just more than two minutes to solve a problem of size $n = 30$, Bentley estimates that Version 1 would require about 10 billion times the age of the universe to run to completion. (He did not perform the experiment.)

Overall, the largest individual speedups were obtained by algorithmic improvements: Version 2 produced a speedup proportional to $n$, and Versions 5, 6, and 8 contributed individual speedups by factors ranging from 3 to 174, depending on problem size. Code tuning efforts in Versions 3 and 4 contributed individual speedups by factors between 2 and 13, again depending on problem size. More importantly, the combined effect of these individual improvements is multiplicative: when $n = 10$, Version 5 is 697 times faster than Version 1; when $n = 20$, Version 8 is 746 times faster than Version 5.

The chapter is organized around two basic approaches to making code run faster.

1. *Reduce instruction counts.* As a general rule, the fewer instructions executed, the faster the code will run. There are two ways to reduce the instruction count for a given code block $B$: either decrease the number of times $B$ is performed or decrease the number of instructions contained in $B$. These techniques are discussed in Section 4.1.
2. *Reduce instruction times.* On modern systems, individual instructions can take varying amounts of time, ranging from nanoseconds to milliseconds. The second approach to tuning involves identifying the time-expensive instructions and reducing their counts (or their times). Section 4.2 surveys ideas for exploiting properties of the memory hierarchy and of multicore architectures to reduce total computation time even though total instruction counts may increase. These

techniques can be applied at the algorithm level, for example, by reorganizing a data structure, or at the code level, for example, by rewriting a loop.

Tuning is not always necessary, or even desirable. Tuning can be antithetical to principles of good software design, because it complexifies code, is harder to maintain, and often exploits narrow assumptions about applications and platforms. Section 4.3 lists some issues to consider when deciding whether or not to undertake a tuning project and proposes a systematic procedure that minimizes errors and maximizes efficiency when the decision is to go forward.

## 4.1 Reducing Instruction Counts

Algorithm tuning has received less systematic treatment than code tuning in the experimental literature; therefore, we start with two case studies to illustrate the basic approach. Section 4.1.1 extends these examples and presents some general guidelines for tuning algorithms.

### Case Study: Bin Packing by Exhaustive Search

The bin packing problem was introduced in Section 3.2: Given a list $L$ containing $n$ weights from the real interval $[0, 1)$, pack them into unit-capacity bins so as to minimize the number of bins used.

Figure 4.1 shows an example of 10 weights packed two different ways. Packing (a) is the result of using the next fit packing algorithm. Next fit works through the list from left to right, maintaining a single "open" bin as it goes. It packs as many weights as possible into the open bin and starts a new bin when the next weight will not fit. Thus (.4, .1) are packed into the first bin, but .6 will not fit, so it starts a new bin, and so forth. The next fit rule packs this list into seven bins, while the

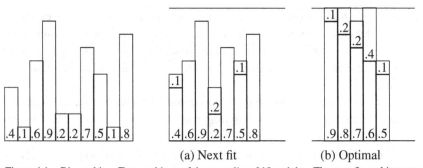

              (a) Next fit                 (b) Optimal

Figure 4.1. Bin packing. Two packings of the same list of 10 weights. The next fit packing uses seven bins, and the optimal packing uses five bins.

```
1 global    list[0..n-1];    // list to be packed
2 global    optcost;         // minimum bin count

3 procedure binPack (k) {
4   if (k == n) {
5       b = binCount();              // use next fit
6       if (b < optcost) optcost = b;
    }
7   else
8     for (i = k; i < n ; i++) {
9         swap (list, k, i);         // try it
10        binPack (k+1);             // recur
11        swap (list, k, i);         // restore it
    }

 }
```

Figure 4.2. binPack. An exhaustive search algorithm for bin packing.

optimal packing (b) uses only five bins to pack the same list. Next fit runs in $O(n)$ time and can never use more than twice as many bins as the optimal packing (since every bin but the last one is at least half-full).

The bin packing problem is NP-hard; that means that no polynomial-time algorithm is known that guarantees to find an optimal packing of every list. In this section we consider an exponential-time exact algorithm that does guarantee to find optimal packings.

The binPack procedure sketched in Figure 4.2 is an example of an algorithm in the *exhaustive search* paradigm, which solves an optimization problem by (exhaustively) checking all possible solutions. The procedure constructs all permutations of the list recursively, using k as a parameter. At stage k, the elements in list[0...k-1] have been fixed in the permutation; the stage considers all remaining elements for position list[k] and recurses to generate the rest of the permutation. Once a permutation is complete (when k == n), the algorithm calls binCount() to build a next fit packing and saves the cost of the best packing found as optcost.

It is not difficult to see that this algorithm must find an optimal packing because that packing can be decomposed into the permutation that would produce it under next fit. The algorithm takes $O(n \cdot n!)$ time to generate all $n!$ permutations and compute binCount for each. Java implementations of binPack and the several variations discussed here are available for downloading from *AlgLab*. The run-time experiments mentioned in this section were performed on the HP platform described in the first timing experiment of Section 3.1.2.

Like most exhaustive search algorithms, binPack is painfully slow: a Java implementation takes a little more than an hour to run through all permutations when $n = 14$. (In contrast, the polynomial-time first fit algorithm in Section 3.2 can pack a list of size $n = 100,000$ in about 0.01 second.)

Here are some ideas for making the exact algorithm run faster via algorithm tuning.

*Branch-and-bound.* The *branch-and-bound* technique is an important tuning strategy for any exhaustive-search algorithm. The idea is to insert a test to compare the minimum cost found so far (optcost) to a lower-bound estimate on the final cost of a partially constructed solution. If the lower bound is greater than optcost, then this partial solution cannot possibly lead to a new optimum, and further recursion can be abandoned. We say that this "branch" of the recursion tree can be "pruned."

Here are three lower bounds that could be checked against optcost at stage k.

- The bin count for a partial list list[0..k] is a lower bound on the bin count for the whole list. Define function binCount(k) to compute the bin count for list[0..k].
- The sum of weights in a list (rounded up) is a lower bound on bin count for the list. For example, if the weights sum to 12.3, at least 13 bins are needed to pack them. Define function weightSum(k+1) to sum the weights in list[k+1..n-1]. The quantity

```
Ceiling (weightSum(k+1) - (1-list[k]))
```

  is a lower bound on bin count for the partial list in list[0..k]. The Ceiling function performs the rounding-up step. The negated second term reflects the possibility that some weights, totaling at most (1 - list[k]), might be packed together with the weight in list[k] and not included in the sum.
- The sum of these two lower bounds is even better. If

```
binCount(k) +
   Ceiling( weightSum(k+1) - (1-list[k]) ) >= optcost
```

  then further recursion on the list can be skipped.

Applying this tuneup to the loop in Figure 4.2 we obtain the following code fragment.

```
8       for (i = k; i<n ; i++) {
9           swap(list, k, i)         // try it
9.1         b = binCount(k);
9.2         w = weightSum(k+1);
9.3         if(b+ Ceiling(w-(1-list[k])) < optcost)
```

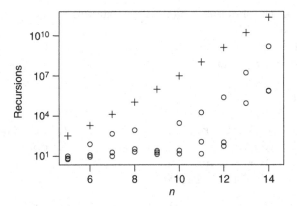

Figure 4.3. Branch-and-bound. The $x$-axis marks problem sizes $n$. The $y$-axis marks total recursive stages executed, on a logarithmic scale. Crosses show the counts for one test of $V0$ at each problem size. Circles show the results of three random trials of $V1$ at each problem size. With branch-and-bound the algorithm executes between $5 \times 10^1$ and $2.3 \times 10^9$ times fewer recursions.

```
10          binPack (k+1);      // recur if needed
11          swap (list, k, i)   // restore it
```

Branch-and-bound adds code that increases the cost of each recursive stage, in hopes of reducing the total number of stages executed. There is no guarantee that the reduction in recursion count will be enough to justify the extra cost of the binCount and weightSum procedures. Experiments can be used to evaluate the trade-off.

Figure 4.3 shows results of an experiment to compare total recursive stages invoked in our original version, called V0, to a branch-and-bound version V1. Since V0 always recurs the same number of times, only one test was performed per problem size. V1 was measured in three random trials at each problem size, using list weights drawn uniformly from $[0, 1)$.

Branch-and-bound is clearly very effective at reducing the total number of recursive stages, although the amount of reduction can vary significantly among trials. At $n = 14$, V0 executed 236.9 billion recursions while V1 executed between 730,000 and 1.59 billion recursions, which represents improvements by factors between 150 and 2200. Overall in these tests counts of recursive stages improved by factors as low as 50 and as high as 230 million.

This reduction in recursion counts translates to important runtime improvements, despite increases in the cost per stage. V0 takes 63 minutes of CPU time at $n = 14$, while V1 has average runtimes near 20 seconds, which represents about a 217-fold speedup.

```
3   binPack (k, bcount, capacity, sumwt) {
4   if (k == n) {
5    if (bcount < optcost)
6        optcost=bcount;
    }
7   else {
8     for (i=k; i<n; i++ ) {
9         swap (list, k, i);              // try it
9.1       if (capacity + list[k] > 1) {   // does it fit?
9.2           b = bcount + 1;             // use new bin
9.3           c = 1 - list[k];
9.4       }
          else {
9.5           b  = bcount;                // use old bin
9.6           c  = c - list[k];
          }
9.7       w = sumwt - list[k];            // update sumwt
9.8       if (b+Ceiling(w-c) < optcost)   // check bound
10            binpack(k+1, b, c, w);      // recur if necessary
11        swap (list, k, i);              // restore it
      }
    }
  }
```

Figure 4.4. binPack V2. This version applies branch-and-bound and propagation.

Branch-and-bound is a special case of *pruning*, which is discussed more fully in Section 4.1.1 under Recursion-Heavy Paradigms.

*Propagation.* Our next tuning strategy focuses on speeding up binCount and weightSum, which together contribute $O(n)$ extra work at each recursive stage. Implementation V2 uses *propagation* to replace these methods with incremental calculations that take only constant time per stage.

The new version is shown in Figure 4.4. To compute the weight sum incrementally we introduce a new parameter sumwt, initialized to equal the sum of the entire list. On line 9.7 the weight in list[k] is subtracted from sumwt and passed to the next recursive stage. Calculation of binCount(k) is propagated by introducing two parameters, bcount and capacity, and performing next fit incrementally during the recursion. Lines 9.1 though 9.6 determine whether the current weight list[k] fits into the current open bin, or whether a new bin is needed. Now that the value of capacity is available, it can be used to give a tighter lower bound on the estimated bin count, so 1-list[k] is replaced with 1-c in the test on line 9.8.

Tests using the Java -Xprof profiler to compare V1 and V2 on identical inputs show that propagation cuts the average cost of each recursive stage in half; that translates to a 50 percent reduction in total running time. The new lower bound test on line 9.8 yields small improvements: about half the time there is no difference in recursion counts, and 90 percent of the time the improvement is less than 20 percent.

**Guideline 4.1** *Propagation: Replace a full computation in each recursive stage with an incremental computation that passes partial results as parameters.*

*Preprocessing.* Our third tuneup involves using an approximation algorithm to find a good packing as a *preprocessing* step, on the theory that a low initial value for optcost will make the branch-and-bound test more effective during the recursion. Version V3 incorporates an approximation algorithm known as first fit decreasing (FFD), which is run before the recursion begins, to find a good initial value for optcost. FFD sorts the weights in decreasing order and then applies the first fit algorithm described in Section 3.2.

As before, preprocessing adds extra cost to the algorithm that may or may not be recovered by reductions in total recursion counts; as before, experiments can inform the cost-benefit analysis.

Figure 4.5 shows results of an experiment designed to assess this trade-off. The $x$-axis shows log recursion counts ($\log_{10} v_2$) for version $v_2$, measured in 30 random trials at $n = 14$. The y-axis shows the log differences in recursion counts

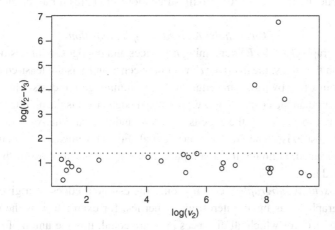

Figure 4.5. Recursion counts. The $x$-axis shows $\log_{10}(v_2)$, and the y-axis shows $\log_{10}(v_2 - v_3)$, in 30 random trials at $n = 14$. Six of the 30 trials produced differences of 0, not shown on this logarithmic graph. The dotted lines mark trials where the difference in recursion counts was below 25.

$(\log_{10}(v_2 - v_3))$ in tests using identical inputs. The $v_2$ recursion count ranges from 14 to $2.5 \times 10^8$, and corresponding differences $v_2 - v_3$ in the graph range from 2 to $6.1 \times 10^6$. Of the 30 trials, 6 resulted in differences of 0 and are not shown on the graph.

Most points are below the dotted line, which corresponds to $v_2 - v_3 = 25$ and represents a very small difference compared to the scale of $V_2$. In three trials the differences were on the order of $10^3$, $10^4$, and $10^7$, giving improvements ranging from 10 percent faster to 15 times faster. Additional tests not shown here suggest that V3 can occasionally, but rarely, run up to 500 times faster than V2.

Profiling and runtime measurements for V2 and V3 show that the time for FFD is microscopically small compared to the recursion code. Considering timing inaccuracies introduced by the Java VM, V3 is observably faster than V2 only when the number of recursive stages is at least 20 percent smaller. The conclusion: preprocessing with FFD adds no significant extra time to `binPack` and, with rare exceptions, makes no significant improvements in recursion counts.

**Guideline 4.2** *Preprocessing: Add work before the algorithm begins, to save work when the algorithm executes.*

Together these three modification – branch-and-bound, propagation, and preprocessing – have produced an implementation V3 that takes between five minutes and three hours when $n = 16$, while the estimated CPU time for V0 is at least two months. This works out to at least a 730-fold speedup due to algorithm tuning.

The next section presents a second case study using an algorithm with very different structure from `binPack`, to illustrate more strategies for algorithm tuning.

### Case Study: A greedy graph algorithm

Given a graph $G = (V, E)$ containing $n$ vertices and $m$ edges, with positive costs $c(x, y)$ on the edges, the *distance* $d(x, y)$ between $x$ and $y$ is the least-cost way to travel from $x$ to $y$ by traversing edges in $G$ and summing their costs. This distance may be less than the cost of edge $(x, y)$ itself: if edge $(x, y)$ is the unique least-cost path from $x$ to $y$, we say the edge is *essential*, and if an alternative path of equal or lower cost exists, the edge is nonessential. For convenience we assume that $G$ is undirected, although the assumption is not necessary to most of the results mentioned here.

The *essential subgraph* $S$ contains only the essential edges of a given graph $G$. Subgraph $S$ has many interesting properties, for example: it is the smallest subgraph of $G$ for which all distances in $G$ are equal; it is the union of $n$ single-source shortest path trees of $G$; and it must contain a minimum spanning tree of $G$. Let $m'$ denote the number of edges in $S$; it holds that $n - 1 \le m' \le m$. Under a general random model with an arbitrary distribution on edge weights in $G$, the expected number of edges $m'$ is $\Theta(n \log n)$.

```
procedure findEssential (G) constructs S
     S.initialize(n)      // Subgraph initially empty
     P.initialize(G)      // Priority queue of edges of G

1    while (P.notEmpty() ){
2        <x, y, cost> = P.extractMin();
3        if (S.distance(x,y) > cost) S.insert(x,y,cost);
     }
```

Figure 4.6. ES. Computing the essential subgraph, $S$, of $G$.

In this section we consider an algorithm called ES that takes $G$ and constructs the essential subgraph $S$. It is not hard to extend the algorithm to solve the all pairs shortest paths problem – to compute all distances in $G$ – in $O(m'n \log n)$ time.

C and Java implementations of the algorithm variations described here can be downloaded from *AlgLab*. All experiments in this section were performed using random complete graphs with edge costs drawn uniformly from $(0, 1)$. Time measurements reported here are of the C implementations, run on the HP platform described in the first timing experiment of Section 3.1.2.

Figure 4.6 shows pseudocode for the main loop of ES. Each iteration of the loop invokes S.distance to return the distance between $x$ and $y$ in the (unfinished) subgraph $S$. If there is no alternative path in $S$, the edge must be essential, so it is inserted in $S$. The correctness of this algorithm is established by noting that edge $e = (x, y)$ can be correctly identified as essential or nonessential by considering only paths of essential edges with costs smaller than $e$.

Our first version V0 implements the priority queue $P$ with an array of edges sorted in increasing order by cost. Function P.initialize takes $O(m \log m)$ time to sort the edges, P.notEmpty is constant time, and P.extractMin takes constant time per edge to work through the sorted array.

Subgraph $S$ is implemented with an adjacency list. Figure 4.7 shows the S.distance function, which uses Dijkstra's well-known single pair shortest path algorithm to find the distance from s to d in S.

The priority queue Ps holds vertices w in order by smallest-known distance from s, denoted w.dist. The status of each vertex goes from unseen, before it is encountered, to inqueue when it is encountered and inserted into Ps, and done when it is extracted from Ps. Each iteration of the main loop extracts a vertex w with minimum distance from Ps. If this is the destination node d, the search ends; otherwise lines 9 to 11 perform the familiar *relax* operation on each neighbor z of w, checking whether a better distance to z via w can be found. If so, z.dist is updated, and Ps.decreaseKey is invoked to update Ps. If there is no path from s to d in S, the function returns distance +Infinity.

```
procedure S.distance(s, d) returns distance from s to d
 1  For all vertices v: v.status = unseen;
 2  Ps.init(s,0);                     // insert s with distance 0
 3  s.status = inqueue;
 4  while (Ps.notEmpty()) {
 5      <w, w.dist> = Ps.extractMin();
 6      w.status = done;
 7      if (w == d) return w.dist;            // found d
 8      for (each neighbor z of w) {
 9          znewdist = w.dist + cost(w,z);    // relax
10          if (z.status == unseen)
11              Ps.insert(z, znewdist);
12          else if (z.status == inqueue)
13              Ps.decreaseKey(z, znewdist);
    }//while
14  return  +Infinity;                        // didn't find d
```

Figure 4.7. S.distance. Dijkstra's algorithm finds the distance from s to d in S.

A quick profiling experiment using the Unix `gprof` utility shows that 78 percent of CPU time is spent executing `S.distance` and the data structure functions it invokes. Therefore, we focus first on tuning strategies for reducing the cost of `S.distance`.

*Memoization.* Dijkstra's algorithm is usually conceived of as executing once, but here it is invoked repeatedly, in alternation with edge insertions to *S*. Our first algorithm tuneup exploits this fact by introducing a matrix to record distances as they are discovered. This is an example of *memoization* – "making a memo" of a result to avoid the cost of recalculating later.

The new version incorporates a global distance matrix D that saves the distance from s to w each time some w is extracted from Ps. Because it is possible for the distance from s to w to decrease via future `S.insert` operations, the value recorded in D is only an upper bound on the true (minimum) distance, which might be discovered later. But sometimes the upper bound is enough to establish whether the edge is essential. Let `ecost` be the cost of edge $(s,d)$ at an invocation of `S.distance`: if `(D[s,d] <= ecost)`, the edge is not essential, and the Dijkstra search can be skipped. If `(D[s,d] > ecost)`, the search takes place. Here is the modified code:

```
procedure S.distance(s, d, ecost) returns
        distance from s to d, or upper bound D[s,d]
```

```
0.1   if (D[s,d] <= ecost) return D[s,d];
1       For all vertices v: v.status = unseen;
2       Ps.init(s,0)                    // insert s with distance 0
3       s.status = inqueue;
4       while (Ps.notEmpty()) {
5           <w, w.dist> = Ps.extractMin();
5.1         if (w.dist < D[s,w]) D[s,w] = w.dist;
6           w.status = done;
```

The S.distance function no longer returns the exact distance from s to d in S; sometimes it returns an upper bound D[s,d] on that cost, but only when that bound proves the edge to be nonessential. This is an example of *finessing* by replacing the expensive "exact" calculation of the distance from s to d, with the upper bound found in D[s,t]. Since the result of S.distance is only used to check whether an edge is essential or nonessential, the bound suffices when it is less than edge cost.

**Guideline 4.3** *Finesse a calculation: Replace an expensive exact calculation with an inexpensive bound or approximation, in such a way that the overall result is unchanged.*

Version V1 implements this tuneup. Memoization adds $O(n^2)$ cost to the algorithm to initialize D but saves the cost of some redundant executions of S.distance. Does the trade-off work?

Our first experiment compares CPU times for versions V0 and V1. The C code was compiled with the highest optimization level (gcc -O3); times were measured with the Unix time command running on the HP platform described in the timing experiment of Section 3.1.2. The random number generator was fixed so that both versions were run on identical inputs. The table that follows shows runtimes in seconds, averaged over 10 random trials at each problem size. Clearly memoization yields an important speedup: V1 runs 48 to 75 times faster than V0 on these problem sizes.

| Runtime | $n = 800$ | $n = 1000$ | $n = 1200$ | $n = 1400$ |
|---|---|---|---|---|
| $v_0$ | 24.11 | 49.04 | 87.57 | 144.97 |
| $v_1$ | .49 | .83 | 1.32 | 1.91 |
| $v_0/v_1$ | 49.20 | 48.24 | 66.34 | 75.90 |

It should be pointed out that all experiments described in Section 4.1.1 are carried out on random uniform graphs with $(0,1]$ edge weights, and the results would be quite different on other graph models. This point is discussed further in Section 4.1.1 under Data Structures and Access Patterns.

**Guideline 4.4** *Memoization: Save results in a table to avoid having to redo the work.*

*Loop abort.* The greedy ES algorithm contains two main loops: the "outer" loop in Figure 4.6 iterates over edges in $G$ and calls S.distance, and the "inner" loop in Figure 4.7 iterates over vertices and invokes operations on Ps. The *loop abort* strategy involves finding a test to stop a loop early rather than letting it run to completion.

For example, the outer loop iterates $m$ times, considering each edge of $G$ in increasing order by cost. With a bound on the cost of the largest essential edge we could modify the main loop in Figure 4.6 to stop early, like this:

```
bound = (global) bound on max essential edge cost

procedure findEssential (G) constructs S
      S.initialize(n) // Subgraph initially empty
      P.initialize(G) // Priority queue of edges of G
1     while (P.notEmpty()){
2          <x, y, cost> = P.extractMin();
3          if (S.distance(x,y) < cost ) S.insert(x,y,cost);
4          if (cost > bound) break;         // loop abort
      }
```

**Guideline 4.5** *Loop abort: Add a test to stop a loop early.*

Experiments using version V1 indicate that this idea could be very effective if a suitable bound can be found: on random uniform graphs the subgraph $S$ is finished after the smallest 2 to 10 percent of edges have been considered; that means that the remaining 90 to 98 percent of edges are nonessential. (This observation applies only to random uniform graphs, but theoretical results mentioned in the Chapter Notes suggest that a similar property holds for general random graphs.) For graphs with uniform edge costs from $(0, 1)$, a bound of $x \in (0, 1)$ on the largest essential edge would reduce the number of outer loop iterations from $m$ to $xm$.

One way to implement the loop abort test is to calculate an upper bound $D(S)$ on the *diameter* of $S$, which is the maximal distance between any pair of vertices in $S$. If ecost is greater than the diameter (or its upper bound), the ES algorithm can stop because all remaining edges must be nonessential.

One way to compute such a bound is to perform a full search of $S$ from vertex s to every other vertex in the graph. Let f be the farthest-away vertex found in that search; twice the distance from s to f is an upper bound on $D(S)$. Any type of search will do: one idea is to rewrite S.distance to perform a full Dijkstra search from s rather than stopping when d is encountered; another is to run a breadth-first search (BFS) from s. The slower Dijkstra search would provide a tighter bound on the diameter, and the faster BFS search would yield a looser bound.

We employ a small pilot experiment for guidance in choosing a good bounding strategy, by adding a full BFS search inside S.distance, to run before the (inner) main loop begins. The full Dijkstra search can be implemented by commenting out the loop abort test on line 7 of the code in Figure 4.7. Here are some observations from an exploratory experiment to evaluate these two strategies.

- Early in the computation when $S$ is unconnected, both searches return $D(S) = \infty$, which is no use in the loop abort test. Later, when $S$ is nearly finished, the bounds returned by these searches yield significant reductions in main loop iterations. For example, at $n = 1000$ the BFS bound is near 0.06 on average; that means that with the loop abort test the main loop executes about 30,000 iterations instead of the full 499,500 iterations, a reduction of 94 percent.
- A full BFS search of $S$ is much faster than a full Dijkstra search. The slightly tighter bounds returned by the full Dijkstra search are not enough to counteract the greater computation time.
- Both BFS and the full Dijkstra search are much more expensive than the partial search (to node d) performed in S.distance. Furthermore, the bounds returned by these searches do not change much from call to call. It is not cost-effective to perform a full search at each invocation of S.distance.

On the basis of these observations, version V2 implements the following search strategy for the loop abort test: (1) Wait until $n$ edges have been added to $S$ to activate the BFS search (so it is more likely to be connected); (2) once the search is activated, in each call to S.distance, check whether BFS has been performed with source vertex s; if not, run the BFS search with s as source. This adds at most $n$ invocations of BFS to the cost of the algorithm. The new code section is sketched in Figure 4.8.

Note the result of the BFS search is memoized on line 0.6. In fact, all distances discovered during BFS search can be memoized (not shown).

Also, if the farthest-away vertex f has distance less than ecost, the edge must be nonessential and the Dijkstra search need not be performed. This test to abort the inner main loop appears on line 0.7.

Another loop abort test can be applied to this inner loop, as follows. Since Dijkstra's algorithm finds vertices in increasing order by distance, each w.dist extracted on line 5 is a lower bound on the distance from s to d. If (w.dist > ecost), then edge (s, d) must be essential: we can abort the Dijkstra search and return the bound w.dist instead of the true distance.

```
bound = (global) bound on max essential edge cost

procedure S.distance(s, d, ecost) returns
          distance from s to d, or upper bound D[s,d]

0.1   if (D[s,d] <= ecost) return D[s,d];
0.2   if (S.edgeCount() >= n) {
0.3          if (s.dfs has not been performed) {
0.4          <f,f.dist> = S.dfs(s);          // f is farthest fror
0.5          if (d*2 < bound) bound = d*2;    // save min bound
0.6          if (D[s,f] > f.dist) D[s,f] = f.dist; // memoize
0.7          if (f.dist <= ecost) return f.dist;   // loop abc
      }

1     For all vertices v: v.status = unseen;
2     Ps.init(s,0)                     // insert s with distance
3     s.status = inqueue;
4     while (Ps.notEmpty()) {
5          <w, w.dist> = Ps.extractMin();
5.1        if (w.dist < D[s,w]) D[s,w] = w.dist;
6          w.status = done;
```

Figure 4.8. BFS search. The BFS search returns the distance from s to the farthest-away vertex f. Twice this distance is an upper bound on the diameter of *S*.

```
4     while (Ps.notEmpty()) {
5          <w, w.dist> = Ps.extractMin();
5.1        if (w.dist < D[s,w]) D[s,w] = w.dist;
5.2        if (w.dist > ecost) return w.dist;   // loop abort
6          w.status = done;
```

This reduces the number of iterations of that loop but also might increase total cost of the algorithm because fewer memoizations would be performed in each call to S.distance.

These two loop abort strategies will be evaluated together with the next algorithm tuneup, called *filtering*.

*Filtering.* Consider the relax operation on line 9 of Figure 4.7. If (z.dist > ecost), there is no need to insert z into Ps because it can not affect the decision about whether edge (s,d) is essential or nonessential. If the (inner) loop abort tuneup mentioned earlier is implemented, the loop will stop before this value can be extracted, anyway. This strategy of *filtering* the data structure saves the cost of some `insert` operations and speeds up other operations by making the priority queue smaller overall.

**Guideline 4.6** *Filtering: Avoid inserting an element into a data structure if the element cannot affect the outcome of the computation.*

Besides memoization we have considered three tuning strategies for ES: loop abort for the outer main loop, loop abort for the inner main loop, and filtering the `Ps` data structure. These strategies interact with one another – for example, the effectiveness of the inner loop abort test depends on whether or not the outer loop abort test is implemented.

As a general rule, the proper way to evaluate tuneups that interact in this way is to use a full factorial design as described in Section 2.2.2. This experimental design permits analysis of the main effects of each tuneup alone, as well as the interaction effects of various combinations. The difficulty is, the design requires $16 = 2^4$ design points – as well as code versions – to test all combinations of the four tuneups. Implementing 16 versions of one program is prohibitively time-consuming in many cases. The design would have to be even bigger to incorporate tests of alternative strategies for bounding the diameter, a variety of input classes and sizes, and other runtime environments.

Fortunately we can apply algorithmic reasoning to eliminate most of these combinations from consideration:

- It is a safe bet that memoization improves computation time in every case, because the cost of storing a number in a table is tiny compared to the cost of a redundant search in $S$. The $O(n^2)$ initialization of the distance matrix represents a very small proportion of other initialization costs. We can cut the design in half by not testing versions without memoization.
- The effectiveness of the outer loop abort test depends on the number of invocations to `S.distance` saved versus the cost of finding the bound on the largest essential edge. The inner loop abort and filtering strategies modify the cost of `S.distance`, which affects the balance between invocation cost and bounding strategy. This experimental study does not try to optimize that balance, so we omit design points that omit the outer loop test, on the principle that few invocations of `S.distance` are better than many invocations, no matter how fast it is.
- The only design points remaining involve the inner loop abort test and filtering, totaling four design points. Exploratory experiments on these four versions of the code suggest that the inner loop abort never improves total computation time and sometimes slows it down: it is better *not* to abort this loop so that more memoization can occur. Experiments also reveal that filtering always provides a small reduction in total computation time.

On the basis of these results, our next implementation V2 incorporates memoization (from V1), filtering, and the BFS search to support the outer loop abort test. Average CPU times (in seconds) for 10 trials at each problem size are shown in the table.

| Runtime | $n = 800$ | $n = 1000$ | $n = 1200$ | $n = 1400$ |
|---------|-----------|------------|------------|------------|
| $v_0$ | 24.11 | 49.04 | 87.57 | 144.97 |
| $v_1$ | .49 | .86 | 1.33 | 1.93 |
| $v_2$ | .24 | .40 | .62 | .91 |
| $v_0/v_2$ | 100.46 | 122.60 | 141.24 | 159.31 |
| $v_1/v_2$ | 2.04 | 2.15 | 2.15 | 2.12 |

V2 runs twice as fast as V1, mostly because of the loop abort test. Although that test cuts about 90 percent of calls to S.distance, the extra cost of the BFS searches means that the speedup is only a factor of 2.

Altogether, these three tuneups have contributed speedups by factors between 100 and 160 over the original implementation of ES.

*Customizing The Data Structure.* Profiling reveals our next target of opportunity: In V2, the Ps.extractMin function takes about 36 percent of computation time, more than any other function. Rather than zooming in on that particular operation, however, we take a wider look at Ps and find ways to *customize the data structure* by matching operation costs to the operation frequencies imposed by the ES algorithm.

Priority queue Ps supports four operations: initialize, extractMin, insert, and decreaseKey. Versions V0 through V2 employ a textbook implementation of Ps using a simple binary heap, together with a location array that stores, for each vertex, its location in the heap. The location array is used in the decreaseKey(z, z.dist) operation, to find vertex z in the heap. Here are some alternative ways to implement Ps.

- **Option 1: initialization vs. insertion.** The original version initializes the heap to contain one vertex s and later performs some number $I$ of insert operations. An alternative is to initialize Ps to contain all $n$ vertices and perform zero inserts later.
- **Option 2: initialization vs. insertion.** Yet another alternative is to use BFS to find all $B \leq n$ vertices reachable from s. Initialize the heap to contain those $B$ vertices and perform zero inserts.
- **Option 3: memoization.** This option memoizes the entire heap, saving it unitll the end of each invocation of S.distance(s,d), and restoring it the next

time the function is called with the same source s. This requires replacing Ps
with an array P[s] to hold separate heaps for each s. Since edges may have
been added to $S$ since the last time P[s] was saved, the heap may not correctly
reflect distances $S$ when restored. Therefore, the restore step must apply the
relax operation to every edge that was added in the interim. This restore step
can be implemented without increasing the total asymptotic cost of the algorithm
(see [24]). With this modification, the cost of initializing and inserting during
each call to S.distance drops to zero, but the restore (relax) step must be
performed for some number $R$ of new edges in each call.

- **Option 4: decrease-key vs. sifting.** The location array finds z in the heap
  in constant time, which is clearly better than a linear-cost search for z. On the
  other hand, the location array must be updated every time a heap element is
  moved by a siftup or siftdown operation. Sifting occurs in the inner loops
  of the insert, extractMin, and decreaseKey operations, and updating the
  location array as well as the heap likely doubles the cost of sifting. If the number
  $K$ of decrease-key operations is small compared to $T$, the number of elements
  sifted, it would be faster to omit the location array. Instead, decreaseKey
  could be implemented by placing a new copy of z in the heap. The extractMin
  would be modified to skip duplicate keys.

The right choice depends on the values of parameters $I$, $B$, $R$, $K$, and $T$ and
on the code costs of these various alternatives. Most of these options interact,
suggesting another factorial design. But before writing $16 = 2^4$ copies of the code,
we use exploratory experiments to measure these parameters and identify the most
promising options.

The first experiment modifies V2 to report the outcome (insert, reject) for each
edge in the graph (with the outer loop abort turned off for the moment). From this
experiment we learn that when ES is applied to a random uniform graph, it works
in two phases. In phase 1, $S$ grows rapidly because most edges are accepted as
essential; in phase 2, when $S$ is completed, all edges are rejected as nonessential.

These two phases produce distinct patterns of access to Ps and different conclusions about which implementation options are best. To take a concrete example, in
one trial with $n = 100$ and $m = 4950$, phase 1 (building $S$) occupied the first 492
iterations. When $S$ was completed, it contained 281 edges; that means that about
40 percent of edges were accepted during phase 1. Phase 2 (when all edges were
nonessential) occupied the remaining 4457 iterations.

Here are some observations about the parameters in these two phases; the
notations $I_1, I_2$ refer to parameter $I$ in phases 1 and 2, respectively.

1. *Options 1 and 2.* In phase 1 the original implementation performs one initialization and $I_1 = 30.9$ inserts per call on average. Option 1 would initialize a

heap of size $n = 100$ and perform zero inserts. Option 2 would perform a BFS search on $B_1 = 51.2$ vertices (on average), then initialize a heap of size $B_1$, and then perform zero inserts. It is a close call: none of these options is likely to be significantly faster than another. In phase 2, however, option 1 is the clear winner: the original version performs $I_2 = 97.1$ inserts on average, which must be slower than initializing a heap of size 100, and the BFS search in option 2 is superfluous since $B = n$.

2. *Option 3.* In phase 1 the original implementation performed $I_1 = 30.9$ inserts and $K_1 = 4.8$ decrease-keys per call on average, totaling $14,907.6 = 492 \times 30.9$ inserts and $2,361.6 = 492 \times 4.8$ decrease-keys. By comparison, option 3 would initialize a heap of size $n = 100$ and perform 0 inserts and no more than $K_1$ decrease-keys per call: this option is clearly worth exploring. In phase 2, option 3 is the clear winner because the cost of the restore operation drops to zero, while the original version performs $I_2 = 97.1$ inserts per invocation.

3. *Option 4.* In phase 1 the average number of decrease-keys per call to s.distance is $K_1 = 4.8$, compared to $T_1 = 159.4$ sift steps: savings would likely accrue from implementing option 4. In phase 2, $K_2 = 40.4$ while $T_2 = 625.6$, so the cost difference is smaller.

With the outer loop abort test, V2 spends about 90 percent of its time in phase 1. The path is clear: option 3 should be explored next, and option 4 is also promising. These conclusions should be valid for random uniform graphs at larger values of $n$, but initialization might change the balance of some parameters at small $n$. If the ES algorithm is to be applied to other input classes, these tests should be rerun to check whether these basic relations still hold.

**Guideline 4.7** *Customize the data structure: select a data structure implementation that best matches its pattern of use.*

The reader is invited to download these programs from *AlgLab* and try the suggested tuneups, invent more tuneups, and extend these experiments to other input classes.

### 4.1.1 Tuning Algorithms

Our two case studies illustrate how algorithm tuning can make code run hundreds and thousands of times faster than a straightforward implementation. Can we apply these ideas to other situations? Where does inspiration come from?

As a general rule, good understanding of cost mechanisms at the abstract algorithm level is needed even to imagine that some of these ideas might pay off: preprocessing works in the bin packing example because analysis shows that FFD is fast and near-optimal for these inputs; the loop abort trick works in the ES

- Recursive paradigms.
    - **Exhaustive enumeration**, also known as **brute force**: solve a problem by generating all possible combinations of solution components. In particular, **exhaustive search** algorithms use exhaustive enumeration to solve optimization problems by generating all possible solutions and saving the best one found.
    - **Divide-and-conquer**: divide the problem into subproblems; recur to solve the subproblems; combine solutions to subproblems.
- Iterative paradigms.
    - **Greedy:** construct a solution to an optimization problem incrementally, selecting the least-cost component to add to the solution at each iteration.
    - **Scanning** and **sweeping** algorithms: iterate over a coordinate space containing geometric components, updating the solution at each iteration.
    - **Dynamic programming:** use one or more nested loops to fill in entries of an array or matrix. Values for new entries are computed from values in previously filled entries.

Figure 4.9. Algorithm paradigms. Algorithm design paradigms represent fundamental categories of algorithmic structures.

code because average-case analysis shows that $S$ is quite small compared to $G$. The algorithm analysis literature is an excellent source of inspiration for finding algorithm tuneups.

Most tuneups do not change the asymptotic bounds but rather involve balancing decreased cost in one section of code against increased cost in another. With some exceptions (such as quicksort), experiments are better suited than abstract analyses for evaluating these types of constant-factor trade-offs. Experiments for this purpose can involve simple runtime tests or measurements of key parameters ($I, K$, etc.) that guide the tuning process.

Inspiration can also be found by considering fundamental algorithmic structures. Some of these structures, better known as algorithm design paradigms, are listed in Figure 4.9. This list provides a handy organizing scheme for our survey of algorithm tuning strategies in the following sections. To learn more about algorithm design paradigms, consult the references listed in the Chapter Notes.

### *Recursion-Heavy Paradigms*

An *exhaustive enumeration* algorithm solves a problem by recursively enumerating all possible solutions or solution components. Exhaustive search algorithms – like

```
1  Quicksort (A , lo, hi )
2      if (lo >= hi ) return;        // Cutoff test
3      p = A[lo]                     // Partition element p
4      x = Partition(A, lo, hi, p)   // Partition around p
7      Quicksort (A, lo, x-1)        // Recur left
8      Quicksort (A, x+1, hi)        // Recur right
```

Figure 4.10. Quicksort. An example of the divide-and-conquer paradigm.

our exact bin packing example – use exhaustive enumeration to solve optimization problems, by generating all solutions and saving the one with best cost. Usually these algorithms run in exponential time, so there is a lot of room for improvement by tuning.

*Divide-and-conquer* is another predominantly recursive paradigm. A divide-- and-conquer algorithm solves a problem by breaking it into subproblems and using recursion to solve the subproblems. Quicksort, the most famous algorithm in this paradigm, is sketched in Figure 4.10 for reference in the following discussion.

What these two paradigms have in common, of course, is a large number of recursive procedure calls, with subproblems passed as parameters to subsequent execution stages. These structures yield three basic approaches to tuning: skip some recursive stages; make recursive computations faster by controlling subproblem sizes; or shrink the cost of individual recursive stages.

*Skip Execution Stages.* The first general approach to tuning recursive algorithms is to implement tests to skip recursive calls when possible. The branch-and-bound technique illustrated in the bin packing case study of Section 4.1 is an example of this idea, whereby a lower bound on the cost of a partially built solution is used as a cutoff to avoid executing some branches of the recursion tree. When exhaustive search is used to solve a maximization rather than a minimization problem, an upper-bound test is required instead.

The effectiveness of branch-and-bound can be boosted using preprocessing to find a good initial solution, which may increase the number of skipped recursions. Another way to improve the effectiveness of the branch-and-bound test is to change the computation order to find low-cost solutions earlier rather than later in the recursion. For example, in BinPack the order in which solutions are tested depends on the order of weights in the input list: the original list order is the very first permutation tested. Execution time might be improved if the initial weight list were reordered by pairing big weights with small weights, so that the first permutation is likely to have very low cost when packed by next fit.

Branch-and-bound and related techniques can be extremely effective in reducing the high cost of exhaustive search. Moret, Bader, and Warnow [26] use branch-and-bound to eliminate more than 99.9 percent of candidate solutions from evaluation in their algorithm for computing optimal phylogenetic trees, producing as much as a 250-fold speedup in some inputs. Bentley [4] observed speedups by factors of 7,500 and more by applying two tuneups – branch-and-bound and changing computation order – to his exact algorithm for the traveling salesman problem.

In the more general context of exhaustive enumeration algorithms, *backtracking* is analogous to branch-and-bound, whereby a partially built solution is abandoned if a test reveals that it cannot possibly lead to a feasible solution. Backtracking can also be enhanced by preprocessing, to eliminate some combinations from consideration, or by changing the computation order so that feasible solutions are likely to be found earlier rather than later.

Branch-and-bound and backtracking are special cases of *pruning*, which involves any kind of test – not just inspection of a partial solution – to eliminate recursive stages. For example, the bin packing code could be pruned by installing tests to check for redundant packings: if two weights `list[k]`, `list[k+1]` can be packed into the same bin by next fit, it is not necessary to recur to check the combination `list[k+1]`, `list[k]`.

Pruning can also be applied to divide-and-conquer algorithms. For example, quicksort (Figure 4.10) can be modified to solve many related problems such as selecting the $k$ largest elements from a set, finding all elements greater than $x$, and so forth. If a quick check reveals that no part of the answer can be found to the left of the partition element after partitioning, then the left recursive call can be pruned.

For another example, consider the classic algorithm [12] to find the closest pair of points in a two-dimensional space, by recursing on points to the left and right of the median $x$-coordinate. Each recursive stage returns and reports the minimum distance $d$ that it found among its subset of points. If a quick scan of the ordered $x$-coordinates of points shows that all points in a given subproblem are at least $d$ apart, the recursion can be skipped.

**Guideline 4.8** *Pruning: insert simple tests to prune recursive calls. Boost the strength of these tests by using preprocessing or by changing computation order.*

*Control Subproblem Size.* The next tuning strategy involves adjusting the sizes of recursive subproblems. One idea is to *filter the subproblem* by removing elements from a subproblem before it is passed to the next recursive stage. For example, the bin packing code could check for weights of size exactly 1.0 or for pairs of weights in adjacent locations (`list[k]`, `list[k+1]`) that add up to 1.0. When these weights are found, they can be packed into single bins and removed from further consideration. This type of filtering can yield considerable speedups in situations where common and easy-to-handle subproblems can be identified.

Quicksort can be modified to filter subproblems by not recurring to sort elements that are identical to the partition element $p$. Bentley and McIlroy [9] describe a "fat partition" procedure that groups elements equal to $p$ together at each level, so that the algorithm recurs on subarrays containing only elements strictly less than or greater than $p$. This variation is much faster than conventional versions of quicksort on arrays containing many duplicates and is not much slower than conventional methods on arrays with distinct elements.

A related idea is to *balance subproblem sizes* in divide-and-conquer algorithms. This technique involves adding extra work in the divide step to ensure that the two subproblems are more nearly equal in size. Even though balancing adds extra cost to each stage, theoretical analysis shows that the total amount of work done may be smaller on balanced subproblems.

A well-known example of this approach is to use median-of-three partitioning in quicksort, whereby the partition element is selected as the median of a sample of three elements from the subarray, rather than as shown on line 3 of Figure 4.10. One way to implement median-of-three sampling is shown in the following:

```
2.1   m = (lo+hi)/2;
2.2   if (A[lo]> A[hi]) swap(lo, hi);
2.3   if (A[m] > A[hi]) swap(m, hi);
2.4   if (A[lo]< A[m])  swap(lo, m);
3     p = A[lo];
```

Even more balance can be achieved by selecting medians of 5-, 7-, and 9-element samples, but at some point the cost of selecting a median from a large sample outweighs the benefits due to better balancing. Finding the "sweet spot" between too much and too little balancing work can be an interesting problem in many applications.

**Guideline 4.9** *Control subproblem sizes: remove elements from subproblems before recurring; add or subtract work to balance subproblems.*

*Shrink Cost Per Stage.* Our third approach to tuning is simply to make each stage of the recursion faster. The propagation technique illustrated in the bin packing case study is an example: an $O(n)$ computation repeated at every recursive stage is replaced with an incremental constant-time computation that passes partial results as parameters.

Another idea is to *hybridize the recursion*, by writing recursive code that is tuned for different problem sizes. Quicksort can be hybridized, for example, by introducing a policy that selects the partition element from a sample of $k = (1, 3, 5, \ldots n)$ array elements, where $k$ is calculated as a function of subarray size $n$. As a general rule, large sample sizes are more cost-efficient when $n$ is large, because better balancing pays off; small samples are best when $n$ is small because median-selection is a smaller proportion of the cost at each stage. Experimental and theoretical results in [22] and [25] suggest that choosing $k$ proportional to $\sqrt{n}$ minimizes total comparisons for partitioning and median-selection in the average-case model.

Another common hybridization trick for quicksort is to switch to insertion sort on small subproblems of size less than some bound $b$, because insertion sort is faster on small arrays. Most recursive algorithms can be improved by this trick because procedure-call overhead makes iteration more efficient than recursion at the smallest subproblems.

**Guideline 4.10** *Hybridize a recursive program to make individual stages faster.*

### Iterative Paradigms

We now consider tuning strategies for algorithms with predominantly iterative structures.

Dynamic programming algorithms contain one or more nested loops that iterate to fill in the entries of an array. There may not be much room for tuning these types of algorithms, since the code is usually fairly sparse in the first place. Speedups may be found by looking at memory access: Section 4.2 shows how patterns of memory references can dramatically affect computation times for dynamic programming and other algorithms that are dominated by memory accesses.

Other iteration-based paradigms include greedy algorithms, such as the essential subgraph example in Section 4.1, and scanning and sweeping algorithms, which are often found in computational geometry. A greedy algorithm constructs a solution to an optimization problem incrementally, selecting a least-cost component from a priority queue and adding it to the solution if it meets feasibility conditions. A scanning algorithm uses iteration to process a set of geometric components (points, lines, polygons, etc.), usually in order by increasing $x$-coordinate. A setlike data structure is often used to maintain a collection of "active" elements during the scan and to build the final solution.

These two paradigms are characterized by a main loop that solves the problem incrementally, by invoking operations on one or more non-trivial data structures. Computation time is highly dependent on the efficiency of the data structures, which are likely to contain the dominant costs in the algorithm. Tuning strategies for these paradigms focus on two approaches: find ways to avoid calling some data structure operations, or make those operations more efficient when called.

*Skip Expensive Operations.* Our first approach to tuning iterative algorithms involves inserting tests to avoid carrying out expensive operations in the main loop, which are typically data structure operations.

The *loop abort* test in the Essential Subgraph is an example of this approach: the bound on graph diameter is used to stop the outer loop early rather than carrying the computation out to its worst-case end, thereby avoiding unnecessary calls to S.distance.

The ES code also employs *memoization* inside S.distance to support a second loop abort test: if the memoized bound D[s,d] is less than ecost, then the entire Dijkstra loop can be skipped. This tuneup only works because it is possible in this context for S.distance sometimes to return an upper bound on distance rather than an exact distance. This is an example of *finessing* the distance computation by replacing the expensive exact calculation (Dijkstra's algorithm) with an inexpensive bound (D[s,d]), in a way that does not affect the outcome of the overall computation. Memoization and finessing are general tuning strategies not limited to iterative algorithms or data structures.

*Filtering* is another idea that uses a quick test to avoid calling the insert operation of a given data structure. In the implementation of S.distance, vertex z was checked before insertion into the Ps priority queue, to see whether it could possibly be part of the eventual solution returned by S.distance; if not, the Ps.insert operation was skipped.

More generally, data structure elements can be filtered incrementally inside the main loop or all at once in a preprocessing step. Filtering saves the cost of the insert and reduces the costs of other operations because the data structure is smaller.

Many examples of these types of tuneups can be found throughout the algorithm engineering literature. Osipov et al. [28] describe an interesting combination of filtering and loop abort to speed up Kruskal's minimum spanning tree algorithm. The standard implementation starts by sorting edges of graph $G$ in increasing order by weight: each time around the main loop, the algorithm pulls an edge from the array and checks a data structure to decide whether to add the edge to the solution tree $T$. The authors observe that in many applications $T$ is likely to contain only the smallest edges of $G$. Therefore, their algorithm avoids sorting the entire list of edges beforehand. Instead it uses a quicksort-style partitioning step to divide the list into low-cost and high-cost edges. The algorithm recurs to build $T$ using the low-cost edges: if $T$ is finished when the recursion returns, the algorithm stops (aborts the main loop/prunes the recursion); if $T$ is not finished, the algorithm removes all edges that fail a feasibility test (filters the data), before recurring on the remaining part of the list. This idea could be applied to speed up the ES algorithm by avoiding the cost of sorting the entire list of edge weights.

Tuning also plays a key role in research efforts to design commercial GPS routing systems. A point-to-point GPS mapping query (How do I go from $A$ to $B$?) is typically answered by a shortest-path search in a graph that represents a continent-sized roadmap. The data files are huge: in one standard benchmark, the

U.S. roadmap is represented by a graph of 23.9 million nodes and 59.3 million edges. Researchers on this problem have applied many strategies, especially preprocessing and filtering, to tune Dijkstra's algorithm for this application. Delling et al. [13] tested several combinations of tuneups and, for example, reduced average query response time on the U.S. map from 3.803 seconds to 0.73 millisecond, which represents a factor of 5,216 speedup.

The second approach to tuning greedy and scanning algorithms is to tune data structure operations from the inside. Of course, data structure efficiency is important to many algorithms, not just those in iterative paradigms.

### Data Structures and Access Patterns

A data structure is defined by the collection of basic operations – such as insert, delete, and lookup – that it supports. Because these operations must work together, data structure tuning is like squeezing a balloon: optimizing one operation may cause the cost of another operation to explode.

The first key to data structure design is to find the right balance of costs among all operations, according to the frequencies with which they are invoked. The second key is to exploit the scenario of repeated accesses to the data set by understanding access patterns such as locality. High locality, for example, means that key accesses arrive in bunches: a key that is accessed once in an operation is likely to be accessed again soon.

*Customize the Data Structure.* Every schoolchild (with a college course in data structures) knows how to reason about operation frequencies – such as number of inserts versus deletes versus lookups in a set abstract data type – in order to choose an implementation with best asymptotic cost. Data structure tuning extends this abstract analysis to incorporate more detailed information about what to expect in a given application.

As illustrated in the Essential Subgraph case study, this approach might start with an experiment to find precise counts of key parameters (in that case, $I$, $P$, $K$, etc.). Experiments can also be used to assess locality in access patterns, to learn typical sizes of data elements, and to find the range and distribution of keys.

*Change the Input Presentation.* Instead of tuning the data structure to match input properties, an alternative approach is to tune the input to match the data structure properties. This involves modifying the *presentation* of the input instance – perhaps by reformatting, filtering, or reordering its elements – in a way that does not change the outcome of the algorithm but that may improve computation time. This is often done as a preprocessing step.

For example, in the GPS mapping application mentioned earlier, Delling et al. [13] observe that the time to answer a query depends on two properties: the length of the path from source s to destination d, which determines the number of iterations in the main loop, and the average vertex degree, which determines the size of the priority queue Ps. They tune the input map in a preprocessing step that adds shortcut information so that fewer iterations are needed.

Input instances can be reordered in different ways depending on context: sometimes *randomizing* the input is best, to guarantee average-case performance; sometimes *sorting* the inputs is best; and sometimes the best order is specific to the algorithm, data structure, or application.

For example, in the bin packing case study the first permutation tested is the original input order; reordering the input by interleaving big weights with small weights, to provide a good initial next fit packing, makes the branch-and-bound test more effective. For another example, researchers working on algorithms that use maps as inputs (such as [2]) have observed that organizing input elements in proximity order, where points close together on the map are close together in the input, can yield substantial runtime improvements.

**Guideline 4.11** *Instead of changing the code to match the input, change the input presentation to match the code.*

*Self-Tuning Data Structures.* The data structure tuning strategies described so far depend on having access to the set of inputs that will be used when the algorithm is run, whether to measure their properties or to modify their presentations.

Unfortunately in many cases the experimenter – who, for example, may be tuning a data structure to be placed in a code repository – does not have the luxury of making assumptions about typical inputs or of running experiments to test their properties. Algorithms and data structures developed for general and public use must be tuned for reasonable performance on *all* inputs, not special classes. Rather than aiming for best performance on known input classes, the goal is to avoid terrible performance on any input.

All of the algorithm tuneups mentioned in the case studies were evaluated using quite narrow input classes. In the bin packing example, experiments were run on lists of random weights drawn uniformly from $(0, 1)$: tuneups like branch-and-bound and preprocessing with FFD might be more or less successful in other situations. Experiments on the essential subgraph algorithm used random graphs with uniform edge weights: the loop abort and filtering ideas, especially, are not necessarily effective on other input classes. These experiments were intended simply to illustrate how to evaluate tuneups, and the results should by no means be considered general.

Tuning these codes for a specific application would require new tests using application-specific input models; tuning code for general use is a much harder problem. It is possible to run tests using a wide variety of input classes, but there is no guarantee that every relevant input property that arises in practice has been checked.

One strategy for coping with this situation is to implement self-tuning data structures that respond to input properties observable at runtime. These properties may be measured explicitly in the code, by sampling the input instance and using statistics about the sample to configure the data structure. Input sampling can be performed as a preprocessing step (before the data structure is initialized) or periodically during the computation for on-the-fly adjustments.

This idea is not limited to data structures but can be applied to algorithms as well. Yaroslavskiy et al. [32], in their study of implementation strategies for quicksort, note that the best choice of partitioning code depends on how many duplicate elements are in the input. Their implementation of a sorting utility for JDK contains two partitioning functions, one that works best on distinct elements and one that worst best when duplicates are present. The median-selection code to choose the partition element also samples the input to decide which partitioning procedure to invoke.

Alternatively, self-adjusting data structures can be built to respond implicitly to patterns of access to their elements. For example a self-organizing list generally works to keep recently accessed elements near the front, to exploit locality of reference. A *hand built cache* is a memory structure that saves recently accessed elements so they can be found quickly by cache lookup instead of by another search of the data structure. If copying or storing elements in a cache is too expensive, a *hotlink* may be used instead: a hotlink is a direct link into a frequently accessed part of a data structure, which saves the cost of a conventional lookup to the popular location.

**Guideline 4.12** *When inputs are not known in advance, consider self-tuning data structures that respond to input properties observable at runtime.*

### 4.1.2 Tuning Code

Many of the algorithm tuning strategies described in Section 4.1.1 – such as pruning, propagation, preprocessing, and memoization – can be applied with equal success to lower-level code structures. The main difference is the scale at which opportunities for tuning are recognized: code tuning looks at loops and procedures instead of algorithm paradigms, and at memory layouts instead of data structures. While algorithm tuning often concentrates on reducing the number of times a code block is executed, code tuning often focuses on making a code block faster by rewriting source code so that the compiler emits fewer machine instructions in the block.

```
    a[0..n-1] contains elements to be sorted

1   for (i = 1; i<n; i++ ) {
        // Invariant:  a[0..i-1] is sorted
        // Invariant:  a[i..n-1] not yet sorted
2       for (j=i;  j>0 && a[j]>a[j-1]  ; j--) {
            //Invariant: a[j] > a[j-1]
3           tmp     = a[j];
4           a[j]    = a[j-1];
5           a[j-1]  = tmp;
        }
    }
```

Figure 4.11.  Insertion sort. The first implementation.

Many code tuning techniques are now routinely applied by optimizing compilers, which are generally accepted as doing a better job than humans can by hand tuning. Indeed, tuning by hand can be counterproductive nowadays because it prevents the compiler from recognizing familiar constructs as candidates for optimization.

Successful code tuning requires a good understanding of how compilers and machine architectures work. Even so, intuition can fail in light of the complexities of modern environments. It is important to test every small change made to the code, to check that it actually speeds up the computation. Run a small experiment measuring runtimes before and after each modification, perhaps with the test code in a loop so that time differences are big enough to measure. It also sometimes helps to inspect the object code to learn which optimizations are automatically applied by the compiler.

Rather than an extensive review of code tuning techniques, which are well covered elsewhere (see references in the Chapter Notes), this section surveys a few popular techniques that are not universally applied by compilers. The discussion is organized around three constructs that tend to have high overhead costs: loops, procedure calls, and memory allocations. Some additional aspects of code tuning are discussed in Section 4.2, which describes costs associated with the memory hierarchy and multicore computation.

*Loops*

Figure 4.11 shows a straightforward implementation of the familiar insertion sort algorithm. The outer loop iterates over elements of array a using index i; the inner loop uses index j to sift each element into proper position in the array.

```
      a[0..n-1] contains elements to be sorted

1     for (i = 1; i < n; i++ ) {
2          // Invariant: a[0..i-1] is sorted
           // Invariant: a[i..n-1] not yet sorted
3          int tmp = a[i];
4          for (j=i; (j>0 && a[j]>tmp); j--) {
               // Invariant: hole is at a[j]
5              a[j] = a[j-1];
6          }
7          a[j] = tmp;
      }
```

Figure 4.12. Insertion sort. This version illustrates code motion out of loop.

A loop in source code can be divided into parts: instructions in the *loop body* and instructions in the *loop header*. A loop header like for (i = 0; i < n; i++), for example, generates machine instructions for initializing i, incrementing i, and comparing i to n, which, together with the branching instruction(s) at the bottom of the loop, are called the *loop overhead*.

*Code Motion Out of Loops.* Our first tuneup involves moving code from inside a loop to outside, to avoid unnecessary repeated executions. Simple cases are easy for the compiler to take care of: for example, an assignment like x = 3; inside a loop body would automatically be moved out by most compilers.

But compilers cannot find every opportunity. In the insertion sort code, for example, we can notice that it is not necessary repeatedly to swap the elements a[j-1] and a[j] on lines 3 through 5; instead we could remove the element at a[i] from the array to make a hole, shift array elements to move the hole to the left, and then insert the element into the hole when the inner loop is finished. The new version is shown in Figure 4.12. This tuneup saves the cost of two assignments per inner loop iteration.

*Sentinels.* One way to move code out of the loop header is to install a dummy value, called a *sentinel*, at the end of the array. A sentinel can be used whenever the loop header contains two termination tests: one for the end of the array and one for some property of the current element. Placing a sentinel with the property that stops the loop at the end allows the two tests to be combined. A version of insertion sort with a sentinel is shown in Figure 4.13.

In this case, the use of a sentinel cuts in half the number of tests performed in the inner loop header. The array a [] must be expanded by 1 to hold the sentinel value, and loop indices must change accordingly.

```
a[1..n]  contains elements to be sorted
a[0]     contains the sentinel value -Infinity

1     for (i = 1; i <= n; i++ ) {
2         // Invariant: a[1..i-1] is sorted
          // Invariant: a[i..n] not yet sorted
3         int tmp = a[i];
4         for (j = i; a[j]>tmp; j--) { //new test
              // Invariant: hole is at a[j]
5             a[j] = a[j-1];
6         }
7         if (j==0) a[j+1] = tmp;
8         else a[j] = tmp;
      }
```

Figure 4.13.  Insertion sort. This version uses a sentinel to stop the inner loop.

Sentinels need not be restricted to use in arrays but can be installed to test for the "ends" of other types of data structures such as the leaves of a binary search tree or the root of a heap.

So do these tuneups really work? The table following shows mean CPU times (seconds) for 10 random trials at three problem sizes, using four C implementations of insertion sort, with/without the code motion and with/without the sentinel. The code was compiled with gcc -O3 (the highest optimization level) and tested using the Unix time utility on the HP platform described in the first timing experiments of Section 3.1.2.

|                        | $n = 40,000$ | 80,000 | 160,000 |
|------------------------|--------------|--------|---------|
| Original               | 0.65         | 2.66   | 10.59   |
| With code motion       | 0.40         | 1.61   | 6.43    |
| With sentinel          | 0.67         | 2.72   | 10.91   |
| With motion + sentinel | 0.30         | 1.22   | 4.88    |

Applying the code motion trick to the original implementation makes it faster, but applying the sentinel to the original makes it slower. Combining both tuneups creates the fastest implementation of the four. This is an example of an interaction effect, described in Section 2.2.2, in the discussion of factorial designs: the sentinel makes performance worse when used alone, but better when used in combination with code motion. This illustrates the importance of using full factorial designs to compare all combinations of alternatives when tuning code.

This table also illustrates a point made at the beginning of this section:

**Guideline 4.13** *Code tuning intuition fails in modern environments. Test every change to check that it really does improve speed things up.*

*More Loop-Tuning Ideas.* With that caveat and exhortation, here is a short list of additional techniques for making loops run faster.

- *Loop fusion.* Combine two side-by side loops like this:

```
for (i=0; i<n; i++) a[i] = i;
for (i=0; i<n; i++) b[i] = a[i];
```

Into one larger loop like this:

```
for (i=0; i<n; i++){
  a[i] = i;
  b[i] = a[i];
}
```

Fusing these two loops saves half the cost of a loop header, which can be very effective if the loop body code is small compared to the header. On the other hand, a loop with too many instructions in its body may interact poorly with the instruction cache and/or the data cache and consequently run more slowly. (Section 4.2.1 has more about locality and memory costs.) In those situations, *loop fission*, which reverses the preceding example, is the more efficient option.

- *Loop unrolling.* A tight loop like this:

```
for (i=0; i<n; i++)    b[i] = a[i];
```

Can be unrolled like this:

```
for (i=0; i < n-4; i++) {
  b[i]=a[i];
  b[i+1]=a[i+1];
  b[i+2]=a[i+2];
  b[i+3]=a[i+3];
}
for(; i<n; i++) b[i] = a[i];
```

Unrolling the loop four times removes three-quarters of the loop overhead cost.

- *Unswitching.* Move a decision from inside a loop:

```
for (i=0; i < n; i++) {
    if (type == 0) sum  += a[i];
    else prod *= a[i];
}
```

To outside the loops:

```
if (type==0)
    for (i=0; i<n; i++) sum += a[i];
else
    for (i=0; i<n; i++) prod *= a[i];
```

This opportunity for code motion may not be noticed by the compiler.

- *Nesting busy loops.* When using nested loops, put the busiest loop on the inside, changing this:

```
for (i=0; i<100; i++)
    for (j=0; j<10; j++)
        foo(i,j);
```

To this:

```
for (j=0; j<10; j++)
    for (i=0; i<100; i++)
        foo(i,j);
```

In the second case, the inner loop header test evaluates to `true` 1,000 times and to `false` 10 times, totaling 1,010 tests. In the first case, the inner loop header test executes 1,100 times.

- *Loop access order.* Section 4.2.1 describes a few more ideas for rewriting loops to achieve efficient patterns of memory access.

**Guideline 4.14** *Tune your loops.*

### Procedures

Every procedure call executed in a program corresponds to several machine instructions. Supposing procedure A calls procedure B, these instructions carry out the following tasks: allocating space on the call stack (a special area of memory) to hold local variables for B; initializing those variables; saving all register values for A; saving A's return address; and copying parameter values from A's local space to B's local space. A return from a procedure creates code to reverse this process. This extra code is called *procedure call overhead.*

The best way to eliminate procedure call overhead, of course, is to avoid calling procedures. This tuning technique can be especially powerful when applied to recursive algorithms, which contain large numbers of procedure calls. Unfortunately, replacing a recursive structure with loops is a notoriously difficult and error-prone process in general.

```
1 perms (double*  a, int k, int n) {
2    int i;
3    if (k == n-1) {
4        printPerm(a, n);
5        return;
6    }
7    for (i=k; i < n; i++) {
8        swap (a, k, i);        // try it
9        perms(a, k+1, n);      // recur
10       swap (a, k, i);        // restore it
11   }
12 }
```

Figure 4.14. Exhaustive Enumeration. This procedure prints all permutations of values in array a.

One exception to this general rule arises when the procedure contains only one recursive call that appears at the end (i.e., no post-recursion code). In this case, it is usually straightforward to rewrite the recursive procedure with a simple loop so that the procedure parameters become the loop control variables. This is called *removing tail recursion*. Some optimizing compilers can remove tail recursion automatically: as always, before trying this tuneup, check the emitted code to see whether it is necessary.

The code in Figure 4.14 uses exhaustive enumeration to generate all permutations of the contents of array a. This generation process is at the heart of the exhaustive search bin packing algorithm described in the case study of Section 4.1. Two tuning strategies are applied here.

INLINING PROCEDURE CALLS. Eliminate procedure call overhead for nonrecursive procedures by inserting the procedure body at the point of invocation, adjusting variable names as necessary. In Figure 4.14 the calls to swap on lines 8 and 10 can easily be replaced with three inline assignments:

```
tmp = a[k];
a[k] = a[i];
a[i] = tmp;
```

This saves two procedure calls per recursive stage in the computation.

*Collapse Procedure Hierarchies.* Another way to remove procedure call overhead in recursive programs is to merge two (or more) stages into one, using a recursion-unrolling technique similar to loop unrolling.

```
1 perms (double*  a, int k, int n) {
2       int i, j;
2.1     double tmp;
3       if (k == n-1) {
4          printPerm(a, n);
5          return;
6       }
6.1     if (k == n-2) {
6.2        printPerm(a, n);
6.3        tmp = a[k]; a[k] = a[k+1]; a[k+1] = tmp;
6.4        printPerm(a, n);
6.5        tmp = a[k]; a[k] = a[k+1]; a[k+1] = tmp;
6.6        return;
6.7     }
7       for (i=k; i < n; i++) {
8          tmp = a[k]; a[k] = a[i]; a[i] = tmp; //swap k
8.1         for (j = k+1; j < n; j++) {
8.2          tmp=a[k+1]; a[k+1] = a[j]; a[j]=tmp; //swap k+1
9                  perms(a, k+2, n);          // recur
9.1          tmp=a[k+1]; a[k+1] = a[j]; a[j]=tmp; //restore k
9.2           }
10         tmp=a[k]; a[k]=a[i]; a[i]=tmp; //restore k
11      }
12  }
```

Figure 4.15. Tuning procedures. The calls to swap are replaced with inline code, saving the cost of four procedure calls per recursive stage. The single for loop is replaced by a nested loop, which cuts in half the number of procedure calls.

In Figure 4.14, the single for loop in lines 7 through 11 that iterates to try all elements in position a[k] can be augmented with a nested loop that tries all elements in positions a[k] and a[k+1]. This trick cuts the number of procedure calls in half by replacing every other recursion with a loop iteration. This tuneup also requires changes to the termination test on line 4 to accommodate even and odd values of $n$.

The new version appears in Figure 4.15. A small experiment to test the four C programs implementing these tuneups produced the CPU times (seconds) shown in the following table. These tests were performed with printing commented out to highlight the effects of code changes.

| | $n = 11$ | 12 | 13 |
|---|---|---|---|
| Original | 1.44 | 17.29 | 224.73 |
| With inline | 1.59 | 19.06 | 247.76 |
| With collapse | 1.29 | 9.39 | 199.52 |
| With collapse + inline | 0.95 | 6.56 | 148.29 |

As before, the individual tuneups interact with one another. Writing the swap code inline was counterproductive when applied to the original code, but the code combining both tuneups is fastest, improving on the original by about 25 percent at $n = 13$.

But the more important story is told in the next table. The programs in the previous tests were complied without optimization, whereas the programs that follow were compiled with gcc -O3 using the highest optimization level.

| | $n = 11$ | 12 | 13 |
|---|---|---|---|
| Original | 0.43 | 6.53 | 65.03 |
| With swap inline | 0.44 | 6.75 | 65.96 |
| With collapse | 0.45 | 2.54 | 82.44 |
| With inline + collapse | 0.47 | 2.77 | 70.94 |

The optimizer was much more successful than hand tuning at speeding up this code. Furthermore, the hand-tuned code interfered with the compiler's ability to find some tuning opportunities. This created small speedups at $n = 12$ but larger slowdowns at $n = 13$. These results support another piece of advice given at the beginning of this section:

**Guideline 4.15** *Optimizing compilers are better than humans at tuning code. Step back and let them work their magic.*

The technique of collapsing procedure hierarchies can be especially effective when applied to the smallest $k$ problem sizes in the recursion, so that recursive calls at the lowest levels are replaced by a brute-force iteration.

*Parameters and Local Variables.* The cost of copying a parameter depends, first, on whether the value is passed *by reference* (via copying a pointer to the value) or *by value* (via copying the value itself), and, second, on whether the value is word-sized or a larger structure. Avoid the fatal combination of pass-by-value and large multielement structures.

If the parameter list contains only word-sized elements, parameter passing typically incurs very low overhead because parameters are stored in registers for fast access. Local variables are also faster to access than global variables because the compiler can place them in registers. If a global value must be updated frequently in some procedure, it sometimes pays to *localize the global value* by copying it to the local context, performing the updates, and then copying it back.

But there is no free lunch: *register spill* occurs when there are too many parameters and local variables for the available registers, and spillover values must be stored in main memory. Register spill causes runtimes to spike upward because main memory accesses are much more expensive than register accesses. When this happens, the right code tuning strategy is to shrink the footprint of local variables as much as possible.

**Guideline 4.16** *Reduce procedure call overhead by removing procedure calls and paying attention to data locality.*

### Objects and Memory Structures

High-level languages provide tools for grouping data elements together as units for easier reference. In Java and C++ this capability is provided by objects; in C the structured record type `struct` provides similar but more limited support.

To monitor memory use in Java: Use the `verbose:gc` setting to look at garbage collection statistics.

Memory space for objects and `struct`s is allocated and deallocated at runtime. In Java the `new` statement is used for object construction, and the garbage collector performs deallocation automatically; in C++ objects are constructed using `new` and deallocated using `free`, and in C the the `malloc` and `free` instructions may be used.

These allocation and deallocation statements have high instruction overhead. Constructing an object or `struct` requires machine instructions to locate the declaration of the object, contact the operating system to request storage space, and allocate and initialize the components. Freeing an object carries the expense of notifying the system. As with procedure calls, the best way to save the overhead costs of object construction is to reduce the number (and sometimes size) of objects constructed. Here are some tips.

- *Avoid object resizing* by allocating a large enough object in the first place. It is usually a good idea to use one system call to request a large block of memory and write special-purpose local code to make use of parts of it as needed. This idea can backfire when only a few elements are needed and cost of initializing the large structure dominates the cost of a few requests.

- *Embrace mutability.* A mutable object can change value after being constructed; an immutable object stays fixed throughout its lifetime. Immutability means that every change to the object must take place via construction of a new object. For example, Java `String` objects are immutable, and every method acting on a String object constructs a new one, whereas `StringBuffer` objects supply almost the same functionality without new constructions. Immutability supports code correctness by eliminating side effects, but mutability can be faster. One way to exploit mutability is to recycle objects by rewriting their contents. For example, in a linked data structure, consider building a list of free (deleted) link elements that can be reused by overwriting data fields and links.
- *Exploit static bindings* by moving initializations, casts and type conversions, and hierarchy searches for objects, from runtime to compile-time operations: the fastest code is no code at all. On the other hand, if a field is accessed frequently, it may be cost-effective to move it from a static to a dynamic context, for better memory locality.

**Guideline 4.17** *Eliminate dynamic memory overhead by right-sizing, reusing, and exploiting static bindings.*

## 4.2 Tuning to Reduce Instruction Costs

The algorithm and code tuning techniques of the previous sections aim at reducing instruction execution counts, under the basic premise that having fewer instructions to execute means smaller execution times. However, on modern architectures the total number of instructions executed can sometimes be less important than the order in which they are executed.

Two factors come into play. First, the time to execute any given instruction depends on where its data values are located in the memory hierarchy; the location of those data elements depends on how and when they were previously accessed. Similarly, program time can depend dramatically on how and when I/O instructions are executed. Second, multicore architectures contain a small number of separate processors that run concurrently. A process may be divided into some number of threads that can be executed in parallel on multicore processors: the amount of parallel speedup that can be realized depends on how the threads are organized and how they communicate.

### 4.2.1 Memory and I/O

Figure 4.16 shows a schematic diagram of the memory hierarchy and the I/O system. The salient properties of the memory management system were described in detail in Section 3.1.4 in the section on time and memory. To recap: when an

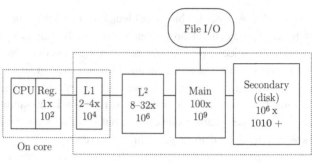

Figure 4.16. Memory and I/O systems. In this simplified diagram, physical memories are arranged in order by distance from the CPU. Access times are shown in units of instruction cycles, and capacities are shown in units of bytes. Real memory systems may contain additional memories not shown in the diagram and have capacities and response times that may vary considerably from the numbers shown here. The I/O system supports access to files on disk.

instruction uses a data word not available in a register, the CPU issues a read or write request to the memory system, together with a virtual address specifying which word is needed. In a similar way, I/O instructions in programs that read or write from files prompt the CPU to issue requests with virtual addresses that are handled by the I/O system. I/O access is typically much slower than access to memory.

When the CPU makes a read request for the word at address $A$, the memory management system locates the data word in the hierarchy, copies it into the next-closer memory and then to the next-closer memory, and so forth, until the data word reaches the CPU. Thus, memory response time depends on how close $A$ is to the CPU when requested. In order to make room for $A$ in the faster memories, the management system may have to choose another word $B$ to evict, that is, move back to a slower memory. The memory system works proactively to promote data in addresses that are likely to be needed soon to the faster memories. Promotion and eviction policies vary from level to level in the hierarchy but are typically based on two principles:

- **Temporal locality:** Once an element is accessed, it is likely to be accessed again soon.
- **Spatial locality:** If a data element is accessed, data elements stored near it in the virtual address space are likely to be accessed soon.

For example, a policy found at all stages of the hierarchy is to move a requested element into faster memory together with a block of adjacent virtual addresses, on the theory that they will be needed soon (spatial locality). These blocks have

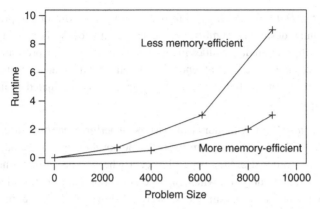

Figure 4.17. Runtimes and the memory system. Program runtimes plotted against problem size exhibit a characteristic "knee" shape as the data outgrow successive memories in the hierarchy. Reducing the data footprint moves the inflection points (crosses) to the right; improving the pattern of memory access moves the points downward.

different names at different points in the memory hierarchy: cache controllers, which manage data movement between caches and main memory, move a *line* of data at a time, and virtual memory (VM) systems, working between main and secondary memory move much larger blocks called *pages*. For another example, VMs typically timestamp page references so that the least-recently used page can be evicted, on the theory that it is least likely to be needed again soon (temporal locality).

The implication of all this for code tuners is that computation time can depend significantly on the size of the virtual address space and on the patterns of memory access used in the program. Bentley [8] points out that program runtimes, when plotted against input size, tend to exhibit a characteristic "knee" shape shown in Figure 4.17. Each bend, or inflection point in a line, corresponds to a point where the capacity of some memory in the hierarchy is exceeded. The two main strategies for writing memory-efficient code are (1) shrinking the footprint of the data, which moves the inflection points to the right, because larger problem sizes can fit into fast memory; and (2) improving the pattern of memory access, which decreases the slope of a given segment.

In contrast to the memory management system, which responds to virtual addresses contained in instructions, the I/O system responds to explicit instructions within a program: open, close, read, and write. Thus the programmer can control when requests are emitted and how many data words are requested at a time.

The next three sections highlight three strategies for tuning code in this context: shrinking the memory footprint, reorganizing data access patterns, and coding for I/O efficiency.

*Shrinking the Data Footprint.* Shrink the memory footprint of the program by removing and redesigning memory elements to occupy less space so that a smaller percentage of program data resides in the slower memories. If a program's virtual address space can be made small enough to fit entirely into cache, or into a small number of pages, the cost of slower memory accesses is eliminated entirely. Here are some tips.

- Avoid *memory leaks.* A memory leak is a type of performance bug – a term coined by Bentley [7] to refer to program errors that do not alter correctness but do create excessive resource use. Memory leaks occur when the programmer neglects to free allocated memory, or, when garbage collection is present, to dereference unneeded data. The program runs slower and slower as it uses more and more memory and in the worst-case scenario can halt the memory system. Memory leaks can can be hard to detect and diagnose. Use `meminfo` and `vmstat` to monitor memory usage in Unix systems or check the Windows Task Manager. A number of commercial memory debugging tools are also available.
- Downsize the input data footprint by changing the presentation in a preprocessing step, for example, by removing unneeded fields, recasting to smaller data types, or removing redundant copies.
- Apply standard techniques of data compression: use *differential encoding* to replace a sequence of similar multiword values with their (smaller) differences; large data fields with many duplicates can be entered into a table and replaced with indices into the table.
- This whole approach is diametrically opposite to the earlier-mentioned strategy of memoizing (described in the essential subgraph case study in Section 4.1). Memoization reduces instruction counts at the cost of growing the memory storage space; shrinking the memory footprint by removing memoization may increase the instruction count but may reduce overall running time because instructions execute faster. The goal is to find the balance point between these two opposing principles. Strategies to shrink memory are likely to be most effective when the footprint is large in the first place.

**Guideline 4.18** *Sometimes less is more: trade space for time. Sometimes less is less: a smaller memory footprint makes code run faster.*

### Tuning for Cache Efficiency

The second approach to reducing memory cost – which can be applied at either the algorithm or the code-tuning level – is to organize the program so that access to memory elements displays as much spatial and temporal locality as possible, since the memory system is designed for optimum performance on these access patterns.

```
// simple matrix multiplication
for (i = 0; i < n; i++)
  for (j = 0; j < n; j++)
    for (k = 0; k < n; k++)
      c[i][j] = c[i][j] + a[i][k] * b[k][i];

// tiled matrix multiplication using 2x2 blocks

for (i =  0; i < n; i += 2)
  for (j = 0; j < n; j += 2)
    for (k = 0; k < n;  k++)
      for (x = i; x < min(i+2, n); x ++)
        for (y = j;  y < min (i+2, n); y++)
          c[x][y]  = c[x][y] + a[x][k] * b[k][y];
```

Figure 4.18. Tiling. Replace array accesses in line-by-line order with array accesses in block-by-block order. Each block should be small enough to fit into a cache line.

We start with some simple rules for writing loops and arrays to achieve good cache performance.

- *Reuse sooner rather than later.* When an array item is accessed, use it repeatedly. For example, use one pass through an array, instead of three passes, to calculate the mean, min, and max statistics.
- *Respect memory layouts.* Loops that iterate through two-dimensional arrays run faster when the scanning order in the loops matches the order in which arrays are laid out in virtual memory. Most modern languages (except Fortran) use row-major order, so that elements A[0, 0], A[0, 1], A[0, 2], A[1, 0], A[1, 1] ... would appear sequentially in memory. A nested loop that traverses such an array should put the first (leftmost) index in the outermost loop. This principle can also be applied to higher-dimensional arrays.
- *Stride-right.* The *stride* or step size of an array is the number of memory addresses between successive elements: an array with stride 1 stores elements in successive addresses. Loops that increment using i++, to match the stride of the array, can be faster than loops that use larger increments. Loop increments that match the cache line size are especially slow.
- *Tiling matrices.* Sometimes matrix computations require both row-major and column-major order, making cache efficiency difficult to achieve. A classic example is matrix multiplication, $C = A \times B$, where matrix $A$ is accessed in row-major order and $B$ in column-major order. *Tiling* can help: Break each matrix into

blocks (each small enough to fit into a cache line) and access the matrices block-by-block. Figure 4.18 shows code for conventional matrix multiplication and tiled matrix multiplication, assuming that a 2x2 subarray fits into a cache line.

- *Fields and arrays.* Is it better to group data fields together in an array of records or separately in a collection of arrays? The answer is either to match the record structure to the access pattern or to match the access pattern to the record structure, keeping in mind cache line sizes. For example, if fields $A$ and $B$ are accessed together in time and small enough to fit in a cache line, locate them together in an array of records and use a single loop to access them. But if $A$ and $B$ are too big to fit together in the cache, put them in separate arrays and access them with two loops. Contrariwise, if two fields are not processed together, put them in separate arrays.

The basic idea here is to exploit the "whack-a-mole" principle: you could score big points in the carnival Whack-a-Mole game if, instead of popping up randomly, the moles exhibited temporal locality (a mole that pops up now is likely to pop up again) and spatial locality (nearby moles pop sooner than faraway moles). For best performance from the memory system, your program should generate array addresses to optimize whack-a-mole scores.

**Guideline 4.19** *The whack-a-mole principle: tune memory accesses to obey spatial and temporal locality.*

This principle can also be applied to algorithm and data structure design. Ladner et al. [20] provide a good illustration in their analysis of cache-efficient binary search. In the standard implementation the search keys are stored in sorted order in an array. The first search probe is at the middle (median element) of the array, the second probe is at one of the two quartiles, and so forth, like this:

| Key | 10 | 20 | 30 | 40 | 50 | 60 | 70 |
|---|---|---|---|---|---|---|---|
| Probes | 3 | 2 | 3 | 1 | 3 | 2 | 3 |

This access pattern has no locality. A better alternative is to organize the array so that the first element probed is at the first position in the array, the second probes are in the next two positions, and so forth, like this:

| Key | 40 | 20 | 60 | 10 | 30 | 50 | 70 |
|---|---|---|---|---|---|---|---|
| Probes | 1 | 2 | 2 | 3 | 3 | 3 | 3 |

This arrangement has good spatial locality and ensures that the array is accessed in increasing index order, although some indices are skipped.

An even better idea is to organize the keys into groups so that each group is contained in the node of a perfectly balanced binary tree. Such a tree can be laid out in memory (like a heap) so that the locations of parents and children can be calculated arithmetically, rather than with explicit pointers. Ladner et al. [20] describe two tree-based implementations of binary search, as follows.

- A **cache-aware** implementation exploits platform-specific knowledge of how many keys can fit into a cache line. In general, an interior node in the tree contains a key stored together with its children and immediate tree descendants, as many as the line will hold. For example, the root node may hold the median and the two quartiles; the children of the root hold the octiles; and so forth. This exploits temporal locality because when $x$ is accessed, its immediate descendants in the search tree will be loaded together with it into the cache. Here is an example layout assuming three keys per cache line.

| Keys | (40, 20, 60) | (10, 30, $x$) | (50, 70, $x$) |
|---|---|---|---|
| Cache loads | 1 | 2 | 2 |

- The **cache-oblivious** version decomposes the tree to exploit spatial locality, without making assumptions about cache capacities. Here is how it works: break the binary tree $T$ into groups according to some level $h$ in the tree ($h$ is a power of 2). The top of the tree forms subtree $T_0$, which has $2^{h/4}$ leaves. The remaining $2^{h/2}$ (disconnected) subtrees form trees $T_1 \ldots T + 2^{h/2}$. Store the trees $T_0, T_1 \ldots$ sequentially in memory, so that nodes likely to be accessed sequentially in time are near one another, and all probes are in increasing order by address.

The authors observe that cache-aware and cache-oblivious variations of this tree structure can improve overall computation time by factors of 2 to 8 over classic binary search, even though the number of elements accessed is identical in all versions.

### Tuning for I/O Efficiency

A large body of research has developed around design of I/O-efficient algorithms, also called external memory or "big data" algorithms. These types of algorithms are critically important when the data set to be processed is too large to fit within main memory and must be accessed on disk using file I/O.

I/O efficiency involves a combination of algorithm tuning – so that data elements are accessed in an order that matches their storage layout – and code tuning – so that source code instructions with unusually high cost overhead can be minimized. Here are some sources of high costs in I/O processing, and what to do about them. References to more resources on I/O efficiency may be found in the Chapter Notes.

- *Minimize open/close operations.* Opening and closing files require scores of machine instructions. To minimize this cost, avoid repeated opening and closing and instead make one pass through the data file whenever possible. Storing data in one big file rather than many small files also reduces open/closing costs.
- *Reduce latency.* Read/write operations create two kinds of time delays: *latency* refers to the amount of time needed to contact the disk and get it ready for data transmission, and *transfer time* refers to the time actually spent moving data elements between disk and main memory. Reduce latency by using a few large data transfer operations – that is, reads or writes with many data elements specified – instead of several small ones.
- *Decouple I/O and instruction execution.* When possible, remove reads and writes from inside the loops so that instructions do not have to wait on I/O operations. I/O buffering and threading can be used to decouple I/O operations from instruction executions by running the two tasks in separate computation threads.
- *Exploit locality.* Data access in files can be optimized in ways similar to data access in memory: organize the data on disk to match the computation order and organize the computation order to make best use of spatial and temporal locality.

This last strategy can lead to dramatic reductions in computation time for I/O-bound applications. Here are two of many examples that may be found in the algorithm engineering literature.

Ajwani, Dementiev, and Meyer [1] describe an external memory breadth-first search (BFS) algorithm that can traverse enormous sparse graphs too big for main memory. They show how to decompose these massive graphs into smaller subgraphs to be stored in files for fast processing in BFS order. On graphs containing $2^{28}$ nodes, their I/O-efficient algorithm takes around 40 to 50 hours (depending on graph type) both to decompose the graphs and to perform the BFS traversal, while conventional methods take 140 to 166 days to traverse the same graphs.

Arge et al. [2] describe a project to develop I/O-efficient algorithms for problems on grid-based terrains. A grid-based terrain is a geospatial data set where each point in the grid is labeled with spatial coordinates (such as latitude and longitude) and an elevation. One problem is to compute the *flow accumulation* points of the terrain – the low points where water will likely flow. Computing the flow accumulation requires initially placing one unit of flow at every grid point and then distributing flow to neighbor points according to their height differences. For a $\sqrt{N} \times \sqrt{N}$ grid this can be done in memory in $O(N \log N)$ by sorting grid points by height, then scanning the sorted points and distributing flows to downhill neighbors. This algorithm is not I/O efficient, however, because sorting destroys the geospatial locality needed to transfer flow from points to their neighbors. In the worst case, processing each point in sorted order would require a read and write for half its neighbors, totaling $O(N^2)$ I/O operations.

The authors show how to organize the computation so that flow distribution can be performed in a single I/O pass. They compare the standard internal algorithm and their I/O-efficient version using five geospatial data sets ranging in size from 12MB to 508MB. On small inputs the internal algorithm runs slightly faster than the external algorithm, but once a threshold based on main memory size is reached, the internal algorithm grinds to a halt, spending all its time thrashing among I/O accesses. On one data set containing 512MB grid points the I/O-efficient algorithm finished in about four hours; the authors estimate that the internal algorithm (halted after four days of computation) would have taken several weeks to finish.

**Guideline 4.20** *Pay attention to the frequency, order, and size of I/O requests in I/O bound computations.*

### 4.2.2 Concurrency

Nowadays every desktop or laptop is a multicore platform with two to eight separate processors (sometimes more) capable of executing code in parallel. The main tool for speeding up algorithms to run on these new platforms is to apply *multithreading*, which splits a given process into two (or more) separate instruction streams: each stream is called a thread. In a perfect world, a process could be split into $p$ threads to run on $p$ processors and finish $p$ times faster than on one processor. Of course, this so-called perfect parallel speedup cannot always be realized, since some parts of a computation are necessarily sequential. Algorithm and code tuning strategies can be applied to achieve partial – but still significant – parallel speedups in many cases.

Finding general strategies for exploiting low-level parallelism is a relatively new area of experimental algorithmic research, and there are more questions than answers about how to proceed. One obstacle to progress is the absence of a general model of parallel computation that reflects real computation times on a wide variety of modern architectures. As a result, an implementation tuned for performance on one platform may require substantial reworking to achieve similar results on another. Even within a single platform, performance can depend dramatically on how the process scheduler maps threads onto processors and on the order in which separate threads are executed: scheduler decisions are impossible to predict yet may have more impact on computation time than any particular tuneup. Finally, inadequate time measurement tools on concurrent system make it difficult to measure properly the effects of any given tuneup.

Although our understanding of best practice in this area is nowhere near fully developed, a handful of general tuning techniques can be identified. The basic idea is to decompose an algorithm into some number of distinct threads that work on separate subproblems (with separate memory address spaces) and do not need to communicate with one another. Threads slow down when information must be shared, because communication requires synchronization, which means that one process is likely to be stuck waiting for another. This is true even when communication takes place via data reads and writes to the same virtual address. The *cache coherence problem* refers to the possibility that processor-specific caches may hold different values for the same element (at the same virtual address), without being aware of one another. If the runtime system does not take steps to ensure cache coherence, the programmer must incorporate synchronization code to the threads: either way synchronization slows down the parallel computation.

Here is a list of algorithm and code tuning strategies for exploiting threading on multicore computation.

- *Divide-and-conquer* algorithms often are natural candidates for paralleliza-tion, since they work by breaking the problem into independent subproblems. Therefore, each recursive procedure call can trigger a new thread that works independently of sibling threads. A small amount of synchronization may be required if the divide-and-conquer algorithm performs a postorder processing step.
- *Branch-and-bound* algorithms can sometimes be structured so that multiple threads can work independently on solution subsets, except for intermittent sharing of their currently optimal solutions. The question is how to balance the synchronization costs of sharing new solutions against the instruction savings from pruning when better solutions are shared.
- Many *array-based computations* are natural candidates for parallel decompo-sition, if the arrays can be separated into independent sections processed in separate threads.
- *Decoupling slow processes*, such as those involving user interfaces and I/O, from the main instruction-heavy computation allows the main thread to avoid being continually interrupted by synchronization requests.
- *Minimize threading overhead.* Thread creation and destruction have high over-head, so a few long-lived threads may run faster than many short-lived threads. When communication among threads is necessary, a few synchronization phases with larger blocks of shared data are more efficient than many small synchronization phases with smaller blocks of shared data.

## 4.3 The Tuning Process

We turn now from the question of how to tune algorithms and code to consider questions of when and why.

Certainly performance considerations should come into play well before implementation – let alone code tuning – begins. The code to be tuned should have "good bones," which can only be obtained by proper decomposition of the system into well-structured components and by choosing the right algorithm to implement in the first place. No amount of tuning can rescue a fundamentally flawed design with poor asymptotic performance from the start.

Furthermore, algorithm and code tuning should not begin until after *all* the code is written. The tune-as-you-go strategy is a recipe for failure: the important performance bottlenecks in a program can only be identified once the code is complete and can be run on realistic-sized inputs.

Start by building a simple, straightforward implementation of the algorithm and apply your best verification and validation skills to ensure that that implementation is correct.

**Guideline 4.21** *Think about performance while working on system design and algorithm design and building correct code. But do not think about tuning until after these steps are completed.*

Once a well-validated implementation is in hand, the next question is whether or not to proceed with the tuning project. Many experts have weighed in on this question:

- *The First Rule of Program Optimization: Don't do it. The Second Rule of Program Optimization (for experts only!): Don't do it yet.* – Michael A. Jackson [17]
- *We should forget about small efficiencies, say about 97% of the time: premature optimization is the root of all evil.* – Donald Knuth (quoting C. A. R. Hoare) [19]
- *More computing sins are committed in the name of efficiency (without necessarily achieving it) than for any other single reason – including blind stupidity.* – William A. Wulf [31]
- *The irresistible appeal of efficient coding's siren song and the the number of programming sailors who crash their programming ships on the siren's rocky shore calls for a code-tuning safety-awareness program.* – Stephen McConnell [23]

Listen to the experts: tuning can be evil, sinful, and a siren's call. Too many people waste too much time on misguided tuning efforts that have little effect on performance. The best code for the application is not always the best-tuned code, because tuning adds complexity and exploits special assumptions about application or platform.

Before starting any tuning project, think carefully about what kind of improvement you can realistically expect. A variation on Amdahl's law – normally applied to assessing potential speedups from parallel computation – can be used to estimate the impact of your tuning effort. Suppose section A of your code can be sped up by a factor of $F$, and section A accounts for a proportion $P$ of total computation time. Then the overall speedup $S$ from tuning is limited to $S = (1 - P) + (1/F) \cdot P$. Section A might run 10 times faster ($F = 10$), but if A represents only 1/10 of the total computation ($P = 0.1$), then total runtime is reduced by only 9 percent ($.91 = (.9 + (.1 \cdot .1))$). Is a speedup from 1 minute to 0.91 minute really worth several days of coding, debugging, and maintenance time? If the answer is no, stop now – the code is fast enough.

**Guideline 4.22** *Tune judiciously. It is a huge waste of valuable human time to build code that is incrementally faster but much harder to validate, debug, and maintain.*

Sometimes the answer is yes. Tuning pays off when running times can be reduced from weeks and months to seconds and minutes, moving the computation from infeasible to feasible. Smaller improvements by factors of 10, or even by 10 percent, can be critically important on code that is run many times over or in real-time applications. Here is a procedure to apply when the decision is to go forward with the tuning project.

1. Call the simple validated implementation Version 0 (V0). Build a collection of testbed instances that spans the range of algorithm performance: worst case, best case, random instances, typical instances from applications, and so forth. Run V0 on those instances, recording both the outputs (solutions) and the computation times. Save these results (and the random number seeds if necessary for exact replication) and make a backup copy of V0. Identify a target at which the code will be deemed "fast enough."
2. Is the current version fast enough for your application? Are the tuning strategies you can think of likely to produce only marginal improvements? If the answer to at least one question is yes, stop. If more tuning is needed, use profiling to inform the decision about what sections of code to focus on.
3. Start by looking for algorithm-scale tuneups. As illustrated in the case studies, these tuneups often involve balancing increased cost in one code section against lower cost in another section. When faced with multiple options that interact, it may be necessary to implement a factorial experiment to evaluate combinations

of options. Simplify the experimental design using operation counts and code profiles to find promising ideas to try first.

Implement one or more tuneups and compare the new versions to V0, using the testbed instances, to check that the code remains correct. Fix the bugs and compare to V0 to see which version is faster. Make a backup copy of the old version and go to step 2.

4. When you run out of ideas for algorithmic tuneups, or when the most expensive code block is part of a data structure, focus on the data structure. Data structure tuning should take place *after* algorithm tuning, because algorithm tuneups change operation frequencies. It is best to consider data structure efficiency as a whole rather than focusing on individual operations. Apply one or more tuneups; check the new version against V0 for correctness and fix the bugs. Then compare the new version to the previous version. If the new code is faster, make a backup copy of the old version and go to step 2.

5. Once your algorithm and data structure tuning ideas are exhausted, it is time to apply code tuning to shrink instruction counts within the dominant code blocks. Follow the previous procedures for ensuring that new versions remain correct and are more efficient; then go to step 2.

6. Programs with high memory access costs or high I/O overhead are candidates for memory-efficient and I/O-efficient tuning techniques. Follow the previous procedures and go to step 2.

It is not clear when the decision about whether to implement threaded or parallel versions of the implementation is best made. On the one hand, switching to a parallel implementation is best done early in the process, because simple implementations are easier to parallelize, and tuning should proceed with individual threads. On the other hand, given the relatively poor measurement tools and the relatively large (but unpredictable) influence of the scheduler, thread tuning can be a difficult and error-prone process. Tuning early exacerbates the problem.

## 4.4 Chapter Notes

This chapter has surveyed a number of techniques for tuning algorithms and tuning code, using illustrations in case studies and from the algorithm engineering literature. Here are some pointers to further reading on these topics.

See [11] or [24] to learn more about properties of the essential subgraph $S$ and the ES algorithm. Frieze and Grimmett [14] have derived an upper bound on the largest essential edge that holds for any graph where edge weights are assigned at random, independent of vertices. Their bound implies that random uniform graphs contain only the smallest $cn \log n$ of $n^2$ edges.

For more on algorithm design paradigms, see any algorithms textbook, such as [12] or [16]. Code tuning, sometimes with algorithm tuning included, has been covered widely. See works by Bentley [3], [4], [5] Bryant and O'Hallaron [10]; Kernighan and Pike [18]; Leiss [21]; Müller-Hannemann and Schirra [27]; and Shirazi [29].

A good discussion of how the memory hierarchy and I/O systems work may be found in Bryant and O'Hallaron [10]. To learn more about tuning techniques for out-of-memory problems, see Gibson et al [15] and Vitter [30]. Here are the tips and techniques developed in this chapter.

4.1  *Propagation: replace a full computation in each recursive stage with an incremental computation that passes partial results as parameters.*

4.2  *Preprocessing: add work before the algorithm begins, to save work when the algorithm executes.*

4.3  *Finesse a calculation: replace an expensive exact calculation with an inexpensive bound or approximation, in such a way that the overall result is unchanged.*

4.4  *Memoization: Save results in a table to avoid having to redo the work.*

4.5  *Loop abort: add a test to stop a loop early.*

4.6  *Filtering: avoid inserting an element into a data structure if the element cannot affect the outcome of the computation.*

4.7  *Customize the data structure: select a data structure implementation that best matches its pattern of use.*

4.8  *Pruning: insert simple tests to skip recursive calls. Boost the strength of these tests by using preprocessing or by changing computation order.*

4.9  *Control subproblem sizes: remove elements from subproblems before recurring; add or subtract work to balance subproblems.*

4.10  *Hybridize a recursive program to make individual stages faster.*

4.11  *Instead of changing the code to match the input, change the input presentation to match the code.*

4.12  *When inputs are not known in advance, consider self-tuning data structures that respond to input properties observable at runtime.*

4.13  *Code tuning intuition fails in modern environments. Test every change to check that it really does speed up the code.*

4.14  *Tune your loops.*

4.15  *Optimizing compilers are better than humans at tuning code. Step back and let them work their magic.*

4.16  *Reduce procedure call overhead by removing procedure calls and paying attention to data locality.*

4.17 *Eliminate dynamic memory overhead by right-sizing, reusing, and exploiting static bindings.*

4.18 *Sometimes less is more: trade space for time. Sometimes less is less: a smaller memory footprint makes code run faster.*

4.19 *The whack-a-mole principle: tune memory accesses to exploit spatial and temporal locality.*

4.20 *Pay attention to the frequency, order, and size of I/O requests in I/O bound computations.*

4.21 *Think about performance while working on system design and algorithm design and building correct code. But do not think about tuning until after these steps are completed.*

4.22 *Tune judiciously. It is a huge waste of valuable human time to build code that is incrementally faster but much harder to validate, debug, and maintain.*

## 4.5 Problems and Projects

Many of the implementations described in this book may be downloaded from the companion Web site *AlgLab*: www.cs.amherst.edu/alglab. Here are a few suggestions for projects using these programs.

1. Suppose you can improve the running time of a given program by a factor of 2 in one day's work, but no more than a factor of 32 (five day's work) can be squeezed out of any given program. Your time is worth $100 per hour. This includes time waiting for a program to finish a computation. Which of the following scenarios is worth the price of a week of algorithm engineering effort?

   a. The program is executed once a day and takes one hour to run.

   b. The program is executed a million times per day, and each run takes one second.

   c. The program is executed once a month and takes one day to run.

2. Download the code for the exact bin packing algorithm from *AlgLab* and apply the additional algorithm tuneups described in the case study. What other tuneups can you think of? Do these tuning strategies work when applied to other types of inputs?

3. Download the code for the essential subgraph algorithm from *AlgLab* and apply more tuneups, especially the heap-memoization idea. How well do the tuneups work? What happens if the algorithm is run on other types of inputs?

4. Can the MCMC algorithm of Chapter 3 be improved by substituting a different data structure (such as a hash table) that better fits the patterns of data access? What operations and costs would you measure to help you answer this question?

Can improvements be found by shrinking the data footprint and/or reordering data access patterns?

5. Apply the algorithm and code tuning strategies in this chapter to any of the programs available in *AlgLab*. How much improvement can you find?

6. Find out which code tuning strategies your favorite optimizing compiler uses. Compile C programs with no optimization and with optimization and compare the assembly language output to look at the differences. How much difference does compiler optimization make to computation time?

7. Build a suite of simple C programs to evaluate techniques for speeding up loop and array accesses. Compare running times at a variety of input sizes and try to locate the performance knees illustrated in Figure 4.17. How much variation do you observe from platform to platform?

## Bibliography

[1] Ajwani, Deepak, Roman Dementiev, and Ulrich Meyer, "A computational study of external-memory BFS algorithms." *Proceedings of the Seventeenth Annual ACM-SIAM Symposium on Discrete Algorithms*, SODA '06, 2006.

[2] Arge, Lars, Laura Toma, and J. S. Vitter, "I/O efficient algorithms for problems on grid-based terrains," *ACM Journal of Experimental Algorithmics*, Vol 6, Article 1, 2001.

[3] Bentley, Jon, *Writing Efficient Programs*, Prentice-Hall, 1982.

[4] Bentley, Jon, "Faster and faster and faster yet," Software Explorations, *Unix Review*, June 1997. (Available from UnixReview.com, web.archive.org).

[5] Bentley, Jon, *Programming Pearls*, 2nd ed., ACM Press/Addison-Wesley, 2000. See especially part II (columns 6 through 10): Performance.

[6] Bentley, Jon, "Industrial-strength data compression: Build or buy?" Power Point talk given at Amherst College, 2011.

[7] Bentley, Jon, "Performance bugs," Power Point slides, 2011.

[8] Bentley, Jon, "Cache-conscious algorithms and data structures," Power Point slides, April 20, 2000.

[9] Bentley, Jon, L. and M. Douglas McIlroy, "Engineering a sort function," *Software–Practice and Experience*, Vol 23, Issue 1, pp. 1249–65, November 1993.

[10] Bryant, Randal E., and David R. O'Hallaron, *Computer Systems: A Programmer's Perspective*, Prentice-Hall, Boston. pp. 46–93. 2003.

[11] Cooper, Colin, Alan Frieze, Kurt Mehlhorn, and Volker Priebe, "Average Case Complexity of Shortest-Paths Problems in the Vertex-Potential Model," in J. Rolim, ed., *Randomization and Approximation Techniques in Computer Science,* LNCS 1269, Springer-Verlag, 1997.

[12] Cormen, Thomas H., Charles E. Leiserson, Ronald L. Rivest, and Clifford Stein, *Introduction to Algorithms*, 3rd ed., MIT Press, 2009.

[13] Delling, Daniel, Peter Sanders, Dominik Schultes, and Dorothea Wagner, "Engineering Route Planning Algorithms," in *Algorithmics of Large and Complex Networks: Design, Analysis, and Simulation*, Springer-Verlag, Berlin, Heidelberg, 2009.

[14] Frieze, A. M., and G. R. Grimmett, "The shortest path problem for graphs with random arc-lengths," *Discrete Applied Mathematics*, Vol 10, pp. 55–77, 1985.

[15] Gibson, Garth A, Jeffrey Scott Vitter, and John Wilkes, "Strategic directions in storage I/O issues in large-scale computing," *ACM Computing Surveys, Special ACM 50th Anniversary Issue: Strategic Directions in Computing Research,* Vol 28, Issue 4, December 1996.

[16] Goodrich, Michael T., and Roberto Tamassia, *Algorithm Design*, Wiley, 2001.

[17] Jackson, Michael, *Principles of Program Design*, Academic Press, 1975.

[18] Kernighan, Brian W., and Rob Pike, *The Practice of Programming*, Addison-Wesley, 1999.

[19] Knuth, Donald E., "Structured programming with goto statements," *Computing Surveys* Vol 6, Issue 4, pp 261–301, 1974.

[20] Ladner, Richard E., Ray Fortna, and Bao-Hoang Nguyen, "A Comparison of Cache Aware and Cache Oblivious Static Search Trees Using Program Instrumentation," in *Experimental Algorithmics*, Springer Lecture Notes in Computer Science, No 2547, pp. 78–92, 2002.

[21] Leiss, Ernst L., *A Programmer's Companion to Algorithm Analysis,* Chapman & Hall/CRC, 2007.

[22] Martínez, Conrado, and Salvador Roura, "Optimal sampling strategies for Quicksort and Quickselect," *SIAM Journal on Computing*, Vol 31, No 3, pp. 683–705, 2001.

[23] McConnell, Steve, "Introduction to Code Tuning," in *Code Complete: A Practical Handbook of Software Construction*, Microsoft Press, 1993.

[24] McGeoch, Catherine C., "All pairs shortest paths and the essential subgraph," *Algorithmica* Vol 13, Issue 5, pp. 426–441, 1995.

[25] McGeoch, Catherine C., and Doug Tygar, "Optimal sampling strategies for quicksort," *Random Structures and Algorithms*, Vol 7, pp. 287–300, 1995.

[26] Moret, Bernard M. E., David A. Bader, and Tandy Warnow, "High-performance algorithm engineering for computational phylogenetics," *Journal of Supercomputing*, Vol 22, pp. 99–111, 2002.

[27] Müller-Hannemann, Matthias, and Stefan Schirra, eds., *Algorithm Engineering: Bridging the Gap between Theory and Practice*, Springer LNCS Vol 5971, 2010. See especially chapter 6: "Implementation Aspects".

[28] Osipov, Vitaly, Peter Sanders, and Johannes Singler, "The Filter-Kruskal minimum spanning tree algorithm." Proceedings of ALENEX 09, Article number 52, Available from: www.siam.org/proceedings/alenex/2009.

[29] Jack Shirazi, *Java Performance Tuning*, O'Reilly, 2000.

[30] Jeffrey Scott Vitter, "External memory algorithms and data structures: Dealing with massive data," *ACM Computing Surveys*, Vol 33 Issue 2, pp. 209–271 2001.

[31] William A. Wulf, "A case against the Goto," *Proceedings of the 25th National ACM Conference,* pp. 791–797, 1972.

[32] Yaroslavskiy, Vladimir, Joshua Bloch, and Jon Bentley, "Quicksort 2010: Implementing and timing a family of functions," Power Point slides. 2010.

# 5

# The Toolbox

Write your workhorse program well; instrument your program; your experimental results form a database: treat it with respect; keep a kit full of sharp tools.

Jon Louis Bentley, *Ten Commandments for Experiments on Algorithms*

They say the workman is only as good as his tools; in experimental algorithmics the workman must often build his tools.

The *test environment* is the collection of programs and files assembled together to support computational experiments on algorithms. This collection includes test programs that implement the algorithms of interest, code to generate input instances and files containing instances; scripts to control and document tests, tools for measuring performance, and data analysis software.

This chapter presents tips for assembling and building these components to create a reliable, efficient, and flexible test environment. We start with a survey of resources available to the experimenter. Section 5.1 surveys aspects of test program design, and Section 5.2 presents a cookbook of methods for generating random numbers and combinatorial objects to use as test inputs or inside randomized algorithms.

Most algorithm researchers prefer to work in Unix-style operating systems, which provide excellent tools for conducting experiments, including:

- Utilities such as `time` and `gprof` for measuring elapsed and CPU times.
- Shell scripts and makefiles. Shell scripting makes it easy to automate batches of tests, and makefiles make it easy to mix and match compilation units. Scripts and make files also create a document trail that records the history of an experimental project.
- I/O pipes for combining input generators, test programs, and analysis tools.
- Filters such as `awk` and `sed` that are used to parse, reformat, and recombine input and data files.

Resources specific to algorithmic experiments are surveyed in the next section.

## Resources for Experimenters

The first tip for building the test environment is to make use of the many resources that are available to you.

**Guideline 5.1** *Stand on the shoulders of giants: use the experimental resources available to you in-house and on the Internet.*

Even if you are implementing from scratch, test code from libraries and repositories can be used for backup implementations in validation tests or measured to compare your new ideas to state-of-the art alternatives. Other resources include instance generators, input testbeds, and tools for program measurement and data analysis.

The following is a short list of resources available on the Internet. There are far too many problem-specific code repositories and testbeds available to be listed here: to find resources for a particular problem or application, follow links on the sites listed here, or try a keyword search using the problem name as key.

1. The *Stony Brook Algorithm Repository* has links to implementations of algorithms for many standard combinatorial problems. The repository can be searched by language or by problem; each implementation referenced in the collection is given a quality rating. www.cs.sunysb.edu/~algorith/.
2. The *DIMACS Implementation Challenges* site contains solvers, generators, and input instances contributed by participants in several DIMACS Implementation Challenges carried out over the past two decades. Each challenge focuses on a different open problem in algorithm research. dimacs.rutgers.edu/Challenges/.
3. *LEDA* is a C++ library of fundamental data types and data structures, as well as implementations of leading algorithms for several problem areas. Some of the software is available only by license agreement, but free and low-cost licenses for academic researchers are available. www.algorithmic-solutions.com.
4. *CGAL*, the Computational Geometry Algorithms Library, provides C++ implementations of data structures and algorithms for problems in two-dimensional (2D) and three-dimensional (3D) computational geometry. www.cgal.org.
5. The *Stanford GraphBase* has resources for experiments on combinatorial problems, especially on graphs. The site contains data structures and source code for many graph algorithms, random generators, structured instances and a list of Open Challenge problems. ftp.cs.stanford.edu, directory pub/sgb.
6. The *INFORMS OR/MS Resource Collection: Computer Programs* contains links to programs and tools for solving optimization problems of interest in the

operations research community, with an emphasis on local search and linear programming. www2.informs.org/Resources/Computer_Programs.

7. The ACM *Journal of Experimental Algorithms* publishes software, data, and input files to accompany published research papers in experimental algorithmics. www.jea.acm.org.
8. The *R Project for Statistical Computing* is an open source software environment for statistics and data analysis, with strong support for exploratory and graphical methods. All of the graphs and statistical analyses in this text were produced using the R package. www.r-prog.org.

Another good source of tools and test files may be the guy in the office down the hall. Experimental research is not performed in a vacuum: find out what others have done and make use of resources available in your workplace or research community.

### 5.1 The Test Program

It is useful to make a conceptual distinction between the *application program* that is implemented for use in a real-world scenario and the *test program* that is built to support experiments. An application program reads input, solves the problem, and writes output; the test program does the same but may have additional code that reads experimental parameters and prints performance statistics. The application program interface is designed for compatibility with the larger application environment; the test program interface is designed to support experiments.

The application and test programs may in fact be identical, but that need not always be the case. Sometimes the two are developed in parallel; sometimes the test program is transferred to application code at the end of an experimental project.

What the two programs have in common is the abstract algorithm that they both implement. The test program becomes a tool for simulating algorithm behavior, and the algorithm becomes the vehicle for interpreting test results and for translating insights from experiments to design and analysis tasks aimed at applications.

The *test apparatus*, sometimes called the "harness" or "scaffolding," is the extra "wrapper code" added to an implementation to support experiments. Sometimes experimental goals dictate that the code be invoked exactly as in the application; that may require placing all the test apparatus outside the source code.

The amount of time and effort to invest in building the test apparatus depends on the project. In experiments where precise and accurate runtime statistics are required, the test program should be bare of apparatus, so that the extra code does not skew runtime measurements. A bare implementation is fine for quick tests of basic properties and features. The apparatus for a pilot study may be small and simple, consisting of just a few counters and a print statement; if necessary, this code can be removed at compile time for timing tests. A workhorse study incorporating multiple experiments and complex designs may need a sturdy apparatus that supports correct results, fast and flexible experiments, and good documentation.

The next few sections survey tips for building the test program and apparatus.

### 5.1.1  Correctness

Above all, the test program must faithfully represent the algorithm being studied. Two key weapons in the war against programmer errors are *validation* and *verification*.

### Validation

Validation testing is a process of checking that the output is a correct solution for the given input. Start by assembling a good variety of input instances for this purpose: include *stress test* inputs (see Section 2.2.1) that exercise extreme and boundary conditions, *coverage* inputs to exercise different execution paths within the program, and *typical* inputs with features that are common in applications.

In order to perform a validation check you need to know what the correct solution is. In many experimental situations – especially when the inputs are large or the problem is NP-hard – it may be difficult to tell whether a given solution is correct. How do you know this coloring really is optimal? How do you know that this is in fact the minimum spanning tree of a 5000-vertex graph? These fundamental difficulties can not always be eliminated, but steps can be taken to increase confidence in program outputs, as follows.

- Create a suite of contrived inputs for which outputs are easy to compute by hand. Examples include inputs with only 0's and 1's (or all 0's) as weights and inputs with optimal solutions known by construction.
- Even with NP-hard problems it is always possible to construct a verifier program that checks that the output meets feasibility conditions. Mehlhorn et al. [13] describe a collection of program checkers for validating solutions to geometric problems.
- Find instances with known solutions in public testbeds.
- Replicate the experiments with a different solver and compare outputs. As mentioned in Section 2.1, the pilot program and the workhorse program should be implemented independently, by separate people working on different platforms. This creates two versions of the test program so that outputs can be compared; software repositories and libraries may also serve as sources of backup programs for replication experiments.

After the initial validation experiment, replication tests should be performed every time the test program is modified. Automating the replication process makes this rule easier to follow; Unix script files and the `diff` utility for finding differences in files are ideal for this purpose.

## *Verification*

While validation involves inspecting inputs and outputs, verification is a formal procedure for checking the code against a set of *assertions* embedded in the code. An assertion is a Boolean expression that makes a claim about the state of the program at a given point during execution.

Although a full discussion of formal verification is outside the scope of this text, figure 5.1 illustrates the basic idea. The figure shows a procedure that inserts x into its sorted position in array A. The array is of size n and when the procedure starts A[0..top] already contains elements in sorted order.

Three types of assertions are shown in comments: *preconditions* on lines 2 to 5, *loop invariants* on lines 9 to 11, and a *postcondition* on line 17.

The preconditions state the properties that must hold when the procedure is called for this code to be correct: the array must exist, the value of top must be

```
1   InsertInArray (A,   n,   top,   x) {
2           // Pre:   A[0..n-1] is defined
3           // Pre:   0 <= top < n-1
4           // Pre:   A[0 .. top] is sorted in increasing ord
5           // Pre:   A[top+1 .. n-1] is free
6           j = top;
7           top++;
8           while (j > 0) {
9                   // Inv:   A[0 .. j] is sorted
10                  // Inv:   A[j+1] is free
11                  // Inv:   A[j+2 .. top] is sorted and > x
12                  if (A[j] > x) A[j+1] = A[j];
13                  else break;
14                  j--;
15          }
16          A[j+1] = x;
17          // Post:   A[0 .. top] is sorted and contains x
18          return A;
19      }
```

Figure 5.1. Verification. Preconditions, postcondition, and loop invariants for inserting x into sorted array A.

between 0 and n-2 (1 less than the maximum array index, to make room for the new element), and the elements in A[0..top] must already be in sorted order. The postcondition describes the condition that is guaranteed to hold upon exiting the procedure.

The loop invariants described the conditions that must hold each time around the loop. Checking correctness with respect to loop invariants involves three questions:

1. *Are the invariants true when the loop is entered the first time?* In this case, the invariant on line 9 follows from the precondition on line 4 and the assignment on line 6: A[0.. top] is sorted, and j is initialized to top. Line 10 follows from preconditions on lines 3 and 5 and the assignment on line 6. The assertion on line 11 regarding A[j+2 .. top] is true because j+2 is greater than top (lines 6 and 7), so no such array elements exist; we say the condition *holds vacuously*.

2. *Assuming the invariants are true at the top of the loop, do they hold at the bottom of the loop?* Imagine inserting lines 9, 10, 11 just after line 14:

```
14.1    // A[0..j] is sorted
14.2    // A[j+1] is free
14.3    // A[j+2 .. top] is sorted and > x
```

Assuming the invariants at the top of the loop hold for the old value of j, we check that the invariants at the bottom hold for the new value of j. Invariant 14.1 follows from line 9 and the decrement on line 14. Invariant 14.2 holds because the assignment on line 12 makes A[j] free, and the decrement on line 14 makes A[j+1] the location of that free element. Finally, invariant 14.3 follows from line 11, plus the comparison on line 12: if A[j] <= x, the code would not have reached the bottom of the loop, because of the break statement. This value is copied into A[j+1], and with the decrement on line 14 the assertion holds for A[j+2].

3. *Do the invariants imply correctness after the loop ends?* Assertions 14.1, 14.2, and 14.3 are true at the loop bottom and therefore are true when the loop terminates. Therefore, the assignment on line 16 is correct, and the postcondition is true.

The simple act of writing out loop invariants in comments and checking these three questions against the code can be powerful insurance against common coding mistakes like off-by-1 errors, omitting initializations, mishandling loop control variables, running off the ends of arrays, and so forth. It also helps to write a procedure or macro to check preconditions at runtime, as shown in the following:

```
void assert(boolean e, String msg){if (!e) print(msg);}

9     assert((0<=top && top<n-1), "Assertion 9 fails");
10    for(i=1; i<=top; i++)
          assert(a[i-1]<=a[i],"Assertion 10 fails");


}
```

**Guideline 5.2** *Apply your best validation and verification techniques to build confidence in test program correctness.*

### *5.1.2 The Interface*

Besides correct, the test program and test apparatus should be designed for ease of use, flexibility, and efficiency. Here are some tips.

#### *Inputs*

Test programs run on two types of inputs: the instance to be solved, and specifications of test parameters such as number of trials and which performance indicators to report. These inputs and specifications may be embedded in the source code or presented at runtime. Each approach has its merits.

Input instances from applications are normally in separate files, of course, but instance generators may be located inside or outside the solver program. Placing the generator inside the test program saves the overhead costs of reading inputs, which can be especially important when huge numbers of inputs are tested or when I/O costs dominate computation costs. If random instances are to be reused in other tests, it is easier to save the random number seeds than the instances in files. If experiments are run on both generated and real instances, it may be simplest to read everything from files so that I/O costs are comparable across test runs.

Placing experimental parameters in the source code is simple and fast, and fine for small projects. The drawback is that frequent changes to the experimental design require frequent changes to the source code; these types of changes are slower to implement, more difficult to automate, harder to document, and more likely to introduce errors, than changes presented at runtime. With the latter convention, the act of running a new test need not be slowed down to the pace of human coding and compiling time. It is faster to create new input files: automating that step is even faster and less error-prone.

**Guideline 5.3** *Test parameters that change frequently should be specified at runtime rather than compile time.*

One approach is to create a little language of keyword-attribute pairs that specify test parameters. The front end code to interpret such a language is easy to modify by changing the keyword list and adding new operations. Example C and Java front ends built along these lines may be downloaded from *AlgLab*.

For example, the sample input file that follows (used in the essential subgraph case study described in Section 4.1) specifies that 3 random graphs of each size $n = 50\ldots90$, incrementing by 20, are to be generated; the random number seed is also specified.

```
trials 3
nmin 50
nmax 90
nstep 20
seed   77271179
```

The source code uses default values when some lines are not present in the input; for example, if no random number seed is given, the system time is used. This basic format can be extended to specify, for example, which performance indicators to report, file formats, and source and destination files.

If several variations of the test program are to be evaluated, each distinct version of the source code should be saved for future reference. In some cases, it is simpler to write separate routines, which can be mixed and matched at compile time using tools such as `makefile`, or at runtime via a driver program that selects the desired combination.

### Outputs

Output files from experiments contain both solutions and reports of performance indicator measurements. These may be written to separate files (`stderr` and `stdout` if convenient) or to a single file. If the latter, include line labels so that solution data can be extracted for validation and performance data can be extracted for data analysis. The Unix `awk` filter is handy for this purpose.

The performance data should be in a format that can be sent directly to the data analysis software package. In the case of the R statistical package that I use, a numerical data matrix is most convenient. Performance data are written one line per trial, with each line containing both the experimental parameters (input size, trial number, code version, etc.) and performance measurements for that trial. This matrix format is also well suited to analysis as an Excel spreadsheet.

Bentley [3] also points out the value of building a "self-describing" data file that contains a complete record of the test parameters that produced it. Descriptions of the input and parameter values not included in the data matrix can be included as comments.

**Guideline 5.4** *Write self-describing output files that require minimal reformatting before being submitted for data analysis.*

For example, in the data file that follows (generated by the input commands shown earlier), the first comment line gives the meaning of each column of data; comments at the end, the test parameters. The first two columns record test parameters (trial number and number of nodes), and the remaining six columns show performance data from each trial.

```
c trial nodes   edges   total   cost rank   treelimit
  0 50    1225    135 0.208441 245   99     0.535475
  1 50    1225    97  0.153967 188   84     0.326501
  2 50    1225    135 0.241896 305   125    0.441828
  0 70    2415    157 0.180725 440   184    0.350588
  1 70    2415    177 0.155560 332   187    0.387239
  2 70    2415    181 0.133144 326   112    0.337195
  0 90    4005    211 0.099920 400   175    0.261381
  1 90    4005    232 0.097191 409   219    0.244378
  2 90    4005    243 0.093865 402   178    0.281792
c nmin 50
c nmax 90
c nstep 20
c seed   77271179
c trials 3
```

Exceptions to this general format may sometimes be necessary; the main idea is to create output files that need a minimal amount of reformatting by hand before they can be analyzed.

### 5.1.3 Documenting the Experiments

Every experiment leaves a trail of files containing input instances, design point specifications, and test outputs. Without *documentation* of every experiment, the project can quickly spiral out control: it becomes impossible to keep track of which outputs go with which code versions and inputs, or even what the numbers mean.

Keep a notebook (electronic or otherwise) open at all times during experiments to jot down notes, reminders, and questions.

My approach to documentation is to run each experiment in a Unix shell script, which creates a record of the input file(s), command line arguments, code versions, and output file(s) used in the experiment. Each script file is saved and recorded by name in the notebook file, which also mentions the question prompting the experiment and describes the file formats. Complex data analyses in R can be preserved as source files and recorded in the notebook. The self-describing output files mentioned earlier are also useful in this regard.

It is equally important to keep track of source code revisions. Especially in algorithm engineering projects, many versions of the source code may be tested in many combinations. The test apparatus may go through several revisions as well, as new designs and measurement strategies are developed.

It helps to incorporate at least a rudimentary system of version control to manage all these changes to source code. Each recompilation represents a revision, which should be described (using source code comments and/or a separate notebook file), given a distinct number or timestamp, and stored in a backup repository for future reference. Gent et al. [8] suggest using a commercial version control software system, especially when test code modules are continually evolving and shared among a group of researchers.

Record-keeping complexity can be reduced, as suggested earlier, with a test apparatus that accepts specifications at runtime rather than compile time.

**Guideline 5.5** *Document your experiments! You should be able to return to your test environment a month later and know exactly how to replicate your own results.*

## 5.2 Generating Random Inputs

Section 2.2.1 surveys the variety of input classes that may be incorporated into algorithmic experiments. Input classes that are generated rather than collected – including random, random structured, and hybrid inputs – require generators to build the instances. This section surveys basic techniques for generating random numbers, permutations and samples, and combinatorial structures that are common in algorithmic experiments.

### 5.2.1 Uniform Random Variates

A *random number generator* (RNG) is a procedure that can be invoked repeatedly to produce a sequence $U_0, U_1, \ldots$ of *random variates* with certain properties described later.

Most operating systems and language libraries contain RNGs based on the *linear congruential* (LC) method. The method uses a (global static) variable s that is initialized with a value called the *seed*. Each time the RNG is called, the procedure applies an arithmetic formula to s, and the result becomes the new value of s that is returned by the procedure.

The example LC procedure shown in Figure 5.2 applies an arithmetic function to s using three constants a, b, and m. (The term *linear congruential* refers to this function family.) The % denotes the modulus operator, which returns the integer

```
static long s;

void rngInitial(long seed)   {s = seed;}

long random() {
   long a = 1664525;
   long b = 1013904223;
   long m = 2^32;
   s = (a*s+b)  %   m;
   return  s;
}
```

Figure 5.2. A random number generator. This is an example of a linear congruential generator.

remainder from dividing (a*s + b) by m. The modulus operation ensures that s is always between 0 and m-1.

The values of a, b, and m must be carefully chosen according to number-theoretic principles to ensure that good random sequences are generated. The combination is from *Numerical Recipes* [16]; others may be found in Knuth [10] and L'Ecuyer [12].

An integer in the range $[0, m-1]$ can be converted to a real number in the range $[0, 1)$ (the bracket notation means including 0 but not including 1) by dividing by $m$. Many software libraries contain generators that use this technique, with $m$ set to a very large number, to return floats and doubles instead of integers and longs. In this section we refer to specific generator types with rngInt(m), which returns a random int or long in $[0, m-1]$, and rngReal(), which returns a random float or double in $[0, 1)$.

Let $U_0$ denote the initial seed value, and let $U_1, U_2 \ldots$ denote the sequence of *uniform random variates* returned by successive calls to a given RNG. Generators of uniform random variates are evaluated according to two properties:

1. *Uniformity.* Each possible integer in $[0, m-1]$ is equally likely to be generated as the next $U_i$.
2. *Independence.* The probability that $U_i$ takes a particular value $u \in [0, m-1]$ does not depend on previous variates $U_0 \ldots U_{i-1}$.

All linear congruential methods, and indeed all computer-based random number generators, fail property 2, because each variate $U_i$ depends exactly on the value of the previous variate $U_{i-1}$. For this reason LC generators are technically called *pseudorandom number generators*, although the distinction is often ignored in common parlance.

Pseudorandom generators are evaluated according to how well they mimic a true (theoretical) source of independent uniform variates. A good RNG has a long *period*, which means it runs for a long time before repeating a value – a maximum period of $m$ is ideal but not always realized. The RNG is also expected to pass tests of uniformity and randomness. A standard collection of statistical tests has been developed to test property 1 and to detect patterns in the $U_i$ sequence that would be unusual in a truly independent source of variates. These tests look at, for example, the lengths of "runs" above and below the mean, the lengths of monotonically increasing and decreasing sequences, distributions of poker hands that encode the variates, and so forth. See Knuth [10] for a survey of these tests.

The linear congruential RNGs available nowadays in most systems are considered adequate for many but not all purposes; see [15] for a survey of common features and problems. Here are some tips for making best use of them.

- Initialize with a big integer seed value, ideally using as many digits as the type allows. Small integer seeds create sequences that start out less random but improve as more variates are generated. If the initial seed value cannot be controlled (because it is set by a procedure external to the test program, for example), run the RNG for several iterations to get past initial conditions.
- The low-order bits of integers generated by LC methods are less random than the high-order bits. To mimic, say, a coin toss with a random sequence of 0's and 1's, do not use a formula based on low-order bits, such as `r = rngInt() % 2`. On some systems this could produce a strictly alternating sequence of 0's and 1's, or a sequence of all 1's. Instead use the high order bits:

    ```
    if (rngReal() < 0.5) r=0; else r=1;
    ```

- Linear congruential generators tend to exhibit patterns of serial correlation (a type of nonrandomness) within short subsequences. For example, assigning $(U_i, U_{i+1}, U_{i+2})$ in sequence to create random points in 3-space can yield sets of points that line up on hyperplanes. To avoid this problem when generating random points in D-space, use different RNG streams with separate seeds for each dimension; apply a combination of scrambling and skipping operations to break up patterns in short sequences; or use a different category of RNG, such as a linear feedback shift register (LFSR). See Knuth [10] for an introduction to LFSR generators.
- A common technique for initializing the seed is to call the (Unix) system `time` command, which returns a long integer recording accumulated clock ticks since some startup date. If two calls to the time command occur in succession, the clock may not have had a chance to advance.

- Linear congruential methods should never be used as a source of random numbers in cryptographic applications, because the generating function is too easy to guess. They can also create problems in experiments that require huge numbers of variates – more than the period allows – and/or a high degree of statistical precision in the results. For these applications alternative generators (more random, but slower) are recommended.

All other categories of random variates for computational experiments are created by algorithms that transform or combine sequences of uniform variates generated by RNGs. Here are two simple one-line transformations.

- To generate an integer $I$ uniformly in the range $[a,b]$ (inclusive), use
  `I = a + (int) (rngReal()*(b-a+1));`
- To generate a real $R$ in the range $[a,b)$ use the formula `R = a + rngReal() * (b-a);`

Even if a given RNG passes all tests of randomness, some small pattern of nonrandomness could be magnified by such a transformation, in such a way that the experimental outcomes are artifacts of the RNG and not reflective of "true" (theoretical) properties. It is always wise to replicate key experimental results by substituting a different RNG and comparing the outputs.

### 5.2.2 Random Permutations

A *permutation* of the integers $1\ldots5$ is a particular ordering, such as $(5, 1, 3, 2, 4)$ or $(1, 2, 3, 5, 4)$. A *random permutation* of size $n$ is generated such that each of the $n!$ possible orderings of the first $n$ integers is equally likely to appear.

Random permutations are common in algorithm studies. Algorithms like Random in Figure 2.3 and SIG in Figure 2.7 in Chapter 2 generate random permutations as a processing step; also, average-case inputs for many standard algorithms and data structures, including quicksort, insertion sort, and binary search trees, are defined in terms of random permutations. A random tour of a graph corresponds to a random permutation of the vertices.

The code to generate a random permutation in array `perm[1...n]` appears in the following. This loop should be implemented as shown: plausible-looking variations, for example, choosing a random index in $1\ldots n$ instead of $1\ldots i$ at each iteration, do not yield outputs that are uniformly distributed.

```
Random Permutation (n) {
    for (i = 1; i<=n; i++) perm[i] = i;    // initialize
    for (i = n; i>=2; i--) {
        r = (int) (rngReal() * i) + 1;    // random in 1..i
```

```
    tmp = perm[i];                         // swap
    perm[i] = perm[r];
    perm[r] = tmp;
  }
  return perm;
}
```

This procedure takes $O(n)$ time to generate a random permutation of $n$ integers.

### 5.2.3 Random Samples

A *random sample* is a subset of $k$ elements drawn from a collection of $n$ elements, such that each possible subset is equally likely to be drawn. We assume here that a sample is drawn from the integers $1 \ldots n$. The random sample may be drawn *with replacement*, which means that duplicates are allowed (that is, we imagine replacing each element after it is drawn from the set), or drawn *without replacement*, which means that duplicates are not allowed.

Random sampling can be used to create a small version of a large data set while preserving its statistical properties or to create a hybrid input instance by sampling from a space of real-world components. Sampling can also be used to create random combinatorial objects with certain types of structures: for example, random samples of vertices could be designated "source" and "sink" in a flow network.

Sampling with replacement is easy: just call the RNG $k$ times. The loop that follows samples $k$ integers with replacement from the integer range $[1 \ldots n]$ in $O(k)$ time.

```
SampleWithReplacement (n, k) {
    for (i=0; i<k; i++)
            sample[i] = (int) (rngReal()*n)+1;
    return sample;
}
```

To generate a sample without replacement when $k$ is much smaller than $n$, use the same loop with a set data structure to reject duplicates, until $k$ distinct integers are collected:

```
SampleWithoutReplacement (n, k) {
    Set S = empty;
    while (S.size() < k) {
            r = (int) (rngReal()*n)+1;     // sample 1..n
            if (!S.contains(r)) S.insert(r);
    }
    return S;
}
```

```
static int k;               // sample size
static int n;               // sample range is [1...n]
static int s = 0;           // selected
static int c = 0;           // considered

int orderedSampleNoReplacement() {
    double  p;
    int nextInt;
    boolean done = false;
    while (!done) {
            p = (double) (k-s)/(n-c);
            if (rngReal() < p) {   // with probability p
                nextInt = c + 1;
                s++;
                done = true;
            }
            c++;
    }
    return nextInt;
}
```

Figure 5.3. Ordered integer samples. Sampling $k$ integers from $1 \ldots n$ without replacement, in increasing order. The next integer in the sample is returned at each invocation of this routine.

If $k$ is near $n$, this loop spends too much time rejecting duplicates toward the end of the process; in this case, it is more efficient to generate a random permutation of $1 \ldots n$ and then select the first $k$ elements of the permutation.

### Ordered Integer Samples

Sometimes the experiment calls for a random sample of size $k$ from $1 \ldots n$, generated without replacement and sorted in increasing order. For example, an ordered integer sample may be used to select from a pool of $n$ real world elements, such as URLs from a trace of network activity, or a directory of test input files. The ordered sample is used in a linear scan through the pool to pull out sampled elements by index.

A simple approach is to generate the sample without replacement as shown previously, and then sort the sample. Sorting takes $O(k \log k)$ time and $O(k)$ space, which may be fine in many situations.

Faster methods are known, however. The algorithm sketched in Figure 5.3, due to Fan et al. [7] and Jones [9], generates a sample of $k$ integers from the range $[1 \ldots n]$, on the fly, returning the next integer in the sample at each invocation.

```
static double k;              // total in sample
static double i = k;          // counter
static double m = 1.0;        // current top of range

double orderedSampleReals() {
    m = m * exp(ln (rngReal()) / i);
    i--;
    return m;
}
```

Figure 5.4. Ordered reals. Generating a sample of $k$ doubles from $[0, 1)$ in decreasing order. The next double in the sample is returned at each invocation of the procedure.

To understand how it works, note that the integer 1 (or any particular integer) should be a part of the final sample with probability $k/n$. If 1 is selected, then 2 should be part of the final sample with probability $(k - 1)/(n - 1)$; if 1 is not selected, 2 should be selected with probability $(k)/(n - 1)$. Let c denote the number of integers that have been considered so far in the selection process, and let s denote the number that have already been selected for the sample. Then the probability of selecting the next integer is equal to $(k - s)/(n - c)$. At each invocation the procedure considers integers in increasing order according to that probability, until one is selected.

This algorithm requires constant space. The time to generate $k$ of $n$ integers is proportional to the last integer generated, or $O(n - n/k)$. This may be preferable to the sample-sort-scan approach when the sample is too large to be stored conveniently in an array; it also may be more efficient if the test program can sometimes stop before the entire sample is generated.

### Ordered Reals

A related problem is to generate a sorted sample of $k$ reals uniformly without replacement from $[0, 1)$. Bentley and Saxe [2] describe an algorithm that creates such a sample on the fly, using constant space and constant time per invocation. Like the preceding method, this algorithm is preferred if the sample is too big to store in advance, or if sorting takes too much time. The algorithm generates the sample variates in decreasing order – for a sample in increasing order, just subtract each variate from 1.0.

The algorithm is shown in Figure 5.4. The idea is first to generate random variate $M_1$ according to the distribution of the *maximum* of a sample of $k$ variates from $[0, 1)$. Once $M_1$ is generated, the next variate represents the maximum $M_2$ of a sample of $k - 1$ variates from $[0, M_1)$, and so forth. The first variate $M_1$ is generated

```
ReservoirSample(k, Pool) {
  // Pre: Pool contains at least k elements
  S.init(empty); // priority queue of pairs with key u

  for (i=1; i<=k; i++) {        // initial sample
    u = rngReal();
    p = Pool.take(i);           // take element i
    S.insert(p,u);
  }
  int n = k+1;
  while (Pool.hasElement(n)) {
    u = rngReal();
    if (u <= S.minKey())    {
      S.extractMin()            // delete old
      p = Pool.take(n);         // take element n
      S.insert(p, u);           // insert new
      n++;
  }
  return S.data();
}
```

Figure 5.5. Reservoir sampling. This procedure returns a random sample of size $k$ from a pool of $n$ elements where the size of the pool is not known in advance.

using the formula $M_1 = U_1^{(1/k)}$, which can be coded as shown in the figure; ln is the natural logarithm function, and exp exponentiates $e$, the base of natural logarithm. Subsequent variates $M_{i+1}$ are scaled by multiplying by $M_i$.

### Reservoir Sampling

The *reservoir sampling* problem is to generate a random sample of $k$ elements from the integers $1 \ldots n$ on the fly, where $n$ is not known in advance.

For example, the experiment may call for $k$ lines to be sampled at random from an input file without prior knowledge of the file size, or of $k$ packets from a router trace without knowing in advance how many packets will pass through the router. An application of reservoir sampling appears in the selection procedure of the markov.c program shown in Figure 3.4, which samples a random array element ($k = 1$) from a subarray $a[i \cdots j]$, without prior knowledge of the subarray size.

The reservoir sampling algorithm due to Knuth [10] is sketched in Figure 5.5. Start by selecting the sample $(1, 2, \ldots k)$, which is the correct choice if $k = n$. If it turns out that $n = k + 1$, a new sample can be constructed from the old one as follows: with probability $1/n$ replace a random element in the current sample with the value $n$; otherwise with probability $1 - 1/n$ do not change the sample.

The algorithm continues this way for each new $n$ in sequence, replacing random elements in the current sample according to appropriate probabilities.

A convenient way to manage these probabilities is to create a pair $(i, u)$ that associates pool element $i$ with a real number $u$ chosen uniformly at random from $[0, 1)$. These pairs are stored in a priority queue $S$ using $u$ values as keys. When the algorithm is finished, the elements tied to the $k$ smallest of $n$ random reals $u \in [0, 1)$ form the sample in $S$.

### 5.2.4 Nonuniform Random Variates

Variates generated from a *nonuniform* distribution have the property that some values appear more frequently than others. Nonuniform data can be used to model a wide variety of real-world phenomena, from patterns of access at Web sites, to population densities in maps, to distributions of file sizes, to lengths of words in text.

Nonuniform distributions are also widely used in robustness tests of algorithms. Many algorithms and data structures, for example, cell-based geometric algorithms, display best performance when the inputs have a uniform or near-uniform distribution; experiments are used to learn how performance degrades when inputs move away from this theoretical ideal.

A *discrete probability distribution* $P = (p_1, p_2, \ldots p_n)$ specifies the probability that each integer $i \in 1 \ldots n$ is likely to appear next in a sequence of random variates $R_1, R_2, \ldots$. For example, the distribution $P = (.5, .3, .2)$ specifies that 1 is generated with probability .5, 2 is generated with probability .3, and 3 is generated with probability .2. Sometimes probabilities are specified by a *probability density function* $p(i)$ instead of a list. For example, the probability density function for the roll of a random die is $p(i) = 1/6$ for $i \in [1 \ldots 6]$. If $P$ is a *continuous* probability distribution, the variates $R_i$ take values in some real range that may be bounded or unbounded. Continuous distributions are usually specified by probability density functions. No matter how the distribution is specified, the probabilities always sum to 1.

We say a distribution $P$ *models* a real-world scenario if the variates generated according to $P$ tend to have the same statistical properties as naturally occurring events in that scenario. The following is a short list of classic scenarios and the distributions that have been used to model their properties. Each distribution corresponds to a family of density functions parameterized by the values in parentheses.

Code for simple generation tasks is shown in the list, but more complicated procedures are omitted here because of space constraints. Precise mathematical definitions of these distributions and generator code may be found in DeVroye's [5] comprehensive and definitive text and in most simulation textbooks, for example, [4], [11], or [17].

- A **Bernoulli trial** is a single event with two possible outcomes A and B, which occur with probabilities $p$ and $1 - p$. This distribution can be used to model, for example, a coin toss ($p = .5$), a random read or write to a memory address, or a random operation (insert, delete) on a data structure. The *Bernoulli (p)* distribution generates a sequence of random outcomes in Bernoulli trials as follows:

```
loop:
    if (p > rngReal())   generate(A);
    else generate(B);
```

The *binomial(t, p)* distribution models the number of failures (B) among $t$ independent Bernoulli trials with success (A) probability $p$. Use this distribution, for example, to generate counts of how many heads and tails are observed in $t$ coin flips.

The *geometric (p)* distribution models the number of initial events B before the first occurrence of A in a sequence of Bernoulli trials: use this distribution to generate, for example, a count of how many reads occur before the next write. The *negative binomial (k, p)* distribution models the number of initial events B before the $k^{th}$ event A. Use this to generate a random count of inserts before the $k^{th}$ delete operation.

- A **Poisson process** is a system where events occur independently and continuously at a constant average rate, for example, clients arriving at a Web site or packets arriving at a router. The discrete *Poisson(λ)* distribution models the number of events (arrivals) occurring in a fixed time interval, where $\lambda$ is the average number of events in the interval.

  Use the continuous *exponential (λ)* distribution to generate random time intervals between successive events in a Poisson process. To generate a random variate $X$ according to this distribution use the formula $X = (-\ln U)/\lambda$, where $U$ is a random uniform real in $[0, 1)$ and ln is the natural logarithm.

- The **normal** $(\mu, \sigma)$ distribution is used to model quantities that tend to cluster around their mean $\mu$; parameter $\sigma$ denotes the amount of "spread" away from the mean. This is the famous bell-shaped curve, used to model situations in which variation from the mean can be interpreted as a sum of many small random errors. Classic examples include positions of randomly moving particles, cumulative rainfalls in a period, scores on standardized tests, and errors in scientific measurements.

  To generate a variate $N$ according to the standard normal distribution with mean $\mu = 0$ and deviation $\sigma = 1$, generate two uniform reals $U_1$ and $U_2$ and apply the formula

$$N = \sqrt{-2\ln U_1}\cos(2\pi U_2).$$

Alternative formulas that are faster and/or more accurate in some cases may be found in the references cited earlier.

- The **lognormal** $(\mu, \sigma)$ distribution describes variables that can be seen as the products, rather than sums, of many random errors – that is, the logarithms of these variates are normally distributed. This distribution is skewed, with a compressed range of low values near the mean and a long tail of high values spread over a larger range. Classic examples found in nature include size measurements of biological phenomena (height, weight, length of hair, length of beak) and financial data such as changes in exchange rates and stock market indices. The lognormal distribution and the related *Pareto* distribution have been used to model file sizes in Internet transactions, burst rates in communication networks, and job sizes in scheduling problems.

- **Zipf's distribution** $(n)$ is commonly used to model discrete distributions arising in the social sciences, such as word and letter frequencies in texts. This distribution has been proposed [1] to model Internet features such as counts of links in Web pages and counts of e-mail contacts. Parameter $n$ denotes the number of distinct elements in the set. Zipf's law states that the frequency of an element is inversely proportional to its rank in a table of frequencies: the most common element occurs with probability $c$, the second with probability $c/2$, the third with probability $c/3$, and so forth. The probability density function is $Z_n(i) = 1/(i H_n)$, where $H_n = \sum_{i=1}^{n} 1/i$ is called the $n^{th}$ harmonic number.

### General Distributions

General methods are also known for generating random variates according to arbitrary discrete distributions where the probabilities $P = (p_1, p_2, \ldots p_n)$ are specified in a list rather than by a function, and distributions (such as Zipf's) where no simple arithmetic transformation is known. Two techniques called the *lookup method* and the *alias method* are sketched here.

The lookup method starts by constructing an array $prob[1 \ldots n]$ containing the cumulative probabilities:

$$prob[k] = \sum_{i=1}^{k} p_i$$

For example, if $P = (.5, .3, .2)$, the array would contain $[.5, .8, 1]$. The cumulative probabilities create a table of breakpoints in the unit interval:

Once the table is built, each random variate *r* is generated by the following loop:

```
double p = rngReal();
for (int r = 1; r < n; r++) if (p < prob[r]) break;
return r;
```

The lookup method takes $O(n)$ initialization time and $O(n)$ time per element generated, worst case; the lookup is fastest if the original probabilities are sorted in decreasing order. Binary search can be applied to improve this to $O(\log n)$ time per element.

The lookup method works well when *n* is fairly small. The alternative *alias method* takes only constant time per element generated, but uses more space. This method starts by building an *alias table* table[1...n] that holds an *alias probability* and an *alias value* for each element. We denote these values table[r].prob and table[r].alias.

The generation code starts with a random real rx, generated uniformly from the real range $[1, n+1)$. This value is separated into its integer part *r* (uniform on $1...n$) and its real part x (uniform on $[0,1)$). The integer *r* becomes the table index, and the real x is compared to table[r].prob. Depending on the comparison, the code generates either *r* or table[r].alias:

```
double rx = (rngReal()*n)+1;   // real on [1..n+1)
int r = (int) rx;              // integer part
double x = rx - r;             // real part
if (x < table[r].prob) return r;
else return table[r].alias;
```

The initialization code to build the alias table is shown in Figure 5.6. The main loop pairs up low-probability elements j with high-probability elements k, so that k becomes the alias for j. The diagram that follows shows how this works for distribution $P = (.5, .3, .2)$. The horizontal line marks the average probability for three elements, equal to $1/3$. In the first step some of the excess probability for element 1 is mapped to form the alias for element 3; in the second step the remaining excess for element 1 becomes the alias for element 2. The three values in table[].alias are $(x, 1, 1)$; the three values in table[].prob are $(1, .9, .6)$, reflecting the cutoffs scaled to $[0, 1)$.

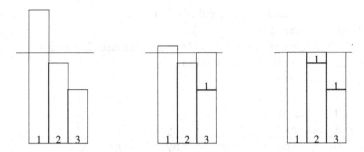

The initialization process starts by creating a set H of elements with higher-than-average probabilities and a set L of elements with lower-than-average probabilities. All probabilities are multiplied by n to simplify the arithmetic, so element i is inserted into H or L according to whether the scaled probability R[i] is more or less than 1.

During the main loop an arbitrary element k is selected from H and an arbitrary element j is selected from L. The table[j] values are assigned, and j is removed from further consideration. The remaining probability for k is calculated; if the result is below average, k is moved from H to L. The initialization step takes $O(n)$ time to build the table; the sets H and L can be implemented with a simple unordered array partitioned around high and low elements.

### 5.2.5 Random Structures and Objects

The collection of known methods for generating random geometric objects (points, lines, etc.) and random combinatorial objects (trees, graphs, networks) is far too large to be surveyed here in any detail. As a general rule these generation methods work by combining techniques for generating numbers, permutations, and samples, as described in the previous section. To illustrate the variety of generation methods available, a short list of techniques for generating random unweighted graphs follows.

- **Random uniform graph** $G(n, p)$. This is an undirected graph on $n$ vertices, such that each of the $n(n-1)/2$ possible edges is generated independently with probability $p$. Start with an empty graph on $n$ vertices. Consider each edge $(i, j)$ in sequence, and with probability $p$ insert the edge in the graph. The following code works for undirected graphs.

```
for (i=1; i<=n; i++)
    for (j=i+1; j<=n; j++)
        if (p > rngReal()) G.insert(i,j);
```

```
prob[1...n] = table of probabilities
for (i=i; i<=n; i++) {
   R[i] = n*prob[i];        //scale probabilities
   if (R[i] >= 1) H.insert(i);
   else L.insert(i);
}
while (H.notEmpty())  {
   k = H.select();        // any element
   j = L.select();        // any element
   table[j].alias = k;    // j is done
   table[j].prob = R[j];
   L.delete(j);

   R[k]= R[k]+(R[j]-1);     // adjust probability
   if (R[k] <= 1) {
       H.delete(k);
       L.insert(k);
   }
}
```

Figure 5.6.  Initializing table values for the alias method.

- **Random uniform graph** $G(n,k)$. To generate a random undirected graph with exactly $k$ edges, assign each edge to an integer $1 \dots m$, where $m = n(n-1)/2$. Draw a sample of size $k$ without replacement from $1 \dots m$ and insert the corresponding sampled edges in the graph.
- **Nearest-neighbor graph** $P(n,k)$. A random (directed) nearest-neighbor graph contains $n$ vertices. Each vertex is assigned to a random coordinate point $(x,y)$ in the unit square. For each vertex, insert edges to its $k$ nearest neighbors, according to some distance metric.
- **Random proximity graph** $P(n,\delta)$. Assign each of $n$ vertices to a random point in the unit square. Then, for each vertex, add an edge to all neighbors within distance $\delta$.
- **Grid proximity graph** $G(n,k,d,e)$. This graph is built in a grid of of $n$ vertices arranged in a $k$ by $n/k$ rectangle: each vertex has edges to $d$ random neighbors within $e$ rows or columns away. Consider vertices row-by-row and column-by-column: if vertex $v_{rc}$ in row $r$, column $c$, has already been assigned $f$ edges, generate $d - f$ additional edges to random neighbors in higher-numbered rows and columns.

- **Random acyclic graph** $G(n,k,d,e)$. The preceding grid technique can also be used to construct a random acyclic graph, by generating $d$ random edges only in "forward" directions $r + 1$ through $r + e$.
- **Random rooted binary tree** $B(n)$. To generate a random rooted binary tree, create a permutation of the integers $1 \ldots n$ and insert them into the tree according to the binary search tree property. These trees are not uniformly distributed because some shapes are more likely than others to occur.

For ideas on how to generate inputs for a specific algorithmic problem, consult the experimental literature or search the Internet for problem-specific input testbeds.

### 5.2.6 Nonindependence

Another category of random generator of interest in algorithm research produces *nonindependent* random variates $R_i$, where the probability that a particular value $r = R_i$ is generated is *supposed* to depend on recently generated values, in some well-defined way.

To take a simple example, suppose data structure $D$ must respond to a random sequence of (insert, delete) operations using random keys. This application requires that an item with key $k$ cannot be deleted unless it has been previously inserted. Thus the probability that $delete(k)$ is generated next in the sequence depends on whether $insert(k)$ has previously appeared. The problem is to generate a random sequence of $insert(k), delete(k)$ operations, for $k \in 1 \ldots n$ such that every $delete(k)$ operation appears after its corresponding $insert(k)$ operation.

One simple approach is to generate a random permutation of doubled elements $1, 1, 2, 2, \ldots n, n$. For each integer $k$ in the permutation, check whether this is the first or second appearance and generate $insert(k)$ or $delete(k)$ accordingly.

Another approach that creates more variety of sequences is to start by generating random line segments on an interval. First create a collection of $n$ random line segments within the real interval $[0, 1)$ by generating a random pair of endpoints $(x_i, y_i)$ for each segment. Assign a random key $k \in 1 \ldots n$ to each segment; label the left endpoint with $insert(k)$ and the right endpoint with $delete(k)$. Sort the labels by coordinates and generate corresponding insert/delete operations. The method of generating endpoints can be adjusted to control how much overlap occurs in the line segments, and therefore the maximum size of the data structure. For example, to ensure that all inserts precede all deletes, generate left endpoints from $[0, .5)$ and right endpoints from $[.5, 1)$.

Another type of nonindependence of interest in algorithm research is *locality of reference*. In many application scenarios a sequence of address references or key requests will exhibit *temporal locality* or *spatial locality* or both. Temporal locality means that if key $k$ appears in the sequence it is more likely to appear again soon; spatial locality means that key values near $k$ are likely to be requested soon.

One simple approach to generating a sequence with locality is to define a probability distribution $D$ on the *differences* between successive keys in the sequence. For example, suppose the problem is to generate a sequence of keys $K_i$ uniformly from the integer range $[1, 10]$. Let $D_i$ denote a sequence of difference variates generated randomly according to some probability function $\delta(d)$. Generate the initial key $K_0$ uniformly at random and generate subsequent keys $K_{i+1}$ according to

$$K_{i+i} = ((K_i + D_i - 1) \% 10) + 1. \tag{5.1}$$

The modulus function $\%$ is used to wrap key values into the range $[0,9]$, and the trick with $-1/+1$ keeps the distribution centered at $K_i$.

An example density function for differences is shown in the following on the left. This function is defined by $\delta(d) = 1/5 - abs(d)/35$ (using the absolute value function *abs*) and is peaked at 0. Assuming that $K_i = 8$, the density function for $K_{i+1}$ using the preceding formula is shown on the right. This probability density is peaked at 8.

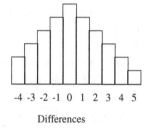

-4 -3 -2 -1 0 1 2 3 4 5                              1 2 3 4 5 6 7 8 9 10

Differences                                          Next key from 8

This difference probability $\delta(d)$ can be easily replaced with another function as appropriate to the model. It can be tricky, however, to find suitable replacement for function (5.1) that constructs $K_{i+1}$ from $K_i$. It is possible to prove a theorem that (5.1) preserves the uniform distribution of the original key: that is, the distribution of every key $K_i$, when averaged over all possible starting keys $K_0$, remains uniform.

This property does necessarily hold when other functions for generating $K_{i+1}$ from $K_i$ are used. The danger is that the distribution of $K_i$ will drift away from uniform as $i$ increases. For example, the scaled function that follows imposes an asymptotic distribution on $K_i$ that is heavier in the middle, so that late in the sequence, 5 is more likely to appear than 1 or 10, no matter how the initial key is generated.

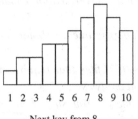

1 2 3 4 5 6 7 8 9 10

Next key from 8

This hazard – that an initially uniform distribution will be skewed via a series of random incremental steps – is not limited to the problem of generating distributions with locality. Panny [14] describes a long history of failed schemes for preserving the initial properties of a random binary search trees, over a sequence of random insertions and deletions. Under the usual definition, a random binary search tree (BST) of size $n$ is created by one of the following equivalent processes: (1) Select a permutation of keys $1 \ldots n$ uniformly at random and insert the keys into the tree in permutation order or (2) generate $n$ uniform reals from $(0, 1)$ and insert them into the tree in generation order.

One common approach to studying insert/delete costs in binary search tree algorithms is to start by generating an initial random BST of size $n$ by method (2) and then to apply a sequence of alternating random insertions and deletions, so that $n$ stays constant. A simple method is to generate an `insert` key uniformly at random from $[0, 1]$, and then a `random` delete key uniformly from the set of already inserted keys. However, this approach fails to preserve the initial distribution of tree shapes; for example, Eppinger [6] showed experimentally that the average internal path length first decreases and then increases over time, a property that was later proved. Because of this phenomenon, the measured performance of a given BST algorithm may be more an artifact of the key generation scheme than of the algorithm itself. Many seemingly reasonable generation schemes have similar flaws; see Panny [14] for tips on avoiding this pitfall.

## 5.3 Chapter Notes

This chapter has addressed two practical aspects of experimental algorithmics: how to develop a test environment that supports correct, efficient, and well-documented experiments; and how to generate random inputs and structures according to a variety of distributions.

Here are the guidelines presented in this chapter.

5.1 *Stand on the shoulders of giants: use the experimental resources available to you in-house and on the Internet.*

5.2 *Apply your best validation and verification techniques to build confidence in test program correctness.*

5.3 *Test parameters that change frequently should be specified at run time rather than compile time.*

5.4 *Write self-describing output files that require minimal reformatting before being submitted for data analysis.*

5.5 *Document your experiments. You should be able to return to your test environment a month later and know exactly how to replicate your own results.*

## 5.4 Problems and Projects

1. Implement your favorite array-based algorithm, such as quicksort, binary search, heapsort, or mergesort. As you write, insert comments with loop invariants into every loop and run through the three verification questions for loop invariants. Can you spot any errors?

2. Design a suite of inputs and input generators to validate the code written for question 1. Include an `assert` procedure in the program and run your tests. Did you find any errors? Swap programs with a friend and run your verification and validation tests on the friend's code. Did either of you find errors that were previously missed?

3. Consider the problem of reformatting the output from a timing utility such as `time` or `gprof` into an input format suitable for your favorite statistical analysis package. How much work must be done by hand? Can you write a formatting tool that is faster and less prone to errors?

4. Revisit an experimental project that you carried out at least a month ago. How much do you remember about the tests? Can you replicate every experiment that you performed earlier? Can you reconstruct the meaning and purpose of every data file? What could you have done to document your experiments better?

5. Implement some of the statistical tests of randomness listed in Knuth [10] or DeVroye [5] and use them to check the random number generator provided by your operating system. Does it pass?

6. Apply tests of randomness to evaluate the sequence of low-order bits generated by the RNG. At what point (what bit size) does the generator start to fail the tests?

7. How would you generate $n$ points uniformly at random in the unit circle? How would you generate $n$ points uniformly on the circumference of the circle? How would you generate $n$ points uniformly inside and on the surface of the unit sphere?

8. Use the lookup method and the alias method to implement a generator for Zipf's distribution. How do they compare, in terms of time and space usage? Read about statistical tests of randomness for nonuniform distributions (for example, in Knuth [10]) and apply those tests to the generators. Do they pass?

9. Many approximation algorithms for NP-hard optimization problems on graphs have a guaranteed bound on solution quality under the assumption that the edge weights obey the *triangle inequality*: that is, for each triangle of edges $(x, y)$, $(x,z)$, $(y,x)$ the sum of weights on two edges is at least equal to the weight on the third edge. This ensures that every edge represents the shortest path between its endpoints. Design and implement an algorithm to generate random graphs that obey the triangle inequality. Does it cover the space of all such graphs? (Note: There exist graphs that obey the triangle inequality that cannot be embedded into geometric space.) Is each such graph equally likely to be generated?

10. In GPS applications, a street or road in a roadmap comprises a sequence of connected line segments that represent its location in a satellite image. Design and implement a suite of random generators that model different types of maps: street grids in cities, superhighways, rural roads, and following various terrains (mountains, rivers, lakes, etc.).

11. Design and implement a random generator for variates that are *both* nonuniform (for example generated by Zipf's distribution) and nonindependent, displaying temporal but not spatial locality. Use it to generate a "text" of random words (strings of varying length determined by Zipf's law) to evaluate your favorite set data structure implementations. How closely does performance on your generated inputs match performance on real words in English text?

## Bibliography

[1] Adamic, Lada A., and Bernardo A. Huberman, "Zipf's law and the Internet," *Glottometrics* Vol 3, pp. 143–150, 2002. Availabel from: www.ram-verlag.de/journal.htm.

[2] Bentley, Jon Louis, and James B. Saxe, "Generating sorted lists of random numbers,"*ACM Transactions on Mathematical Software*, Vol 6, No 3, pp 359–364, September 1980.

[3] Bentley, Jon Louis, "Ten Commandments for Experiments on Algorithms," in "Tools for Experiments on Algorithms," in R. Rashid, ed., *CMU Computer Science: A 25th Anniversary Commemorative*, ACM Press Anthology Series, 1991.

[4] Bratley, Paul, Bennet L. Fox, and Linus E. Schrage, *A Guide to Simulation*, Springer-Verlag, 1983.

[5] DeVroye, Luc, *Non-Uniform Random Variate Generation,* Springer-Verlag, New York, 1986. Available from: cg.scs.carleton.ca/~luc/rnbookindex.html for an open-copyright Web edition.

[6]  Eppinger, Jeffrey L., "An empirical study of insertion and deletion in binary search trees," *Communications of the ACM*, Vol 26, Issue 9, September 1983.

[7]  Fan, C. T., Mervin E. Muller, and Ivan Rezucha, "Development of sampling plans by using sequential (item by item) selection techniques and digital computers," *Journal of the American Statistical Association*, 57, pp. 387–402, 1962.

[8]  Gent, Ian P., Stuart A. Grant, Ewen MacIntyre, Patrick Prosser, Paul Shaw, Barbara M. Smith, and Toby Walsh, *How Not to Do It*, Research Report 97.27, School of Computer Studies, University of Leeds, May 1997. Available From: www.cs.st-andrews.ac.uk/~ipg/pubs.html.

[9]  Jones, T. G., "A note on sampling a tape file," *Communications of the ACM*, Vol 5, No 6, p. 343, June 1962.

[10]  Knuth, Donald E., *The Art of Computer Programming:* Vol 2, *Seminumerical Algorithms*, Addison Wesley, 1981.

[11]  Law, Aberill M., and W. David Kelton, *Simulation Modeling and Analysis*, 3rd ed., McGraw-Hill, 2000.

[12]  L'Ecuyer, Pierre, "Tables of linear congruential generators of different sizes and good lattice structure," *Mathematics of Computation*, Vol 68, No 225, pp. 249–260, January 1999.

[13]  Mehlhorn, Kurt, Stefan Näher, Michael Seel, Raimund Seidel, Thomas Schilz, Stefan Schirra, and Christian Uhrig, "Checking geometric programs or verification of geometric structures." *Proceedings of the Twelfth Annual Symposium on Computational Geometry* SGC'96, pp. 159–195, 1996.

[14]  Panny, Wolfgang, "Deletions in random binary search trees: A story of errors," *Journal of Statistical Planning and Inference*, Vol 140, Issue 8, pp. 2334–45, August 2010.

[15]  Park, Stephen K., and Keith W. Miller, "Random number generators: Good ones are hard to find," *Communications of the ACM*, Vol 31, Issue 10, pp. 1192–1201, October 1988.

[16]  Press, William H. et al. *Numerical Recipes: The Art of Scientific Computing*, 3rd ed., Cambridge University, Press 2007. An electronic book is available from the publisher at www.nr.com.

[17]  Ripley, Brian D., *Stochastic Simulation*, Wiley Series in Probability and Mathematics, Wiley & Sons, 1987.

# 6

# Creating Analysis-Friendly Data

For each of us who appear to have had a successful experiment there are many to whom their own experiments seem barren and negative.

*Melvin Calvin, 1961 Nobel Lecture*

An experiment is not considered "barren and negative" when it disproves your conjecture: an experiment fails by being inconclusive.

Successful experiments are partly the product of good experimental designs, as described in Chapter 2; there is also an element of luck (or savvy) in choosing a well-behaved problem to study. Furthermore, computational research on algorithms provides unusual opportunities for "tuning" experiments to yield more successful analyses and stronger conclusions. This chapter surveys techniques for building better experiments along these lines.

We start with a discussion of what makes a data set good or bad in this context. The remainder of this section surveys strategies for tweaking experimental designs to yield more successful outcomes.

If tweaks are not sufficient, stronger measures can be taken; Section 6.1 surveys *variance reduction techniques*, which modify test programs to generate better data, and Section 6.2 describes *simulation shortcuts*, which produce more data per unit of computation time.

The key idea is to exploit the fact, pointed out in Section 5.1, that the *application program* that implements an algorithm for practical use is distinct from the *test program* that describes algorithm performance. The test program need not resemble the application program at all; it is only required to reproduce faithfully the algorithm properties of interest. Most of the techniques described here exploit the laboratory setting and involve changes to test programs that could not work in application scenarios.

Figure 6.1 illustrates the difference between successful and unsuccessful outcomes in this context. Panels (a) and (b) show the results of two experiments

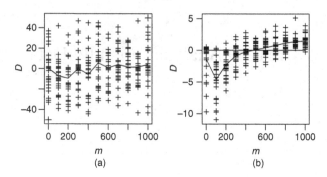

Figure 6.1. Inconclusive versus analysis-friendly data (a) large variance; (b) small variance. The data points in Panel (b) give a clearer view of the relationship between $m$ and the average cost $D(m)$ because the variance in data in each column is small compared to the change in mean between columns.

described later in this chapter, to study the average-case cost of a function $D(m)$. Each column of data represents 25 independent trials at levels $m = 1, 101, 201, \ldots 1001$. The lines connect the sample means in each column. The mean is known to change from negative to positive as $m$ increases: the experimental problem is to find the crossover point $m_c$.

The sample means have the same theoretical average in both experiments, but the data in panel (a) yield little insight about the location of $m_c$, while the data in panel (b) give good support for a conclusion that $m_c$ is somewhere between 400 and 500. The difference can be seen by comparing the scales on the $y-$axes. In panel (a) the points in each data column are spread between $-50$ and $+50$, which is a much larger range than the incremental change in means from column to column. In panel (b) the points are tightly clustered around their means, so the change is easier to see.

The data in panel (b) are more analysis-friendly because they give a clearer view of the relationship between $m$ and the mean cost $\overline{D}(m)$. In fact, the view is so clear that no sophisticated data analysis is needed – a look at the graph is sufficient to find the crossover point. As the Nobel scientist Ernest Rutherford put it [1]: "If your experiment needs statistics, then you ought to have done a better experiment."

The change in sample means is called the *response* of this cost to changes in $m$. The amount of spread, or dispersion, of the points away from their means depends on the *variance* in the data sample. A data sample is analysis-friendly when variance is small compared to the response in the mean. The principle is the same whether the data show a functional relationship or a simple cost difference with respect to some parameter.

**Guideline 6.1** *For best views of how average cost depends on parameters, work to magnify response and minimize variance.*

## Designs for Good Views

Section 2.2 shows how experimental designs – which involve selecting performance indicators, parameters, factors, and design points – can be developed to support specific experimental goals, such as comparison of design options or analysis of functional trends.

Experimental designs can also be developed to improve the data analysis. Of course, the data analysis tail must not wag the algorithm analysis dog: sometimes the right experimental design for the problem at hand simply does not produce easy-to-analyze results. But many designs can be improved for better views of the relationship between parameters and performance.

Figure 6.2 shows an example. Panels (a) and (b) present results of two experiments to study a cost function $C(n)$. The underlying function is the same in both panels, but the experimental designs differ in the range, spacing, and number of levels of $n$, and in the number of random trials. Suppose the goal is to determine whether the average cost $\overline{C}(n)$ is linear in $n$. The data in panel (a) are inconclusive, but panel (b) shows the ideal experimental outcome: a clear view of the cost function with strong support for linearity.

Here are some do's and don'ts for designing better experiments with an eye toward clear views.

- *Do run more trials.* Variance in a data sample is inversely proportional to sample size. Many standard techniques of data analysis become stronger and more reliable when applied to larger samples: as a rule of thumb, reliability increases in proportion to the square root of sample size.
- *Do expand the range of n values.* If the response of $C(n)$ to $n$ is small compared to variance, try magnifying the response by increasing the range of $n$ levels in the experimental design.

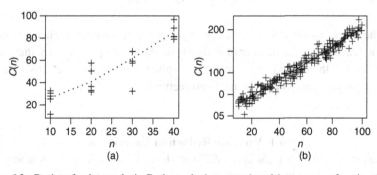

Figure 6.2. Designs for data analysis. Both panels show samples of the same cost function $C(n)$. Which data set would you rather analyze to decide whether $C(n)$ is a linear function of $n$?

- *Don't summarize prematurely.* The sample mean and sample variance are just two of many possible statistics that might be used in an analysis; the right choice depends on distributional properties of the sample. Test programs should aways report the "raw data" showing results of each trial, so the distribution can be examined during data analysis. (Section 7.1.1 surveys alternative statistics and when to use them.)
- *Do "right size" the data sample.* Avoid experiments that produce too many or too few data points to be analyzable. For example, when testing an iterative algorithm it may be impractical to report solution cost $S(i)$ at every iteration, because the resulting data set would be too large. To shrink a too-big data set to manageable size, either *sample* it by reporting $S(k)$ at reasonably spaced intervals or *summarize* it by reporting the average of each batch of $k$ values. (Summarizing within a trial is different from summarizing across random trials.)
- *Don't use "lossy" performance indicators.* Suppose the experimental goal is to study a ratio $R = X/Y$ of two performance indicators $X$ and $Y$. If the test program reports $X$ and $Y$, then $R$ can be directly calculated, as well as other quantities such as $X - Y$ or $(X - Y)/X$, which may be useful during data analysis. If the experiment simply reports $R$, the values of $X$ and $Y$ cannot be recovered. The test program should report measurements that maximize the information content of each trial.
- *Do prefer narrow performance indicators.* A narrow performance indicator focuses closely on one component of algorithmic performance, for example, a count of a single operation. A wide performance indicator, such as a count of total instructions executed or CPU time, represents an aggregate cost. Narrow performance indicators represent simple relationships that are generally easier to model and analyze.

**Guideline 6.2** *Design your experiments to maximize the information content in the data: aim for clear views of simple relationships.*

These options are not available in every experiment, of course. There is usually a practical limit on the number of trials and on the largest problem size that can be measured. If the data will not cooperate despite your best design efforts, consider the techniques surveyed in the next two sections.

### 6.1  Variance Reduction Techniques

A variance reduction technique (VRT) modifies the test program in a way that reduces variance in the measured outcomes, on the theory that less variance yields better views of average-case costs. These techniques really do *reduce variance* in data: if the goal of the experiment is to understand variance as it occurs naturally, do not apply VRTs.

To illustrate how these techniques work, Section 6.1.1 presents a case study to compare two algorithms for a problem in dynamic searching. The first experiment utilizes two straightforward implementations of the algorithms and reports both mean costs and some statistics to assess variance. Next, three variance reduction techniques, called *common random variates*, *control variates*, and *conditional expectation*, are applied, and the outcomes are compared to those from the first experiment. Some tips on applying these VRTs to general algorithms are also presented. Section 6.1.2 discusses some additional VRTs and their general application.

### 6.1.1 Case Study: VRTs for self-organizing sequential search rules

The *self-organizing sequential search problem* is to maintain a list of $n$ distinct keys under a series of $m$ requests for keys. The cost of each request is equal to the position of the key in the list, which is the cost of searching for the key using a linear search from the front. Figure 6.3 shows an example list containing keys $1 \ldots 6$ in positions 1 through 6: a request for key 3 in this list would have cost 5.

The list is allowed to reorder itself by some rule that tries to keep frequently requested keys near the front to reduce total search cost, but the rule must work without any information about future requests. Two popular rules, illustrated in Figure 6.3, are:

- **Move-to-Front** (MTF): After key $k$ is requested, move it to the front of the list, and shift everything between one space back.
- **Transpose** (TR): After key $k$ is requested, move it one position closer to the front by transposing with its predecessor.

Nothing happens if $k$ is already at the front of the list. Transpose is more conservative since keys change position incrementally, while MTF is more aggressive in moving a requested key all the way to the front. Which rule does a better job?

| List: | 5 | 2 | 1 | 6 | 3 | 4 | Request = 3, Cost = 5 |
|---|---|---|---|---|---|---|---|
| | 1 | 2 | 3 | 4 | 5 | 6 | |

| MTF: | 3 | 5 | 2 | 1 | 6 | 4 |
|---|---|---|---|---|---|---|

| TR: | 5 | 2 | 1 | 3 | 6 | 4 |
|---|---|---|---|---|---|---|

Figure 6.3. Self-organizing sequential search. The request for key 3 has cost 5 because that key is in position 5 in the list. The MTF rule moves the requested key to the front of the list; the TR rule transposes the key with its predecessor.

*Average-Case Experimental Analysis*

We develop some notation to analyze these rules. Suppose requests are generated independently at random according to a probability distribution $P(n) = p_1, p_2, \ldots p_n$ defined on $n$ keys. The *request cost* for key $k$ in position $L[i]$ in a given list is equal to its position $i$. The *average list cost* for list $L$ depends on the request costs and request probabilities for each key:

$$C(L) = \sum_{i=1}^{n} i \cdot p_{L[i]}. \tag{6.1}$$

The *average cost* of a rule is the expected cost of the $m^{th}$ request, assuming that $L$ is initially in random order (each permutation equally likely) and that the rule is applied to a sequence of random requests $R_i$, $i = 1 \ldots m - 1$, generated according to distribution $P(n)$. Let $\mu(n, m)$ denote the average cost of MTF and let $\tau(n, m)$ denote the average cost of TR in this model.

The experiments described here measure costs for requests drawn from *Zipf's* distribution, which has been used to model naturally occurring phenomena such as frequencies of words or letters in texts. This distribution, denoted $Z(n)$, is defined over the integers $1 \ldots n$. The probability that key $k \in 1 \ldots n$ is requested next is given by

$$p(k) = \frac{1}{k H_n}, \tag{6.2}$$

where $H_n$ is the $n^{th}$ *harmonic number*, defined by $H_n = \sum_{j=1}^{n} 1/j$. (Multiplying by $H_n$ scales the probabilities so they sum to 1.) A picture of Zipf's distribution for $n = 9$ is shown in the following.

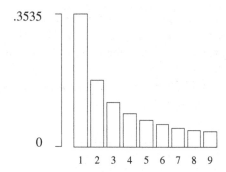

Key 1 is generated with probability $p_1 = 0.3535$. Key 2 appears half as often as key 1, key 3 appears one-third as often as key 1, and so on.

```
SequentialSearchTest (n, m, R, trials) {
  for (t=1; t<= trials; t++) {
    L = randomPermutation (n);
    for (i=1; i<=m; i++) {
      k = randomZipf(n);
      for (j=1; L[j] != k; j++);
      cost = j;
      reorder(R, L, j); // R = MTF or TR
    }
    printCost(R, t, n, m, cost);
  }
}
```

Figure 6.4. Sequential Search test code. This test program prints the cost of the $m^{th}$ request in each trial, assuming keys are generated according to $Z(n)$ and the list is reordered by either MTF or TR.

There are no known formulas for calculating $\mu(n,m)$ and $\tau(n,m)$ under this distribution, so we develop experiments to study these average costs. A test program for this purpose is sketched in Figure 6.4. In each random trial, the code generates an initial list L that contains a random permutation of the keys. Then it generates a random sequence of keys according to Zipf's distribution: for each key, it looks up the request in the list, records the cost, and reorders the list according to the rule. At the end the program reports the cost of the $m^{th}$ request.

Code to generate random permutations may be found in Section 5.2.2 of this text, and two methods for generating random variates according to Zipf's distribution are described in Section 5.2.4. C language test programs for both MTF and TR can be downloaded from *AlgLab*.

The experiment runs $t$ random trials of this program at each design point $(n,m)$. The *random variate* $M_i(n,m)$, which can take any value in $1 \ldots n$, denotes the cost of MTF reported in the $i^{th}$ trial at this design point. The *sample mean* at a design point, denoted $\overline{M}(n,m)$, is the average of $t$ outcomes:

$$\overline{M}(n,m) = \frac{1}{t}\sum_{i=1}^{t} M_i(n,m). \tag{6.3}$$

The *expectation* $E[M_i(n,m)]$ of a random variate such as $M_i(n,m)$ is the weighted average of all possible outcomes, with each outcome weighted by its (unknown) probability of occurring. Since we assume these variates are generated according to some distribution with mean $\mu(n,m)$, it must hold that

$$E[M_i(n,m)] = \mu(n,m). \tag{6.4}$$

We say that variate $M_i(n,m)$ is an *estimator* of $\mu(n,m)$, because its expectation equals $\mu(n,m)$. The sample mean $\overline{M}(n,m)$ from an experiment is likely to be close to $\mu(n,m)$, and it is sometimes possible to quantify how close.

We will also be interested in the *sample variance*, a statistic that describes the dispersion of points away from their mean, defined by

$$Var(M(n,m)) = \frac{1}{t} \sum_{i=1}^{t} (M_i(n,m) - \overline{M}(m,m))^2. \tag{6.5}$$

Let $T_i(n,m)$, $\overline{T}(n,m)$, and $Var(T(n,m))$ denote the analogous quantities for the Transpose rule.

Although experiments are developed here to study theoretical questions, it is worth pointing out that self-organizing search rules, especially MTF, are of interest in many practical contexts. For example, most caching and paging algorithms keep track of elements in least-recently-used (LRU) order, which is identical to MTF order. When used in applications that require lookups in linearly organized data, these algorithms are sometimes more efficient than even binary search, for example, when the key distribution is skewed toward a small number of frequent requests, or when the request sequence exhibits temporal locality. Most of the variance reduction techniques illustrated here apply equally well to theory-driven or application-driven experiments.

### The First Experiment

Rivest [15] showed that for any nonuniform request distribution such as Zipf's distribution, Transpose has lower asymptotic cost, but Move-to-Front reaches its asymptote more quickly. We know that $\mu(n,1) = \tau(n,1)$ because the initial list is randomly ordered; furthermore, Rivest's result implies that there is a crossover point $m_c$ such that

$$\mu(n,m) < \tau(n,m) \quad \text{when } 1 < m < m_c$$

$$\mu(n,m) > \tau(n,m) \quad \text{when } m_c \leq m.$$

Our first experimental goal is to locate the crossover point $m_c$.

Figure 6.5 shows the outcome of the first experiment, measuring $M_i(50,m)$ and $T_i(50,m)$ in 25 random trials at each design point $n = 50$ and $m = 1, 101, 201, \ldots 1001$. The lines connect the sample means $\overline{M}(50,m)$ and $\overline{T}(50,m)$ at each $m$. Unfortunately there is too much variance in the data to locate $m_c$.

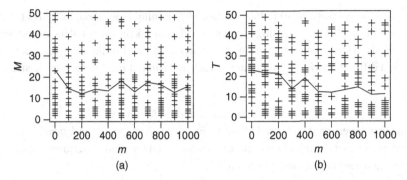

Figure 6.5. The cost of the *mth* request. Panel (a) shows measurements of request costs $M_i(50, m)$ for Move-to-Front; panel (b) shows measurements of request costs $T_i(50, m)$ for Transpose. Both experiments take 25 random trials each at $m = 1, 101, 201 \ldots 1001$, with requests generated by Zipf's distribution on $n = 50$ keys. The lines connect sample means in each column of data.

The sample means and sample variances for the rightmost data columns in each panel ($n = 50, m = 1001$) appear in the following table. These statistics are calculated according to formulas (6.3) and (6.5).

Statistical methods for expressing our confidence in how well the sample means estimate the distribution means $\mu(n, m)$ and $\tau(n, m)$ are described in Section 7.1.2. One method is to calculate *95-percent confidence intervals* for $\overline{M}(n, m)$ and $\overline{T}(n, m)$, which are also shown in the table. If certain assumptions about the data sample hold, the confidence intervals will contain the true means, $\mu(50, 1001)$ and $\tau(50, 1001)$, in 95 out of 100 experiments.

|      | Mean | Var    | 95% Conf.       |
|------|------|--------|-----------------|
| MTF  | 15.6 | 159.75 | [10.64, 20.56]  |
| TR   | 11.4 | 195.83 | [5.91, 16.89]   |

The huge variance in the data creates wide confidence intervals with ranges near 10, which indicate that $\overline{M}(n, m)$ and $\overline{T}(n, m)$ might be as far as $\pm 5$ from their true means. Since the confidence intervals overlap, we cannot say with any certainty whether $\mu(50, 1001) < \tau(50, 1001)$ at this point.

It should be pointed out that the "certain assumptions about the data" mentioned previously and explained in detail in Section 7.1.2 only partially hold in these experiments. Confidence intervals are reported here for comparison purposes, to illustrate how variance reduction yields stronger results. Do not place too much confidence in these confidence intervals for estimation purposes.

It is always possible to reduce variance by running more random trials at each design point: that is, increasing $t$ is guaranteed to shrink the ranges of the confidence intervals. The variance reduction techniques illustrated in the next few sections take a different approach by reducing variance without increasing sample sizes.

### *VRT 1: Common Random Numbers*

The first experiment measured Move-to-Front and Transpose in *independent* trials; that means that the initial random permutations and the random request sequences were generated separately in each test.

The *common random numbers* VRT can be applied to any algorithmic experiment when the following two properties hold:

1. The goal of the experiment is to compare the differences in costs of two (or more) algorithms.
2. There is reason to believe that the costs of the algorithms are *positively correlated* with respect to some random variate in each trial. Positive correlation means the cost of one algorithm is likely to be high when the cost of the other is high, and vice versa.

Under these circumstances, measuring cost differences in paired trials with matching random variates should yield outcomes with less variance than measuring differences using independent random variates.

We can apply this idea to MTF and TR by noting that search costs are identical when list orders are identical, and similar when list orders are similar. Since both rules try to keep frequently requested keys near the front of the list, the costs of the $m^{th}$ request are positively correlated in the sense that frequently requested keys are likely to be near the front and infrequently requested keys are likely to be near the back of both lists. We can induce more correlation by running the two rules on identical rather than separate request sequences, so that list orders are more likely to be similar at time $m$.

The next experiment runs MTF and TR using common random numbers. The variates $M_i(n,m)$ and $T_i(n,m)$ denote the cost of the $m^{th}$ request in the $i^{th}$ trial as before, with the understanding that in trial $i$, the initial list order and the sequence of $m$ requests are the same for both rules.

To evaluate this approach, let $\delta(n,m) = \mu(n,m) - \tau(n,m)$ denote the difference between mean rule costs. By Rivest's result, we know that $\delta(n,1) = 0$ and

$$\delta(n,m) < 0 \quad \text{when } 1 < m < m_c$$

$$\delta(n,m) > 0 \quad \text{when } m_c \leq m.$$

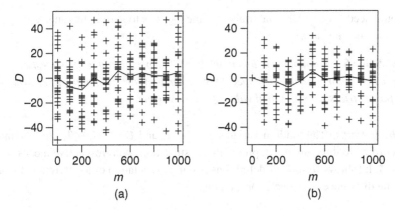

Figure 6.6. Common random numbers. Panel (a) shows the cost difference between TR and MTF on independent request sequences; panel (b) shows the cost difference on common request sequences. Overall variance in panel (b) is about half that in panel (a); at $m = 1$ variance is zero.

In this new notation the experimental goal is to find the point $m_c$ where $\delta(n,m)$ changes from negative to positive. Let

$$D_i(n,m) = M_i(n,m) - T_i(n,m)$$

denote the cost difference in trial $i$, and let $\overline{D}(n,m)$ denote the average difference over all trials at design point $(n,m)$.

Panel of Figure 6.6 shows the results of measuring $D_i(n,m)$ in independent trials as in the first experiment, and panel (b) shows the results of paired tests with matching initial list orders and request sequences. The sample means, sample variance, and 95-percent confidence intervals for the rightmost data columns in each panel appear in the following table.

|  | $\overline{D}(50,1,001)$ | Var(50,1,001) | 95% Conf. |
|---|---|---|---|
| Independent | 4.20 | 456.42 | [-4.17, 12.57] |
| Com. Ran. Num. | -3.00 | 206.75 | [-8.64, 2.63] |

The expectation of the mean $\overline{D}(n,m)$ does not change in the two experiments, but the variance in the data is visibly smaller. Panel (b) shows that $D_i(n,1) = 0$ since initial list orders are identical; that means that variance is zero. In the rightmost column, variance is cut in half and range of 95% confidence intervals reduces from 16.77 to 11.28. Even though $\overline{D}(50,1001)$ is negative in the second experiment, this VRT is not quite enough to obtain a definitive answer about $m_c$, since the interval $[-8.64, 2.64]$ contains both negative and positive values. This experiment would need fewer additional trials than the first one to shrink the range enough to answer the question.

**Guideline 6.3** *Common random numbers: When performance of two test subjects is positively correlated with respect to some random variate, compare performance in paired trials with identical values for that variate.*

*Why It Works.* The random variates $M_i$ and $T_i$ and $D_i = M_i - T_i$ are generated according to three unknown probability distributions with respective means $\mu$, $\tau$, and $\delta$. It follows from their definitions that the expectation of a difference is equal to the difference of expectations, that is:

$$\delta = E[D_i] = E[M_i - T_i] = E[M_i] - E[T_i] = \tau - \mu.$$

By definition (6.2) the *sample variance* of $M_i$ is the average squared distance from the mean:

$$Var(M_i) = \frac{1}{t} \sum_{i=1}^{t} (M_i - \overline{M})^2$$

and the variance of $T_i$ is calculated similarly. The variance of the difference $D_i$ is defined as follows:

$$Var(D_i) = Var(M_i - T_i) = Var(M_i) + Var(T_i) - 2Cov(M_i, T_i).$$

The *covariance* term $Cov(M_i, T_i)$, defined in Section 7.2, is a measure of the similarity of $M_i$ and $T_i$ when matched pairwise across trials: if $M_i$ tends to be high when $T_i$ is high, and low when $T_i$ is low, covariance is positive; if one tends to be high when the other is low, covariance is negative; and when there is no relationship (the variates are uncorrelated), covariance is zero.

If experiments are run on MTF and TR using independent request sequences, it must hold that $Cov(T_i, M_i) = 0$. But if experiments are run using identical inputs, and if $M_i$ and $T_i$ have positive covariance, then the negated covariance term shrinks the value of $Var(D_i)$. This is the phenomenon illustrated in Figure 6.6. Note that if the costs of these two rules were negatively correlated, application of common random numbers would increase the variance in the difference.

In the general context of algorithm experiments, the common random numbers VRT may be applied to two or more algorithms tested on identical inputs, as illustrated here, or to one algorithm tested under different input, design, or environmental conditions. The common random variate could be anything that might be considered a noise parameter (see Section 2.2), which causes measurements to vary from trial to trial – it need not be random in the sense of "randomly generated." This includes properties of the input instance, the initial configuration of a data structure, a random number sequence internal to the algorithm(s), or even the test environment in which experiments are run.

If there is reason to believe that two cost measurements are likely to be positively correlated in matched trials respecting that random variate, a comparison of cost differences in matched trials is likely to give better results than a comparison of differences in independent trials. Usually there will be no proof available that covariance is positive (if you understand the algorithms well enough to analyze their covariance structure, why are you doing experiments?), but a small pilot experiment to check for correlations can provide guidance.

### VRT 2: Control Variates

Instead of exploiting correlation to compare two outcomes, the *control variates* VRT exploits positive correlation to adjust an outcome by moving it closer to its expectation. The technique is illustrated here using the Transpose rule, although it can also be applied to MTF. Suppose now the experimental goal is to estimate $\tau(n,m)$ using measurements of mean costs $\overline{T}(n,m)$.

In general, the control variate VRT can be applied to a variate $T_i$ when another random variate $R_i$ can be identified for which two properties hold:

1. $R_i$ is positively correlated with $T_i$.
2. The expected value $\rho = E[R_i]$ can be calculated.

When these properties hold, we say that $R_i$ is a control variate for $T_i$ and define a new variate $T_i'$ by

$$T_i' = T_i - c(R_i - \rho),$$

with a constant $c$ described later. By definition, $E[R_i] - \rho = 0$, which implies that $E[R_i - \rho] = 0$. Therefore, $E[T_i'] = E[T_i] = \tau$, no matter what value $c$ has, so this new variate is also an estimator of $\tau$. Furthermore, it holds (see [2]) that

$$Var(T_i') = Var(T_i) + c^2 Var(R_i) - 2Cov(T_i, R_i).$$

If the sum of the second and third terms is negative – that is, if there is enough positive correlation between $R_i$ and $T_i$ to dominate the variance in $R_i$ – then the adjusted cost $T_i'$ will have smaller variance than $T_i$. It turns out that variance in $T_i'$ is minimized by setting

$$c = Cov(T_i, R_i)/Var(R_i).$$

Intuitively, this VRT adjusts each $T_i$ to be closer to its expectation by subtracting out the discrepancy between the control variate $R_i$ and its known expectation $\rho$. When $R_i$ is higher than average, the corresponding higher-than-average $T_i$ is

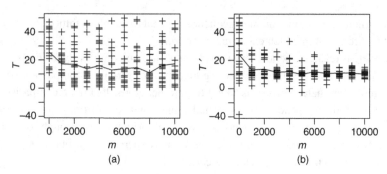

Figure 6.7.   Control variates. Panel (a) shows measurements of $T_i(50,m)$, with no control variate and panel (b) shows measurements of $T_i'(50,m)$ using the control variate $R_i(50,m)$. The lines connect sample means in each column. The data in panel (b) have smaller variance; therefore, the sample means are better estimators of $\tau(n,m)$.

adjusted downward; when $R_i$ is lower than average, $T_i$ is adjusted upward. The variate $T_i'$ has smaller variance than $T_i$ when $T_i$ and $R_i$ are positively correlated.

To apply this VRT to our Transpose rule, let $R_i(n,m)$ be the value of the key requested at time $m$. We can argue that $R_i$ is likely to be positively correlated with $T_i$ because Zipf's distribution assigns probabilities to keys in decreasing order. Therefore, the optimal list order is $[1, 2, 3, \ldots n]$, so the value of key $k$ is equal to its position in the optimal list. Since Transpose aims to create low-cost lists, the position of a given key in the list is likely to be correlated with its value. This correlation is stronger when $m$ is large because the average list cost for TR improves over time.

The average cost of searching the optimal list under Zipf's distribution is easily calculated by

$$\rho(n) = \sum_{i=1}^{n} \frac{i}{i\,H_n} = \frac{n}{H_n}.$$

At $n = 50$ this works out to $\rho(50) = 11.113$. A quick experiment shows that $c = 0.871$ is a good choice of coefficient here; therefore, we define the new estimator of $\tau(n,m)$ as

$$T_i'(n,m) = T_i(n,m) - 0.871(R_i(n,m) - \rho(n)).$$

This variate has (provably) the same expectation as $T_i(n,m)$, but (arguably) smaller variance.

The next experiment modifies the test program to report both the original Transpose cost $T_i(n,m)$ and the adjusted cost $T_i'(n,m)$. The results are shown in Figure 6.7. Panel (a) shows $T_i(50,m)$, and panel (b) shows $T_i'(50,m)$, measured in 25 trials at $m = 1, 1001, \ldots 10001$. These levels are higher than in previous experiments to highlight this effect at large $m$.

Although the overall range of $T_i'(n,m)$ in panel (b) is larger because the adjusted cost $T_i'$ can be negative, and variance in $T_i'(n,m)$ is maximized at $m = 1$ when the list is in random initial order, the reduction in variance at higher values of $m$ is dramatic. Statistics for the two rightmost data columns appear in the following table.

|  | Mean | Var | 95% Conf. |
|---|---|---|---|
| $T_i(50, 10001)$ | 17.48 | 263.68 | [11.11, 23.85] |
| $T_i'(50, 10001)$ | 10.36 | 4.28 | [9.55, 11.17] |

Variance is 62 times smaller when this VRT is applied, and the range of the confidence intervals shrinks from 12.74 to just 1.62. This suggests that the estimate $\overline{T}'(50, 10001) = 10.36$ is off by no more than about 16 percent.

**Guideline 6.4** *Control variates: Adjust variate $T_i$ toward its expectation by subtracting the discrepancy between another variate $R_i$ and its known expectation $\rho$.*

*Applications To Other Algorithms.* More generally in algorithmic problems, a control variate like $R_i$ can be anything that is positively correlated with algorithm cost $T_i$, such as a property of the input, of an internal state of the algorithm, or of a simpler algorithm run on the same input. As before, a proof that $R_i$ and $T_i$ are positively correlated is not likely to be available, but a small experiment can be used to test that property.

Here are some hints on where to look for control variates in algorithmic experiments.

- Data structure experiments often start with a random initial data structure $D_0$ that is subjected to a sequence of $m$ random operations. If the average cost $\delta_0$ of the initial configuration can be calculated, and if average cost at time $m$ is likely to be correlated with initial cost (that is, if the cost of the data structure changes incrementally over time), then $Cost(D_0)$ is a control variate for $Cost(D_m)$. To estimate the cost at time $m$, measure the adjusted cost $Cost'(D_m) = Cost(D_m) - c(Cost(D_0) - \delta_0)$. For example, the initial cost of a random binary search tree may serve as a control variate for the cost after $m$ random insert/delete operations.
- This idea can also be applied to tests of an iterative heuristic that generates a solution $S_i$ at time $i$ by making an incremental change to $S_{i-1}$. The initial solution $S_0$ may serve as a control variate for $S_i$ if its average cost can be calculated.
- Much is known about expected values of properties of random graphs. For example, given a complete graph $G$ with random edge costs generated according

to an arbitrary distribution $F$ with $d = F(0) > 0$, the expected cost of the minimum spanning tree (MST) of $G$ approaches a constant near $1.202/d$ [7]. The cost of the MST of a graph may be used as control variate for the cost of a TSP tour if the two are positively correlated. Results like this provide a pool of possible control variates for algorithms on random graphs.

- In the bin packing case study described in Section 3.2, the problem is to pack a list $L_n$ containing $n$ random weights from the range $(0, 1)$ into unit-capacity bins so as to minimize the $B(L_n)$, the number of bins used. Let $S(L_n)$ denote the sum of all the weights in the list. The bin count $B(L_n)$ is positively correlated with $S(L_n)$, and the mean $\sigma = S(L_n)$ can be calculated whenever $L_n$ is randomly generated. Thus the weight sum is a control variate for bin count. Instead of measuring $B(L_n)$, measure the difference $B'(L_n) = B(L_n) - c(S(L_n) - \sigma)$ and enjoy reduced variance in the results.

- In experiments using real-world data, the mean $\rho$ corresponds to an average over a large pool of real-world instances, which may be impossible to calculate. Borogovac and Vakili [6] point out that control variates can be effective when an exact mean $\rho$ is replaced with an empirical estimate, or with an upper or lower bound. They show how to adjust the calculation of the substitute variate $T_i'$ in these circumstances.

- Whether or not $\rho$ is known, it is sometimes useful simply to redefine the cost of an algorithm by subtracting out a control variate. Bentley et al. [5] describe an experimental study of bin packing algorithms that adopts empty space $E(L_n) = B(L_n) - S(L_n)$ as the measure of solution cost instead of bin count $B(L_n)$. Experimental results for one cost can be arithmetically translated to imply results about the other, but $E(L_n)$ is friendlier to data analysis because variance is smaller. This is sometimes called *indirect estimation* in the VRT literature.

- Johnson, McGeoch, and Rothberg [8] describe a similar use of indirect estimation in a study of the traveling salesman problem: instead of measuring tour cost $T(G_i)$ on a graph of $n$ vertices, they measure $T'(G_i) = T(G_i) - HK(G_i)$, which corresponds to the excess over the Held-Karp lower bound $HK(G_i)$ on tour cost.

### VRT 3: Conditional Expectation

Next we apply the *conditional expectation* variance reduction technique, sometimes called *conditional Monte Carlo*, to the Move-to-Front rule. This VRT conceptually splits an experiment into two phases: first, generate a random state $S$, and second, generate a random sample of the cost of that state.

Using this approach, we can think of one trial of the Move-to-Front rule as consisting of a first phase that generates a sequence of $m - 1$ requests to obtain a random list order $L$ (the state of the algorithm after $m - 1$ requests), followed by

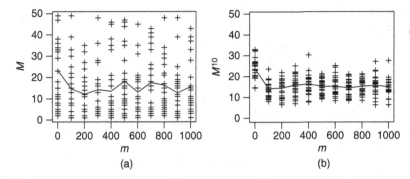

Figure 6.8. Conditional Expectation with 10 extra samples. Panel (a) shows samples of $M_i(50,m)$ from the first experiment. Panel (b) shows samples of $M_i^{10}(50,m)$, which reports the average cost of $r = 10$ requests on the $m^{th}$ list in each trial.

a second phase that generates the $m^{th}$ random request, looks it up in the list, and reports its cost. The random variate $M_i(n,m)$ depends both on the particular list order $\ell$ and on the particular request $k$.

Conditional expectation works by concentrating extra effort in the second phase to reduce variance in the estimation of the cost per state. Two applications of this VRT are illustrated here.

First, instead of generating one request in the second phase, we can modify the code to generate $r$ random requests and record their costs *without changing the list order* each time. The new variate $M_i^r(n,m)$ reports the average costs of $r$ requests on the same list, instead of just one. This average cost has the same expectation as the cost of one request and is guaranteed to have lower variance.

Figure 6.8 presents the result of applying this technique to MTF. Panel (a) shows $M_i(50,m)$ in 25 independent trials at each level of $m$, and panel (b) shows measurements of $M_i^{10}(50,m)$ in 25 independent trials, where each data point represents the average of $r = 10$ requests on the final list order. Since the first phase dominates the computation time, increasing the cost of the second phase by a factor of 10 has negligible effect on total running time. Statistics for the last columns of data are as follows.

|  | Mean | Var. | 95% Conf. |
|---|---|---|---|
| $M_i(50,1001)$ | 15.60 | 159.75 | [10.65 , 22.55] |
| $M_i^{10}(50,1001)$ | 15.00 | 17.61 | [13.35, 16.65] |

Variance is 9.07 times smaller in this table; on average the variance will be 10 times smaller. The range in confidence intervals decreases from 9.91 to 3.3; on average the range will shrink by a factor of $3.17 = \sqrt{10}$.

```
SequentialSearchTest(n, m, R, trials) {
  for (t=1; t<=trials; t++) {
    L = randomPermutation (n); // Phase 1
    for (i=1; i<=m-1; i++) {
      k = randomZipf(n);
      for (j=1; L[j] != k; j++);
      reorder(R, L, j);      // R=MTF or TR
    cost = 0;                // Phase 2
    for (i=1; i<=n; i++)
      cost += i * prob[L[i]];
    }
    printCost(R, t, n, m, cost);
  }
}
```

Figure 6.9. Sequential search test code Version 2. This test program implements the conditional expectation VRT.

Our second example of conditional expectation applied to MTF is even more effective. The next experiment simply replaces the second phase that generates random requests for the list with an explicit calculation of the average list cost under Zipf's distribution, using the cost formula (6.1) given at the beginning of this section applied to the list order $\ell$:

$$C(\ell) = \sum_{i=1}^{n} i \cdot p_{\ell[i]}.$$

The new test program is sketched in Figure 6.9; this code uses an array prob[1...n], which contains request probabilities on keys 1...n under Zipf's distribution.

The calculation of average list cost takes $O(n)$ time, which is more than the average cost to perform a search for one request or even 10 requests. The extra time pays off, however, in the dramatic reduction in variance seen in Figure 6.10. Panel (a) shows all three costs $M_i(n,m)$, $T_i(n,m)$, and $D_i(n,m)$ from the original experiment, and panel (b) shows measurements of $M_i^c(n,m)$, $T_i^c(n,m)$, and $D_i^c(n,m)$, the results of applying the second conditional expectation technique using exact calculation of average list cost. The overall reduction in variance is reflected in the smaller confidence intervals for the rightmost data columns shown in the table.

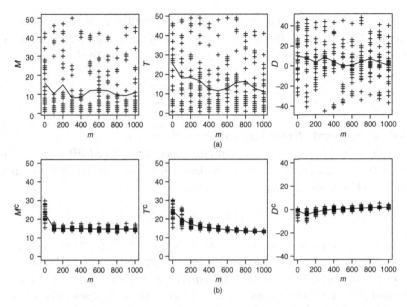

Figure 6.10. Conditional expectation with exact costs. Panel (a) shows measurements of $M_i(50,m)$, $T_i(50,m)$, and $D_i(50,m)$ from the first experiment. Panel (b) shows measurements of these costs after application of conditional expectation with exact computation of average list cost.

|  | $\overline{M}(50,1001)$ | | $\overline{T}(50,1001)$ | | $\overline{D}(50,1001)$ | |
|---|---|---|---|---|---|---|
| Before VRT | 15.6 | [10.6, 20.6] | 11.4 | [5.9, 16.9] | 4.2 | [-4.2, 12.6] |
| After VRT | 14.6 | [14.3, 15.0] | 12.2 | [12.0, 13.4] | 1.5 | [1.1, 1.9] |

Figure 6.1 from the beginning of the chapter shows the difference data on an easier-to-read scale. It is now possible actually to see the faster convergence of MTF predicted by Rivest [15]. We can locate the crossover point $m_0$ somewhere between $m = 401$ and $m = 501$. More experiments focused on that region, together with the common random numbers VRT, could be applied to get a tighter estimate of the location of $m_c$.

**Guideline 6.5** *Conditional expectation: When the computation of an average cost can be split into two parts – generate a random state, then estimate the cost of the state – add extra work to reduce or eliminate variance in the second part.*

*Why Conditional Expectation Works.* Let $L_i$ be a random variate in the experiment that takes a value corresponding to a particular list order $\ell$ after the $m - 1^{st}$ request in trial $i$.

The *conditional expectation* of $M_i$, given that the list $L_i$ is in the order $\ell$, is denoted $E[M_i | L_i = \ell]$. This is the average cost of searching over all positions $j$ in a list ordered by $\ell$. Let $M_i^\ell$ denote a random variate calculated this way:

$$M_i^\ell = E[M_i | L_i = \ell] = \sum_{j=1}^{n} j p_{\ell[j]}.$$

Both $M_i(n,m)$ and $M_i^\ell(n,m)$ are estimators of $\mu(n,m)$.

In the second application of conditional expectation to the MFT rule, the sampling step is replaced with a direct calculation of $M_i^\ell$ as in the preceding formula. It always holds (see [2]) that

$$Var(M_i) \geq Var(M_i^\ell).$$

Therefore, direct computation of the average list cost $M_i^\ell(n,m)$ in each trial is guaranteed to have smaller variance than a single measurement of $M_i(n,m)$.

In the first application of conditional expectation, the test program generates $\ell$ in the first phase and in the second phase generates $r$ random requests to construct a random sample of request costs for $\ell$. This is equivalent to estimating $M_i^\ell(n,m)$ by random sampling. Such an estimate based on a sample of size $r > 1$ is guaranteed to have less variance than an estimate based on a sample of size one, as in the original experiment. The second approach is more effective than the first in reducing variance but cannot always be applied to general computational problems.

Both variations on the conditional expectation VRT should be considered in general algorithmic experiments whenever the following circumstances arise:

1. The experiment can be split into two phases: generating a random "state" and then generating a random variate to estimate the average cost of the state.
2. Either (1) it is cost-effective to generate extra random samples in the second phase, to reduce variance in the estimation of average cost of the state; or (2) the average cost of the state can be directly calculated by traversing its elements.

This scenario is common in data structure experiments, where the purpose of the experiment is to measure the average cost of the data structure over a sequence of $m$ random operations. Instead of reporting the cost of the $m^{th}$ operation, report the cost of many operations on the same configuration of the data structure. For example, to evaluate an algorithm for performing insertions and deletions in binary trees, start by generating $m-1$ random insert/delete operations and then traverse the BST to compute directly the average cost of the next insert or delete.

Another example arises in analysis of heuristic search algorithms, which operate by stepping through a space of solutions. The solution at time $m$ represents a state: instead of reporting the cost of a single solution at time $m$, sample the average cost of many solutions reachable from the solution at time $m - 1$. If sample variance within a single trial is a large component of variance among separate trials, this VRT will be effective. As always, there is no a priori guarantee that the technique will work, but a small pilot experiment can provide guidance.

### 6.1.2 Additional VRTs

We have seen three variance reduction techniques – common random numbers, control variates, and conditional expectation – that worked to reduce variance in the outcomes of the Move-to-Front and Transpose experiments. This section describes four more techniques that may be useful to computational experiments in general, but not to tests of sequential search rules.

### Antithetic Variates

Suppose algorithm $A$ takes a single input $U_i$ drawn uniformly at random from the real interval (0,1), and the cost variate $A_i$ is positively correlated with $U_i$. Instead of generating $t$ independent samples of $A_i$, the *antithetic variates* technique generates $t/2$ pairs of samples using $U_i$ and the antithetic input $U_i^* = 1 - U_i$ to obtain antithetic costs $A_i$ and $A_i^*$. The mean of each pair $A_i^a = (A_i + A_i^*)/2$ is reported as the trial outcome.

For example, instead of generating 10 random uniform inputs,

$$[.53, .27, .65, .05, .33, .27, .91, .53, .98, .45],$$

and computing average cost on the basis of outcomes $A_i$ in 10 trials

$$\overline{A} = \frac{1}{10} \sum_{i=1}^{10} A_i,$$

this approach would generate five pairs of antithetic inputs $(U_i, U*_i)$,

$$[(.53, .47), (.65, .72), (.05, .95), (.33, .64), (.27, 73)]$$

and compute the average of mean antithetic costs

$$\overline{A^a} = \frac{1}{5} \sum_{i=1}^{5} A_i^a.$$

Since $U_i$ and $U_i^*$ each obey the uniform distribution, the expectations are the same in both cases. If $U_i$ and $A_i$ are positively correlated, then the $A_i^a$ variates have smaller sample variance than the $A_i$ variates, even though there are only half as many.

In some cases it may be more appropriate to define antithetic uniforms by $U_i$ and $U_i^* = (U_i + 1/2)\mathrm{mod}\,1)$, if the correlation in algorithm $A$ indicates that this would work better.

At first glance this technique does not apply to our sequential search rules because they do not take uniform variates as inputs, but rather variates distributed by Zipf's rule. On the other hand, the Zipf generator (and any generator of nonuniform variates) does take uniform variates as input.

It is possible to generate antithetic pairs of requests $R_i$ and $R_i^a$ from antithetic uniforms $U_i, U_i^a$ using the *lookup method* of generation described in Section 5.2.4. This method creates an array of break points representing cumulative probabilities in a distribution. For example, the probability distribution $D = (.5, .3, .2)$ on integers 1, 2, 3, would be represented by a table $T = (.5, .8, 1)$ of break points, as shown in the following diagram.

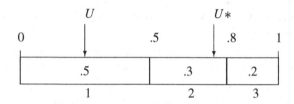

Two table lookups with antithetic uniforms $U_i = 0.25$ and $U^* = 0.75$ would yield antithetic Zipf variates $Z_i = 1$ and $Z_i^* = 2$. Using this lookup method to generate antithetic variates guarantees that $Z_i$ and $Z_i^*$, when considered separately, are each generated according to the Zipf distribution; this is necessary so as not to skew the experimental results.

Use of antithetic variates in the MTF and TR experiments should produce a reduction in variance. However, the test programs originally developed for this problem use the alternative *aliasing method* to generate random requests, which does not lend itself to generation of antithetic request sequences.

### Stratification and poststratification

Suppose an input instance $I$ contains $n$ uniform random numbers from the range $[0, 1)$. This range can be divided into, say, 10 "strata," $[0, .1), [.1, .2) \dots [.9, 1)$, and the expected number of variates in each stratum is known to be $n/10$. The stratification VRT would replace a random sample of $n$ numbers from $[0, 1)$ with a semirandom instance that contains exactly $n/10$ numbers from each stratum.

In our sequential search example, we could generate a random sequence of $m = 137$ requests according to Zipf's distribution with $n = 5$, by first generating the following quantities of each request key so that the proportions are exactly correct:

| Variate | 1 | 2 | 3 | 4 | 5 |
|---------|-----|-----|-----|-----|-----|
| Count | 60 | 30 | 20 | 15 | 12 |

A random permutation of these numbers could then serve as the request sequence in each trial. An experiment that measures search costs using lists containing exactly the expected number of variates in each strataum will have smaller sample variance than one that generates random requests in the standard way.

The problem with applying this approach to Zipf's distribution in general is that for many values of $m$ the expectations of the strata are not integral. Simply rounding those numbers up or down before generating the sequences creates biased inputs that will skew the cost measurements.

This problem can be solved using a trick similar to that described for antithetic variates discussion, by pushing stratification into the random number generator. To create a stratified list of $m = 100$ requests according to Zipf's distribution, first generate a stratified list of 100 uniforms: 10 from $[0,.1)$, 10 from $[.1,.2)$, and so forth. Then use a random permutation of the stratified uniform variates to create a stratified sample of Zipf variates by the lookup method.

A related VRT called *poststratification* is similar to the control variates technique, in the sense that a cost variate $A_i$ is adjusted towards its mean according to the deviation of another variate $S_i$ from its mean (assuming that the two variates are positively correlated). In this case the other variate $S_i$ is associated with the input and represents deviation from expectation within a stratum. Suppose, for example, algorithm $A$ takes input $I$ containing $n$ random numbers drawn uniformly from $(0,1)$, and $A_i$ is correlated with $S_i$, which represents how many numbers in $I$ are above the mean 0.5. The adjusted cost $A_i^*$ would be calculated by $A_i^* = A_i - c(S_i - n/0.5)$, for a constant $c$ that can be selected empirically.

### Importance Sampling

This VRT is applicable when the mean cost is dominated by some very expensive but rare event. A single experiment may not generate enough random trials for the rare event to be observed, so the sample mean $\overline{M}$ consistently underestimates the true mean $\mu$. Importance sampling adjusts the distribution of generated events so that the rare event occurs more frequently (thus reducing variance in the estimate) and then reweights the output measurements to correct the adjustment to the distribution. For details see any textbook on simulation, for example, [2] or [12].

**Guideline 6.6** *Consider a variety of variance reduction techniques, including antithetic variates, stratification, poststratification, and importance sampling.*

## 6.2 Simulation Shortcuts

Simulation shortcuts reduce variance by making the test program run faster. Faster code means that more data samples can be collected per unit of computation time. More data means less variance, and less variance is guaranteed to improve many statistical measures of confidence in estimates of means.

The algorithm and code-tuning techniques of Chapter 4 also make test programs run faster; however, the techniques described here exploit special circumstances of the "laboratory" scenario in which test programs are run and as a general rule cannot be applied to application programs running in real-world situations.

Two categories of shortcuts – called *overloading* and *modeling tricks* – are illustrated here using our sequential search case study. To simplify the discussion the shortcuts are applied to the first versions of the test programs for MTF and Transpose, sketched in Figure 6.11. But in most cases the shortcuts apply as well to later versions that incorporate the variance reduction techniques.

### *Trial Overloading*

The term *overloading* is used in programming language design to refer to an operator or function that can have multiple meanings; here the term is coined to

```
MTF(n,m,trials) {                    Transpose(n,m,trials) {
  for(t=1; t<=trials; t++){            for(t=1; t<=trials; t++){
    L = randomPermutation(n);           L = randomPermutation(n);
    for (i=1; i<=m; i++){               for (i=1; i<=m; i++){
      r = randomZipf(n);                  r = randomZipf(n);
      for (j=1; L[j]!=r; j++);            for (j=1; L[j]!=r; j++);
      c = j;                             c = j;
      tmp = L[j];
      while(j>1){                        if (j != 1) {
          L[j] = L[j-1];                   tmp = L[j];
          j--;                             L[j] = L[j-1];
      }                                    L[j-1] = tmp;
      L[1]=tmp;                          }
    }                                  }
    printCost(M,t,n,m,c);              printCost(T,t,n,m,c);
  }                                  }
}                                  }
```

    (a) MTF                                  (b) Transpose

Figure 6.11. Original test programs for MTF and Transpose.

refer to a test program that reports measurements for multiple design points in one trial.

Our original experimental design to evaluate the MTF and Transpose takes $t = 25$ random trials at levels $n = 50$ and $m = (1, 101, 201, \ldots 1001)$, totaling 11 design points. This design requires running $625 = 25 \times 11$ tests of each algorithm. A faster strategy is to fix the largest design point ($n = 50$, $m = 1001$) and to modify the test code to report the intermediate request costs at $m_d = 1, 101, \ldots$ in one trial. This tactic of overloading each trial to report costs for all levels of $m$ produces the same 625 data points in 1/11 of the time.

To push this idea further, the two test programs could also be modified to report costs for multiple levels of $n$ as shown in the following example.

| 5 | 2 | 4 | 6 | 3 | 1 |
|---|---|---|---|---|---|
| 1 | 2 | 3 | 4 | 5 | 6 |

n = 5: Request = 3, Cost = 5
n = 4: Request = 3, Cost = 3
n = 3: Request = 3, Cost = 2

Suppose the last ($m^{th}$) request is for key 3. In the full list the request cost is 5. The cost of this request in the sublist of keys $(1 \ldots 4)$ is 3, because key 3 is third from the front among sublist keys; similarly the cost of the request among the sublist of keys $(1 \ldots 3)$ is 2. More generally, if the $m^{th}$ request is for key $r$, then for each $k$ between $r$ and $n$, the cost of that request within the sublist of keys $(1 \ldots k)$ can be calculated.

Note, however, that the $m^{th}$ request for keys from $(1, n)$ is not the $m^{th}$ request for keys from $(1 \ldots k)$. Instead it is the $m_k^{th}$ request, equal to the number of requests for keys in $(1 \ldots k)$ that have appeared in the request sequence. Each $m_k$ is a random variate that depends on the particular request sequence.

To implement this second overloading scheme, the test program uses an array rcount[1...n] to hold request counts for every key. After the last request for key $r$, the code reports the request count $m_k$ and the request cost among sublist keys, for each $k \in r \ldots n$.

The code sketch in Figure 6.12 shows how to modify the MTF program to incorporate both overloading strategies. The program reports costs for every $p^{th}$ request, which corresponds to overloading the design points $m = 1, p + 1, 2p + 1, \ldots$. Furthermore, assuming the last request is for key $r$, the program reports, for each key $k = r \ldots n$, the request costs and request counts for sublists of $L$ containing keys in the range $(1 \ldots k)$.

**Guideline 6.7** *Overloading: rewrite the test program to output cost measurements for multiple design points in one trial.*

```
MTF (n, m, p, trials) {
  for(t=1;t<=trials; t++){
    rcount[1..n] = 0;              // initialize request cou
    L = randomPermutation(n);
    for (i=1; i<=m; i++){          // generate m requests
      r = randomZipf(n);
      rcount[r]++;                 // count request r
      for (j=1; L[j]!=r; j++);     // search in list
      cost = j;
      if (i mod p == 1)
          printCost(M,t,n,i,cost); // overload m
      tmp = L[j];                  // move to front
      while (j>1) L[j] = L[j-1];
      L[1]=tmp;
    }
    printCost(M,t,n,m,cost);       // report mth request

    for (i=2; i<=n; i++)           // compute sublist costs
       rcount[i]=rcount[i]+rcount[i-1];
    cost[r..n] = 1;
    for (i=1; i<=n; i++) {         // for each list item
       k = L[i];
       if (k >= r)                 // compute cost
         for (j=i-1; j>= 1; j--)
           if (L[j]< k)cost[k]++;
    }
    for (k=r; k<n; k++)
        printCost(M,t,k,rcount[k],cost[k]); // overload n
  }
}
```

Figure 6.12. Overloading. The MTF test program is modified to report costs for multiple values of *m* and *n* in one trial.

*Possible Drawbacks.* The first overloading scheme, which overloads parameter *m*, leaves the choice of which design points $m_d$ to report entirely up to the experimenter; furthermore, there is no additional time associated with this change to the test program. There appears to be no downside, but overloading is not always cost-free.

For example, the second scheme, which overloads parameter *n*, adds $O(n^2)$ extra time to the test program; the extra computation time becomes worthwhile only when $m >> n$. More generally, overloading may be too expensive to be worth implementing.

Also in the second case, the range of valid costs depends on the final request $r$; that means the experimenter has less control over which costs are reported. Running several trials of this test program will produce relatively more data points for large lists ($k \geq r$) and relatively fewer data points for small lists ($k < r$).

Uneven sample sizes can change the outcome of some types of data analysis. For example, a linear regression analysis performed on the overloaded data set would likely give different results than if the sample contained the same number of replicates at every level of $n$. It may be possible to "rebalance" such a sample by discarding some data points, but that does raise the question of whether overloading is worth the trouble in the first place.

Another possible drawback of trial overloading in any experiment is the loss of independence in the sample data. Overloading $m$ and $n$ induces correlation: for example, if request cost at time $m_d$ is higher than average, because the list is in some rare-but-expensive order, the cost of the next request at time $m_d + 1$ is likely to be higher than average as well. If all 625 trials are run separately (as in the original experiment), then data analysis can proceed with the standard assumption that all data points are independent of one another.

Whether or not correlation makes a difference to the data analysis depends on what analysis technique is used. Lack of independence is problematic for some classic methods of inferential statistics – such as hypothesis testing, regression analysis, and calculations of confidence intervals. For example, a standard hypothesis test applied to assess the difference between $cost(n,m)$ and $cost(n,m+1)$ would give different results for independent versus overloaded samples, and the latter results would be incorrect because assumptions of independence do not hold.

Correlation can be reduced by spacing the overloaded design points further apart – reporting the cost of every 100th request is better than reporting the cost of every 10th request – but in general it is difficult to know how much spacing might be sufficient.

Correlation and imbalance in data samples are less problematic for other categories of data analysis, especially exploratory and graphical methods, where few a priori assumptions are made about the data.

*General Application.* Algorithmic experiments offer many opportunities for using overloading to increase the amount of data generated per trial; a few examples are listed in the following. Whether or not overloading is appropriate for a particular experimental project depends on the goals of the project (do the extra data help the analysis?) and on the type of data analysis that will be applied (does validity depend on assumptions of data independence?).

- Section 2.2.2 describes an experimental design for an iterative-improvement heuristic called SIG. As a factor-reduction strategy the "number of iterations" parameter is overloaded: the test program is modified to report both solution cost and the iteration count every time the solution improves. Instead of running separate trials at several levels, this factor is set to one high level, and the program reports trace data so that it is possible to reconstruct what would have been the outcome had other levels been set. Iterative-improvement heuristics and online algorithms present similar opportunities for reporting costs at several iterations in each trial.

- Kershenbaum and Van Slyke [11] describe an experiment to study spanning trees in random graphs. The goal is to estimate $h(p)$, the probability that a spanning tree exists in a random graph $G(n, p)$ containing $n$ vertices, such that each edge appears with probability $p$. Instead of generating $k$ random graphs for each design point $p = p_1, p_2, \ldots p_k$ and recording the existence of a spanning tree in each, the authors generate one complete weighted graph $H$ with edge weights drawn uniformly at random from $(0, 1)$. This graph "encodes" unweighted graphs as follows: if an edge has weight $w$ such that $w \leq p_i$, the edge is considered to be present in graph $G(n, p_i)$. Let the random variate $W$ denote the largest weight in the minimum spanning tree of $C$. Graph $G(n, p_i)$ contains a spanning tree exactly when $W \leq p_i$. In this way one random trial is overloaded to generate data for all probabilities $p = p_1, p_2, \ldots p_k$.

- Many experimental studies of LRU-style caching algorithms (for example, [4]) employ overloading to report hit/miss ratios for multiple cache sizes $C_1, C_2, C_3 \ldots C_k$ in each trial. The test program constructs a single full-sized list of elements and runs the caching policy on the full list. If a requested element $e$ is within distance $D$ from the front of the list, that access is considered a "hit" for every cache such that $D \leq C_i$, and a "miss" for every cache with $D > C_i$.

- The cost of a recursive algorithm on a problem of size $N$ is usually computed in a postorder fashion by summing costs over all recursive stages. Each stage corresponds to a smaller problem size $n$, and the cost of solving the smaller problem can be reported by the test program. Applying this idea to quicksort, for example, a single trial could report cost for the main problem size $N$, as well as two problems of size about $n/2$, four problems of size near $n/4$, and so forth. A straightforward implementation of this idea would yield a total of $2N$ cost measurements, about half of them on problem size $n = 1$, which is too much: a cutoff or randomized filter could be applied to omit reports at small problem sizes.

```
MTF (n,m,trials) {                  Transpose(n,m,trials) {
  for (t=1; t<=trials; t++) {         for (t=1; t<=trials; t++) {
    time = randomPerm(n);               L=randomPerm(n);
    tstamp = n+1;                       for (i=1; i<=n; i++)
                                          loc[L[i]] = i;
    for (i=1; i<=m-1; i++){            for (i=1; i <= m; i++){
      r = randomZipf(n);                 r = randomZipf(n);
      // No Lookup:                       // Constant Lookup:
      time[r] = tstamp++;                c = loc[L[r]];
    }                                   if (c != 1) {
    // Reconstruct List:                  tmp = L[c];
    r = randomZipf(n);                     L[c] = L[c-1];
    rt = time[r];                         L[c-1] = tmp;
    c = 1;                                loc[L[c]] = c;
    for (i=1; i<=n; i++)                  loc[L[c-1]] = c-1;
      if (time[i] > rt) c++;            }
                                      }
    printCost(M,t,n,m,c);             printCost(T,t,n,m,c);
  }                                 }
}                                 }
```

|          (a) MTF          |          (b) Transpose          |

Figure 6.13. Sequential search modeling tricks. These MTF and Transpose test codes use modeling tricks to record request costs in constant time per request.

### *Modeling Tricks*

A *modeling trick* exploits special properties of the test environment that may not be available in real applications, to simulate the cost of the algorithm in less time than would be required by direct implementation. Two examples of modeling tricks using our sequential search test codes are illustrated in Figure 6.13.

First, the MTF program can be rewritten to exploit the fact that keys appear in the MTF list in order by most recent request: the first key in the list was most recently requested, the second key was second-most recently requested, and so forth. Instead of searching and re-ordering the MTF list for each request, it is only necessary to record time stamps for each key and to reconstruct the list order at the end. The cost of the $m^{th}$ request for key $r$ can be easily computed by counting how many keys have later time stamps than $r$. Figure 6.13 panel (a) illustrates this idea. This modeling trick yields a significant improvement in computation time, from worst case $O(nm)$ to $O(m)$. Assuming requests are generated by Zipf's distribution, the average cost of the original test program is $O(m \log n)$ to generate each data point, while the shortcut version takes just $O(m)$ time to generate the same point.

Second, the Transpose test program can be rewritten so that the location of request key $r$ is found by array lookup rather than a sequential search. The new version uses a `loc` array indexed by request keys, to record the location of keys in L. The transpose operation requires updating two entries in L and in `loc`. This modeling trick also reduces the cost of the test program for Transpose from $O(nm)$ worst case to $O(m)$ worst case, and from $O(m \log n)$ average case (Zipf's distribution) to $O(m)$.

**Guideline 6.8** *Modeling tricks: exploit information available in a laboratory context, to simulate an algorithm more efficiently than can be done by direct implementation.*

Bentley et al. [4] describe a similar modeling trick in experiments to test variations on an LRU-based software cache for use in a telecommunications product. Their application involves lists of size $n = 10,000$ and request sequences of size $m = 10^7$. Their test program stores the keys (which are (client, address) pairs) in a doubly linked list so that the Move-to-Front operation is constant-time, and they use a hash table indexed by keys to perform constant-time lookups into the list. With this implementation they can also apply trial overloading to test different cache sizes in each trial. They remark that straightforward experiments in their real application environment would have taken about a day to perform, whereas their simulation experiments were completed in about 15 minutes. This shortcut and modeling trick had the additional benefit of being transferable to their application code, to yield a software cache that is constant time per request.

Another remarkable modeling trick is demonstrated in Bentley's [3] experiments to calculate the exact average comparison cost of quicksort, assuming partition elements are selected at random. First, he points out that the cost of Quicksort can be simulated without actually sorting, by generating the random partition element location at each stage, as follows:

```
qCost (lo, hi) {
  if (lo >= hi) return 0;
  sum = hi-lo+1;
  m = randomInt(lo,hi);
  sum += qCost(lo, m-1) + qCost(m+1, hi);
  return sum;
}
```

Even with this modeling trick the computation of the exact average-case cost takes exponential time because every possible random outcome must be tested:

```
exCost(lo, hi) {
    if (lo >= hi) return 0;
    n = hi-lo+1;
    sum = 0;
    for (m=lo; m<=hi;  m++)
        sum += exCost(lo, m-1) + exCost(m+1, hi);
    return n-1 + sum / n;
}
```

Memoization reduces this to a quadratic procedure:

```
exCost (N) {
    ex[0] = 0;
    for (n=1; n<=N; n++) {
        // n = hi - lo + 1
        sum = 0;
        for (m=1; m=n; m++)
            sum += ex[m-1] + ex[n-m+1];
        ex[n] = n-1 + sum/n;
    }
}
```

He reduces this further to a linear-time computation. Finally he notes that the generation code can be represented by a recurrence formula

$$C_0 = 0$$

$$C_n = (n-1) + \frac{1}{n} \sum_{i=1}^{n} C_{i-1} + C_{n-i},$$

which has solution $C_n = (n+1)(2H_{n+1} - 2) - 2n \sim 1.386n \log_e n$, where $H_n = 1 + 1/2 + 1/3 + \ldots 1/n$ denotes the $n^{th}$ harmonic number [10]. This sequence of modeling tricks shrinks the time to compute the exact average-case cost of quicksort from exponential to constant time.

## 6.3 Chapter Notes

Computational experimenters have unusual opportunities for adjusting test programs to generate data samples that are easier to analyze. The key idea is to find ways to reduce variance in the output. Two basic approaches were surveyed in this chapter. The first approach is to apply variance reduction techniques (VRTs) that have been developed in the field of simulation. The second is to apply simulation shortcuts, which exploit the experimental scenario to generate more sample points per unit of computation: a larger sample sizes automatically reduces variance in the output.

To learn more about variance reduction techniques, their theoretical justifications, and applications to simulation experiments, see any textbook on simulation, such as [2], [9] or [12]. See also the survey article by by L'Ecuyer [13]. The discussion of variance reduction techniques applied to algorithms for self-organizing sequential search is an updated version of the survey published previously in [14].

The following guidelines were presented in this chapter.

6.1  *For best views of how average cost depends on parameters, work to magnify response and minimize variance.*

6.2  *Design your experiments to maximize the information content in the data: aim for clear views of simple relationships.*

6.3  *Common random numbers: when performance of two test subjects is positively correlated with respect to some random variate, compare performance in paired trials with identical values for that variate.*

6.4  *Control variates: adjust variate $T_i$ toward its expectation by subtracting the discrepancy between another variate $R_i$ and its known expectation $\rho$.*

6.5  *Conditional expectation: when the computation of an average cost can be split into two parts – generate a random state, then estimate the cost of the state – add extra work to reduce or eliminate variance in the second part.*

6.6  *Consider a variety of variance reduction techniques, including antithetic variates, stratification, poststratification, and importance sampling.*

6.7  *Overloading: rewrite the test program to output cost measurements for multiple design points in one trial.*

6.8  *Modeling tricks: exploit information available in a laboratory context, to simulate an algorithm more efficiently than can be done by direct implementation.*

### 6.4  Problems and Projects

C language implementations of the Move-to-Front and Transpose test programs (implementing the variance reduction techniques described in this chapter) are available for downloading from *AlgLab*.

1. What happens if you apply combinations of variance reduction techniques described in this chapter? Modify the MTF and TR test programs to evaluate promising combinations – how much variance reduction can you achieve?
2. Does the control variates VRT work as well for MTF as it does for TR? Does conditional expectation work as well for TR as it does for MTF?

3. The conditional expectation VRT, when applied to MTF and TR, requires $O(n)$ time to traverse the list and compute expected list cost. The original implementation requires only the time needed to search the list. For which combinations of $(n, m)$ does the reduction in variance outweigh the increased computation cost?

4. Run more experiments to locate the crossover point $m_c$ more precisely, for several values of $n$. How confident are you that your analysis is correct to within, say, $\pm 2$? What would you do to increase your confidence in that result? Can you find a function to describe how $m_c$ depends on $n$?

5. What properties of the request distribution $P(n)$ would make $m_c$ easier and harder to analyze? Replicate the experiments in this chapter using different request distributions: how much does the effectiveness of these VRTs depend on the distribution?

6. Implement the antithetic variates idea described at the beginning of Section 6.1.2 (this requires rewriting the random number generator to use the lookup method). How much variance reduction do you observe in MTF and TR? Is it worth the increase in total computation time?

7. Apply stratification and poststratification to MTF and TR. How well do they work?

8. Which variance reduction techniques can be combined with which simulation speedups? Implement some promising combinations and evaluate their effectiveness.

9. Download the Iterated Greedy (SIG) code described in Section 2.2.2, from *AlgLab* and apply some of the variance reduction techniques and simulation shortcuts described in this chapter.

## Bibliography

[1] The quote is attributed to Rutherford in Bailey, N. T. J., *The Mathematical Approach to Biology and Medicine*, Wiley 1967, 23.

[2] Bratley, Paul, Bennet L. Fox, and Linus E. Schrage, *A Guide to Simulation*, Springer-Verlag, 1983.

[3] Bentley, J. L., "The most beautiful code I never wrote," in Andrew Oram and Greg Wilson, eds., *Beautiful Code*, O'Reilly Media, 2007. A video of a talk at Google is Available from http://video.google.com/videoplay?docid=-103178950 1179533828#.

[4] Bentley, Jon, Duffy Boyle, P. Krishnan, and John Meniers, "Engineering little algorithms into a big system." Power Point Slides, 2011.

[5] Bentley, J. L., D. S. Johnson, F. T. Leighton, and C. C. McGeoch, "An experimental study of bin packing." *Proceedings of the 21st Annual Allerton Conference on Communication, Control, and Computing,* pp. 51–60, 1983.

[6] Borogovac, Tarik, and Pirooz Vakili, "Control Variate Technique: A Constructive Approach," in S. J. Mason, R. R. Hill, L. Mönch, O. Rose, T. Jefferson, and J. W. Fowler, eds., *Proceedings of the 2008 Winter Simulation Conference*, IEEE, 2008.

[7]  Frieze, Alan M., "On the value of a random minimum spanning tree problem," *Discrete Applied Mathematics*, Vol 10, pp. 47–56, 1985.

[8]  Johnson, David S., Lyle A. McGeoch, and Edward E. Rothberg, "Asymptotic experimental analysis for the Held-Karp Traveling Salesman bound." *Proceedings of the 7th Annual ACM-SIAM Symposium on Discrete Algorithm*, pp. 341–350, 1996.

[9]  Kleijnen, Jack P. C., *Design and Analysis of Simulation Experiments*, International Series in Operations Research and Management Science, Springer, 2008.

[10]  Knuth, D. E., *The Art of Computer Programming:* Vol 3, *Sorting and Searching*, Addison-Wesley, 1973.

[11]  Kershenbaum A., and R. Van Slyke, "Computing minimum spanning trees efficiently." *Proceedings of the 25th ACM Conference*, pp. 518–527, 1972.

[12]  Law, Averill M., and W. David Kelton, *Simulation Modeling and Analysis*, 3rd ed., McGraw-Hill, 2000.

[13]  Pierre L'Ecuyer, "Variance reduction's greatest' hits." *Proceedings of the 2007 European Simulation and Modeling Conference*, pp. 5–12, 2007.

[14]  McGeoch, Catherine C., "Analyzing algorithms by simulation: variance reduction techniques and simulation speedups," *ACM Computing Surveys*, Vol 24, No 2, pp. 195–212, June 1992.

[15]  Rivest, Ronald, "On self-organizing sequential search heuristics," *Communications of the ACM*, Vol 19, No 2, pp. 63–67, February 1976.

# 7
# Data Analysis

Really, the slipshod way we deal with data is a disgrace to civilization.

*M. J. Moroney, Facts from Figures*

Information scientists tell us that data, alone, have no value or meaning [1]. When organized and interpreted, data become *information*, which is useful for answering factual questions: Which is bigger, $X$ or $Y$? How many $Z$'s are there? A body of information can be further transformed into *knowledge*, which reflects understanding of how and why, at a level sufficient to direct choices and make predictions: which algorithm should I use for this application? How long will it take to run?

*Data analysis* is a process of inspecting, summarizing, and interpreting a set of data to transform it into something useful: information is the immediate result, and knowledge the ultimate goal.

This chapter surveys some basic techniques of data analysis and illustrates their application to algorithmic questions. Section 7.1 presents techniques for analyzing univariate (one-dimensional) data samples. Section 7.2 surveys techniques for analyzing bivariate data samples, which are expressed as pairs of $(X, Y)$ points. No statistical background is required of the reader.

One chapter is not enough to cover all the data analysis techniques that are useful to algorithmic experiments – something closer to a few bookshelves would be needed. Here we focus on describing a small collection of techniques that address the questions most commonly asked about algorithms, and on knowing which technique to apply in a given scenario. References to additional resources in statistics and data analysis appear in the Chapter Notes.

## Categories of Data Analysis

The premise underlying any report of experimental results is, *If you perform the same experiment, your outcomes will be similar to mine.* This premise is based on the assumption that my experiment and your experiment both draw a random data sample $X = (x_1, x_2 \ldots x_t)$ from the same underlying probability distribution. The distribution is defined by a *probability density function* $f(x)$ (usually unknown) that describes the probability that a particular element $x$ will appear in the sample. The contents of one sample may be different from those of the next, but they have some features in common because they are from the same source. Data analysis is applied to describe, quantify, and sometimes explain those common features.

To take a concrete example, the *normal distribution* with mean $\mu$ and standard deviation $\sigma$ is defined by the following probability density function:

$$f_{\mu,\sigma}(x) = \frac{1}{\sqrt{2\pi\sigma^2}} e^{-\frac{(x-\mu)^2}{2\sigma^2}}. \tag{7.1}$$

This function has the familiar bell-curve shape shown in Figure 7.1, which extends infinitely in both directions. Parameter $\mu$ describes the mean (center) of the function, and parameter $\sigma$ describes how widely the points are spread around their mean; in this example, $\mu = 0$ and $\sigma = 1$.

Here is an example of a claim we could make about any sample $X$ drawn from this distribution: since 68 percent of the area under the curve is within distance $\pm\sigma$ from $\mu$, we expect that roughly 68 percent of the points in $X$ will be in the range $[-1, 1]$.

Some data analysis techniques focus on understanding and describing the data sample $X$, and others on characterizing the underlying density function. There are four main areas of data analysis:

- *Descriptive statistics* is concerned with providing concise descriptions of the essential properties of a data sample.

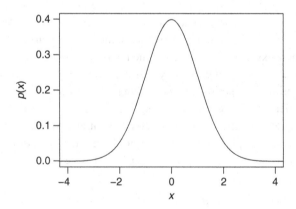

Figure 7.1. The normal distribution. This is the probability density function for the Normal distribution with $\mu = 0$ and $\sigma = 1$.

- *Exploratory data analysis* focuses on discovering patterns and relationships in the data.
- *Graphical data analysis* emphasizes the use of graphs and visualization techniques to understand the sample. Graphs can be used for descriptive or exploratory purposes.
- Methods of *inferential statistics* start with formal assumptions about the general shape of the density function. Inferences are made about properties of the density function, and the soundness of those inferences is also evaluated. *Computer-intensive inferential methods* can sometimes be applied to boost the power of inferential methods.

The data analysis techniques described in this chapter sample from all of these areas, to address the questions and scenarios that are most common in algorithm studies.

### Categories of Data

Data analysis starts with an awareness that different categories of data have different properties, as follows.

- *Categorical data* are qualitative rather than quantitative. For example, the categorical outcomes (success, failure) might be reported in tests of an algorithm for constraint programming. Experimental parameters can also be categorical, such as (hash table, binary search tree), to describe implementation choices for a set data structure.
- *Ordinal data* can be ranked (first, second, third) but have no scale, so arithmetical transformations have no meaning. An example is relevance rankings for pages returned by an Internet search algorithm.
- *Interval data* can be represented on a scale with no natural zero point, so ratios are not meaningful. An example is a temperature: the statement "Today is twice as hot as yesterday" has no natural meaning because *twice* is an artifact of the scale (Centigrade or Fahrenheit). It is hard to find examples of interval data in algorithmic problems.
- *Ratio data* are numerical data with a natural zero point, so ratios and other arithmetic transformations have meaning. This type of data is most common in algorithmic experiments.

The category dictates which data analysis techniques can be applied. As a general rule, ratio data support the widest choice and most powerful analysis techniques.

Often in algorithmic experiments, the experimenter has some control over what category of outcome is reported by the test program: choose ratio data when possible, but never by omitting information.

For example, a test program could be designed to report categorical results (success, failure) for each instance or to report the percentage of successes in *t* trials. The second approach loses information, because the percentage can be derived from the categorical data, but not vice versa.

**Guideline 7.1** *Test programs should report outcomes as ratio data whenever possible, but not at the price of lost information.*

Tukey [16] points out that ratio data can be further broken into subcategories:

- *Counts and amounts* are accumulated totals of discrete and continuous quantities, respectively. They are always positive and often bounded at the low end but unbounded at the high end.
- *Ratios and proportions* result from dividing one number by another. A proportion represents part of a total and ranges between 0 and 1, while a ratio can be greater than 1. Ratios and proportions are always positive. *Counted fractions* are ratios with small integer denominators.
- *Differences* represent the distance between pairs of numbers and can be positive or negative.

As we shall see, sometimes the subcategory also dictates the choice of analysis technique.

## 7.1 Univariate Data

A univariate data sample is a set of scalar numbers that represent outcomes from an experiment. In this section we consider techniques for analyzing univariate data. Section 7.1.1 surveys common descriptive statistics and their properties, and Section 7.1.2 presents some techniques of inferential statistics.

### *7.1.1 Descriptive Statistics*

Descriptive statistics is an area of data analysis concerned with finding concise summaries of key properties of data samples, in a way that does not distort or omit important details. These key properties always include, at least:

- A measure of the *location*, or central tendency of the data.
- A measure of *dispersion*, or how much spread there is away from the center.

Dispersion is just as important as location when summarizing data, especially when conveying your results to others. As mentioned earlier, the premise behind any report of experimental results is "If your experiment is like mine, your results will be similar." If you report that the sample mean is 56.78, with no further information, the reader has no context for interpreting the meaning of "similar": should she expect to see results within ±0.05 or within ±50 of that mean?

**Guideline 7.2** *Location and dispersion are the yin and yang of data summaries; do not report one without the other.*

If the data are well behaved, simple *summary statistics* will suffice. Unusual or complicated data sets are harder to summarize and may require special treatment.

This section reviews the standard summary statistics and their merits; we also consider how to detect unusual properties in data distributions and how to choose appropriate descriptive statistics.

### Common Summary Statistics

Suppose you have a sample of $t$ numbers representing measurements from $t$ tests of algorithm $X$, denoted $(x_1, x_2 \ldots x_t)$. The *ranked* data, denoted $X^r = (x_{(1)}, x_{(2)} \ldots x_{(t)})$, correspond to the values of $X$ sorted in nondecreasing order. For example, a sample of size 6 might look like this:

$$X = (15, 31, 3, 12, 29, 22)$$

$$X^r = (3, 12, 15, 22, 29, 31)$$

We say $x_{(r)}$ is the $r^{th}$-*order statistic* of $X$: in this example the first-order statistic is 3 and the third-order statistic is 15. The order statistics $x_{(1)}$ and $x_{(t)}$ are more familiarly known as the *minimum* and *maximum* of the sample.

Here are five common summary statistics and their definitions. The first two are statistics of location, and the last three are statistics of dispersion.

- The sample *mean* is defined by

$$\overline{X} = \frac{1}{t} \sum_{i=1}^{t} x_i. \tag{7.2}$$

- The sample *median* is the middle-order statistic:

$$\text{Med}(X) = x_{(t+1)/2}. \tag{7.3}$$

If $t$ is even, the definition of *median* is ambiguous: here we adopt the convention that a fractional-order statistic is equal to the average of the two numbers with nearest ranks. Thus the median of $X$ in the preceding example is $18.5 = (x_{(3)} + x_{(4)})/2$. Half the data are above the median and half the data are below it.

- The sample *variance* is defined by

$$\text{Var}(X) = \frac{1}{t} \sum_{i=1}^{t} (x_i - \overline{X})^2. \tag{7.4}$$

| Algorithm | Mean | Median | Var | St. Dev. | IQR |
|-----------|------|--------|-----|----------|-----|
| A | 104.56 | 102.36 | 391.28 | 19.78 | 19.61 |
| B | 100.52 | 100.98 | 1796.01 | 42.38 | 67.15 |
| C | 144.66 | 139.29 | 2675.85 | 85.81 | 33.24 |
| D | 67.25 | 28.99 | 7363.56 | 51.73 | 66.88 |
| E | 108.74 | 86.67 | 2828.39 | 53.18 | 92.93 |

Figure 7.2. Summary statistics. Five statistics for five hypothetical algorithms. Each statistic is calculated on a sample of $t = 50$ data points.

- The sample *standard deviation* is the square root of the variance:

$$sd(X) = \sqrt{Var(X)} \qquad (7.5)$$

- The *interquartile range* (IQR) is the difference

$$IQR(X) = x_{(3t/4)} - x_{(t/4)}. \qquad (7.6)$$

These two order statistics are known as the *third quartile* and *first quartile* of the data set, respectively (using the averaging convention mentioned earlier for fractional ranks). Half the points in the sample lie within the IQR.

Figure 7.2 summarizes results of a hypothetical experiment to test five imaginary algorithms named A through E. The statistics were calculated in each case on samples containing random outputs from $t = 50$ trials of each algorithm.

Variance is shown in the table for completeness but omitted from the discussion that follows: standard deviation is somewhat easier to interpret here, and the remarks that follow about standard deviation apply as well to variance. Some differences between the two are discussed in Section 7.1.2.

This table is hard to understand. Comparison of the means suggests that D is about 33 percent better than A and B. But comparison of the medians suggests that D is more than 70 percent better than A or B: Just how good is D, exactly? Similarly, comparison of standard deviations suggests that C has twice as much dispersion as B, but comparison of the IQRs suggests the opposite. In row A, the standard deviation and IQR are quite similar, but in row B the standard deviation is smaller than the IQR, and in row C the reverse is true. Many more apparent contradictions can be found in this table: which interpretation is the right one? More importantly, how can one set of data produce such different interpretations?

The problem is, some of the statistics in this table are not appropriate to the data sets they describe – instead of providing accurate descriptions of location and

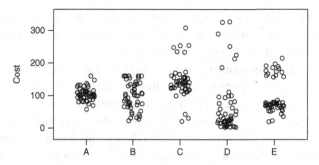

Figure 7.3. Four algorithms. This jittered scatterplot shows 50 measurements each in random trials of algorithms A through E.

dispersion, they obscure some features of the data and introduce ambiguities in interpreting the results. To understand these issues we need to look at the raw data.

### Looking at Distributions

Figure 7.3 shows a *jittered scatterplot* of data samples A through E, plotted side by side. *Jittered* means that a small amount of random variation was added to the $x$-coordinate of each point: jittering spreads out the plotting symbols and removes overlap, making some properties easier to see. A few properties that affect our choice of summary statistics are listed in the following.

- Samples A and B appear to be *symmetric*, with dispersions evenly balanced around their means. A has less dispersion than B.
- Sample C is also symmetric, but it has *outliers* – a few isolated extreme values – at both the high and low ends.
- Data set D is not symmetric; rather, the points are densely clustered at the low end and spread out with a long tail at the high end. The data are *skewed to the right*; a sample with the tail in the other direction would be "skewed to the left." D may also have outliers at the high end; there is no standard definition of what constitutes an outlier, so this is largely a judgment call.
- Data set E is *bimodal*, with two distinct centers of location.

These properties affect our choice of summary statistics in the following ways.

*Symmetry.* Nearly any statistic of location works fine for symmetric data samples like A and B. Symmetry is why the means and medians in rows A and B are nearly identical in the table in Figure 7.2. Our choice of statistics of dispersion, however, depend on additional properties not visible in this scatterplot, which are discussed later in this section.

*Outliers.* Data set C is symmetric except for outliers at the high and low ends. The choice of which summary statistics to apply to a sample containing outliers depends on our understanding of what caused them.

In data from one experiment, outliers might be due to measurement error. In another experiment, òutliers might be observed because the data are from a *fat-tailed* probability distribution, which described later in this section under Kurtosis. When data are sampled from such a distribution, there is a good chance that values far from the center will be in the sample, but these points are rare enough to appear disconnected from the main body sample. Taking more random trials would "fill in" the apparent gaps between outliers and the rest of the sample.

If outliers are solely due to measurement error, they should be discarded, since they do not reflect any property of the algorithm being studied. It is important when reporting experimental results, however, to mention that some measurements were discarded, specify how many, and explain why.

If the outliers are a natural reflection of algorithm performance, and likely from a fat-tailed distribution, they should remain in the sample. But as a general rule, the mean and standard deviation are not good summary statistics for this type of data.

A statistic is called *robust* if it does not change much between different samples drawn from the same distribution. A statistic that is not robust does a poor job of summarizing, because it fails to predict what outcomes will be observed by others. The mean and standard deviation statistics are not robust to outliers, because outliers tend to fluctuate in number and magnitude and to pull these statistics along. The median and IQR are robust because they are based on ranks and not magnitudes.

For example, if just four of the top outliers of sample C are absent from the next sample, the mean drops from 144.66 to 134.12, a difference of 10, while the median drops from 139.3 to just 137.9, a difference of less than 2. Similarly the standard deviation changes from 51.73 to 37.91, a difference of almost 13, while the IQR moves from 33.24 to 30.71, a difference of less than 3.

Another good alternative statistic for sample C is the *trimmed (p) mean*, which discards the top and bottom $p$ percent of the data and computes the mean of what remains. If $p = \lfloor k/t \rfloor$, the trimmed mean is defined by

$$\overline{X}^p = \sum_{r=k+1}^{t-k} x_{(r)}. \tag{7.7}$$

To obtain a robust statistic, choose $p$ large enough to discard the *maximum* number of outliers likely to appear in repeated experiments.

*Skew* The right skew in sample D pulls the sample mean upward toward the tail, but the median does not tend to move because it is based on ranks. This difference prompts careful consideration of which meaning of "center" is best suited to the analysis. Either might be appropriate to a given algorithmic question.

Both the standard deviation and the IQR are intended for use on symmetric distributions. They can be misleading when applied to skewed data sets, since the dispersion they describe is too big on one side and too small on the other. Some alternative descriptive techniques for skewed distributions are discussed later in this section.

*Bimodality.* Sample E has two distinct centers of location, an important fact that is obscured by all five summary statistics. As a general rule, the best strategy for dealing with bimodal (or higher-modal) data samples is to summarize their groups separately, together with information about the size of each group.

|        | Size | Mean   | Median | St. Dev. | IQR   |
|--------|------|--------|--------|----------|-------|
| Low E  | 36   | 77.36  | 81.51  | 15.35    | 18.81 |
| High E | 14   | 189.47 | 186.79 | 16.78    | 25.49 |

If there is no clear gap between groups in a given data sample (and if it is not possible to label the data by group in the test program), it can be very difficult to decide which points belong to which center. In this case *any* statistic of location could be misleading, and it may be safer to eschew summary statistics in favor of graphical displays.

A jittered scatterplot cannot display all of the distributional properties of interest here, however. Figure 7.4 shows *empirical distribution plots* of samples A, B, C, and D. An empirical distribution plot is constructed by simply plotting the points in increasing order by rank. Diagonal sight lines connecting the extremal values are superimposed on each graph.

These graphs reveal more information about the distributions, which is discussed in the next few sections.

*Kurtosis.* The data in panel (a) of Figure 7.4 have a spiral shape, which shows that the data are more densely concentrated near the center and less dense near the ends. Compare this to the sample in panel (b), which follows a straight line (except for a few identical points at the top). The spiral shape in panel (a) is characteristic of data drawn from a normal or near-normal distribution.

The term *kurtosis* describes the "pointiness" of a density function, that is, how dense it is near its center compared to its extremes. It is possible to calculate an

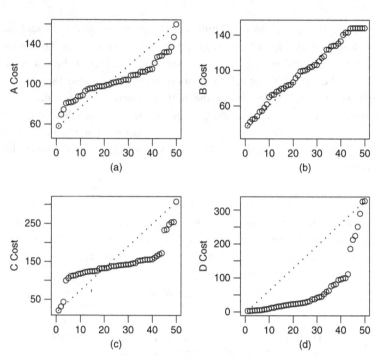

Figure 7.4. Empirical distribution plots. Panel (a), from algorithm A, shows the characteristic spiral shape of a normal distribution. Panel (b), from algorithm B, conforms to a uniform distribution, except for several identical points at the top. Panel (c), from algorithm C, shows a near-normal symmetric distribution with outliers; panel (d), from algorithm D, shows a skewed distribution with outliers. Diagonal sight lines connect the extremal values.

*excess kurtosis statistic* $\kappa$ for a symmetric data sample, which measures how closely the distribution of the sample resembles a normal distribution in this respect:

$$\kappa(X) = \frac{\sum_{i=1}^{t} (x_i - \overline{X})^4}{sd(X)^4} - 3. \qquad (7.8)$$

(Sometimes this statistic is defined without subtracting the constant 3.) The three density functions that follow illustrate this property.

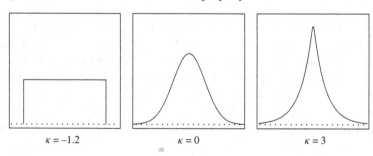

The *uniform* distribution on the left has no bump at all in its center; samples from uniform distributions have negative kurtosis near $\kappa = -1.2$. The normal distribution is shown in the center: samples from normal distributions have kurtosis near 0, no matter what values the parameters $\mu$ and $\sigma$ take. Samples from the *double exponential distribution* (two back-to-back exponential functions) on the right have positive kurtosis near $\kappa = 3$.

Sample A, which has the spiral shape characteristic of a normal distribution in panel (a), has $\kappa = 0.31$, which is close to 0. Sample B, which resembles a uniform distribution, has $\kappa = -1.18$. A data set with positive kurtosis would display a more pronounced spiral than panel (a), with a smaller horizontal center and larger vertical arms.

Kurtosis affects our choice of summary statistics in two ways. First, a distribution with positive kurtosis is said to have *fat tails*: since the peak around the mean is more acute than in the normal distribution, a larger proportion of the density function is pushed into the tails. As mentioned earlier, fat tails in a density functions are associated with outliers in data samples, which deserve special consideration.

Second, kurtosis affects our interpretation of the standard deviation statistic. The *empirical rule* states that 68 percent of the data in a sample fall within one standard deviation of the mean ($\overline{X} \pm sd(X)$), 95 percent fall within two standard deviations, and 99.7 percent are within three standard deviations of the mean. This handy rule is a reason for preferring the standard deviation statistic to variance, since it makes these rough boundaries easy to compute.

The standard deviation and variance statistics are otherwise quite similar in their properties, and equally suitable for summarizing data. (However, they do have distinct properties when used for other purposes, as discussed in Section 7.1.2.)

But the rule breaks down if the data are not normally distributed. Inspection of the data with an empirical density plot or computation of the excess kurtosis statistic can be used to detect this problem, as illustrated in the following table.

|   | $\kappa$ | Mean | St. Dev. | 99.7 percent | Range |
|---|---|---|---|---|---|
| A | 0.31 | 104.56 | 19.78 | [ 45.2, 163.9] | [58.0, 160.0] |
| B | -1.18 | 100.52 | 42.38 | [-26.6, 227.6] | [22.6, 160.0] |
| C | 1.92 | 144.66 | 51.72 | [-10.4, 299.8] | [20.9, 308.0] |

Applying the empirical rule to sample A ($\kappa$ near 0), we get an estimate about the range of 99.7 percent of the data that nicely matches the actual sample range (containing 100 percent of the points). On the other hand, applying the rule to sample B, we obtain an estimated range that is much larger than the actual range. The outliers in sample C pull $\kappa$ to a high positive value, and the Empirical Rule fails again. (The statistic should not be applied to skewed data sets like D.)

**Guideline 7.3** *The Empirical Rule: in a sample from a normal distribution, 68 percent of the data fall within $\pm\sigma$ of the mean, 95 percent fall within $\pm 2\sigma$ of the mean, and 99.7 percent fall within $\pm 3\sigma$. Check that your data are indeed normally distributed before applying this rule.*

If you use the standard deviation statistic in a report of experimental results, the default assumption will be that the Empirical Rule applies. If it does not, either explain how the sample deviates from a normal distribution or choose another statistic.

*Censored Data.* The straight-line pattern in panel (b) suggests that sample B resembles a uniform distribution, except for six points at the top that are all equal to 160. This sharp break from the general trend raises questions: does algorithm B have a natural upper bound of 160 in its cost function, or is this evidence of a *ceiling effect*?

A ceiling effect is a limitation of the experiment that prevents accurate measurement of costs above some upper limit. Ceiling effects are examples of a more general problem known as *data censoring*. Censoring occurs when, instead of an accurate measurement of every outcome, the experiment returns upper or lower bounds on some measurements. In algorithmic experiments data censoring may be caused by some limitation of the test program, the runtime environment, or the experimental design.

For example, a ceiling effect occurs when a predetermined limit on total computation time is set ("Run until a solution is found or one hour has elapsed"): as a result, some time measurements are replaced by the time limit, which is a lower bound on their true values. Another example of censoring occurs when process times are smaller than the system clock resolution and are reported as 0. Censoring can also occur without ceilings or floors: for example, a test program might occasionally halt for external reasons, producing *left-censored* runtimes that are lower than true runtimes, even though no maximum time limit was reached.

Data analysis is difficult when there is no way to tell which measurements are censored, if any. Fortunately, algorithmic experiments are so highly controlled that it is usually possible to identify the culprit data points and to know whether the reported measurements represent under- or overestimates.

If the six high measurements of 160 in sample B are not due to censoring but rather are intrinsic to the algorithm, they should be included in the data analysis.

But, on the other hand, this unusual property should be mentioned and not hidden in summary statistics.

Censored data may or may not be included from sample statistics, depending on the situation. Here are some tips.

- If the data are randomly censored – that is, there is no correlation between a value and whether or not the value is censored – then the censored data points can usually be omitted with little harm.
- If ceiling or floor effects are present, the mean $\overline{B}$ is a misleading statistic, whether the censored data are left in or removed: in either case, the mean is more an artifact of the experiment than of the test subject. In this situation use the median, or else the trimmed (p) mean defined earlier in this section under Outliers.
- Like the mean, the standard deviation is not suitable for data with ceiling and floor effects. The IQR is more robust, as long as it does not contain the censored points. (If censored data points make up more than 25 percent of the sample, it is time to run a new experiment.)

*Skew.* The right-skew in sample D appears as convexity in the empirical distribution plot of panel (d). Left-skewed data would have a concave shape. A *sample skewness* statistic can be calculated as follows:

$$ss(X) = \frac{\frac{1}{n}\sum_{i=1}^{n}(x_i - \overline{X})^3}{sd(X)^{3/2}}. \tag{7.9}$$

A symmetric distribution has $ss(X) \approx 0$, a right-skewed distribution $ss(X) > 0$, and a left-skewed distribution $ss(X) < 0$.

As mentioned earlier, both the standard deviation and the IQR are misleading statistics of dispersion for skewed data because "dispersion" is normally understood as being the same on both sides of the center. If it is not, a better idea is to summarize dispersion separately on each side.

One common approach is to report the *hinges* of the data set, which are the five order statistics $(x_{(1)}, x_{(n/4)}, x_{(n/2)}, x_{(3n/4)}, x_{(n)})$ corresponding to the minimum and maximum, the two quartiles, and the median.

Figure 7.5 shows six *boxplots (or box-and-whisker plots)* for A through E, the latter split into two groups. Each boxplot is a visual representation of the hinges: the bar in the middle marks the median, and the box edges mark the first and third quartiles. Each *whisker* extends to the outermost data point that is within distance 1.5(IQR) from the box edge (a common rule of thumb for marking outliers), and the remaining data points are drawn as individuals. The boxplots are shown in order of increasing medians, so that visual comparisons are easier.

Because they are summaries, boxplots obscure some data features and reveal others. For example, differences in kurtosis are hidden, as are the six top points in

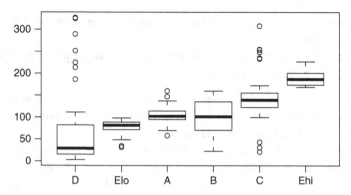

Figure 7.5. Boxplot summaries. These boxplots show the hinges of samples A through E (E is split into two groups).

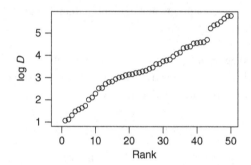

Figure 7.6. Transformation. An empirical density plot of data set D after logarithmic transformation.

B. This graph also reveals some new observations: for example, the third quartile of D is below the first quartiles of A, B, and Ehi, suggesting that $D$ has lowest cost nearly half the time. On the other hand, D also has the highest costs of all five algorithms.

### Data Transformation

An alternative strategy for coping with skewed data is to *transform* the sample by applying a function to each value. For example, Figure 7.6 shows an empirical density plot for our skewed data set D, after application of a *logarithmic transformation* using the function $d_i' = \log_e(d_i)$.

Compare this to panel (d), which shows the empirical distribution of the untransformed data. Logarithmic transformation pulls the long tail toward the middle and makes the resulting sample symmetric. In fact, the transformed data appear to have a uniform distribution: statistics of location will agree on where the center is, and statistics of dispersion are adequate to describe both sides of the center.

If the sample mean $\overline{D}'$ is calculated on log-transformed data and then mapped back to the original scale via exponentiation,

$$\overline{D}^* = exp\left(\frac{1}{t}\sum_{i=1}^{t} \ln d_i\right) \qquad (7.10)$$

the result $\overline{D}^*$ is called the *geometric mean* of D. The geometric mean is an alternative statistic to the sample mean defined in formula (7.2), which is technically called the arithmetic mean. It is more robust to outliers than the arithmetic mean and is often a good choice for summarizing skewed data. The geometric mean is considered more appropriate for summarizing data in the form of ratios and proportions and samples from lognormal distributions (i.e., the logarithms of the data obey a normal distribution). It cannot be used with samples containing negative or 0 data values.

It can be shown that in any data set the geometric mean is bounded above by the arithmetic mean: $\overline{D}^* \leq \overline{D}$. For this particular sample $\overline{D}^* = 32.31$ and $\overline{D} = 67.25$.

Logarithmic transformation is one of a class of *power transformations*, described by a parameter $\theta$, that may be applied to a data set X to adjust for skew.

$$x_i^\theta \text{ for } \theta > 0$$
$$\log_e x_i \text{ for } \theta = 0 \qquad (7.11)$$
$$-x_i^\theta \text{ for } \theta < 0$$

If the data are right-skewed, apply transformations with $\theta \leq 0$. If the data are left-skewed, use transformations with $\theta < 0$; the negative sign keeps transformed data in the same relative order as the original sample.

**Guideline 7.4** *Apply logarithmic transformation, or more generally a power transformation, to impose symmetry in a skewed data sample.*

As we shall see in later sections, not only are transformed data easier to summarize, but transformation simplifies and improves many other types of data analysis as well. Mosteller and Tukey [13] point out that counts and amounts are nearly always right-skewed and easier to analyze if first reexpressed by logarithmic transformation.

### The Right Tool For the Job

Let us move away from hypothetical data sets A through E to apply this discussion of appropriate summary statistics to some a real data. Figure 7.7 shows a jittered

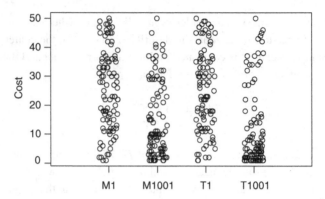

Figure 7.7. Four data samples. M1 and M1001 describe the cost of the MTF algorithm at times $m = 1$ and $m = 1001$. T1 and T1001 describe the Transpose algorithm at the same times. Each sample contains $t = 100$ points.

scatterplot of four measurements of the Move-to-Front and Transpose algorithms for sequential search, which were the subject of a case study described in Section 6.1.1.

Here are some options to consider when deciding how to summarize these data sets.

- *Statistics of location*: arithmetic mean, median, trimmed mean, and geometric mean.
- *Statistics of dispersion*: standard deviation, variance, and interquartile range.
- *Additional statistics*: kurtosis, skew, hinges, and boxplots.
- *Other properties to consider*: outliers, bimodality, and censored data.
- *Strategy*: Apply data transformation to remove skew before summarizing.

We start by looking at empirical distribution plots for these four data samples, in Figure 7.8. Panels (a) and (b) show MFT costs at $m = 1$ and $1,001$, and panels (c) and (d) show Transpose at $m = 1$ and $1,001$. The two data sets for $m = 1$ appear to be uniformly distributed: in fact, it can be proved that the first request obeys a uniform distribution because the list is initially in random order. The two samples for $m = 1,001$ are right-skewed.

Our choice of summary statistics is informed by these properties and by the goals of the analysis. In particular, if one sample is to be compared to another, we need summary statistics that are common to both. Here are some applications of this principle.

1. To compare the data in panels (a) and (b) choose statistics that work for both uniform and skewed distributions. Any of the statistics of location we have

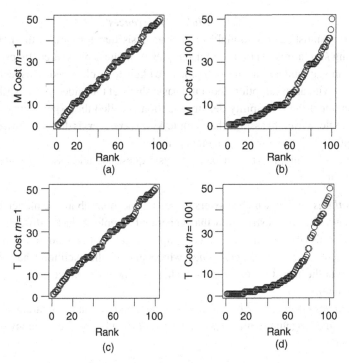

Figure 7.8. Empirical distribution plots for MTF and Transpose at sample points $m = 1$ and $m = 1001$. (a) MTF $m = 1$, (b) MTF $m = 1,001$, (c) TR $m = 1$, (d) TR $m = 1,001$.

considered could be used here. Because of asymmetry in (b), hinges might be the best choice for comparing dispersion. The same reasoning applies when comparing panels (c) and (d).

2. Comparisons of the data in panels (b) and (d) could be improved and simplified by logarithmic transformation, which would impose symmetry on both samples. If analysis proceeds on the untransformed data, hinges or boxplots could be used as summaries.

3. To compare any of these data sets to known *theoretical results* for these algorithms (see Section 6.1.1 for examples), use summary statistics that match the theory. In this case, the arithmetic mean should be applied, including the skewed data samples.

**Guideline 7.5** *Consider these properties when deciding how to summarize a data sample: symmetry, outliers, skew, bi- or multimodality, kurtosis, and data censoring.*

### 7.1.2 Making Inferences

Inferential statistics is a subfield of data analysis that formalizes the notion of observing similar results in different samples from the same source, by providing bounds and guarantees on what outcomes are likely to be observed. This methodology starts with an assumption about the basic shape of the underlying distribution; in this context the probability density function is called the experimental *model*. For example, we might assume that sample $X = x_1, x_2, \ldots x_t$ is drawn from a normal distribution with unknown parameters $\mu$ and $\sigma$.

The most common types of data analysis questions addressed by inferential methods are

- *Hypothesis testing,* which answers yes-or-no questions about the model: is there evidence that the distribution that generated sample $X$ has a different mean than the distribution that generated sample $Y$? Inferential techniques also yield statements of *statistical significance*, which quantify the likelihood that the result of a hypothesis test is due to random chance rather than an intrinsic property of the model.
- *Parameter estimation*, which aims at finding good estimates of parameters such as $\mu$ and $\sigma$, together with *confidence intervals* that bound the accuracy of those estimates.

These types of results only hold if assumptions about the basic shape of the model are true. There is no way of knowing whether the model correctly describes the underlying distribution, but analysis techniques are available for assessing the validity of the assumption as well.

The next section illustrates this approach to the problem of estimating the distribution mean $\mu$.

### Estimation and Confidence Intervals

Assume that data set $A$ from the previous section can be modeled by a normal distribution with (unknown) mean $\mu$ and standard deviation $\sigma$. Recall that the empirical distribution plot (Figure 7.4) and the kurtosis statistic (equation (7.8)) both suggest that this assumption is reasonable, since sample $A$ appears to be close to a normal distribution. Our first goal is to estimate $\mu$ and to assess the quality of that estimate.

The best way to estimate $\mu$ from data set $A$ is to compute the sample mean defined by formula (7.2): here we have $\overline{A} = 104.56$. The next step is to assign a level of "confidence" to this estimate, which describes how close we think $\overline{A}$ really is to $\mu$. There are many ways to define confidence, and most depend on how much dispersion is in the sample.

The *standard deviation of the sample* defined by formula (7.5) is not, in fact, the best choice for estimating parameter $\sigma$. This statistic is a *biased estimator* because it systematically underestimates $\sigma$ when calculated on finite-sized samples. Instead we use the *sample standard deviation* defined by

$$ssd(A) = \sqrt{\frac{1}{t-1}\sum_{i=1}^{t}(a_i - \overline{A})^2}. \tag{7.12}$$

This estimator is also biased, but less so than $sd(A)$. The sample variance $ssd(A)^2$ is an unbiased estimator of true variance $\sigma^2$ and is therefore the preferred statistic when making inferences about variance.

For each sample of size $t$ drawn from the population, we can calculate a sample mean $\overline{A}$. The distribution of sample means, over all possible samples of size $t$, is called the *sampling distribution of the mean*. The central limit theorem states that, no matter what distribution the sample $X$ has, the sample means will have a normal distribution. Furthermore, the standard deviation of this distribution, called the *standard error of the mean*, often shortened to *standard error*, is equal to

$$\sigma_{\overline{A}} = \frac{\sigma}{\sqrt{t}}. \tag{7.13}$$

Note that, like parameters $\sigma$ and $\mu$, the standard error is an unknown property of the model, not of the sample.

*Confidence Intervals.* The standard error can be used to define *confidence intervals* for $\mu$, which are used to assess how far a sample mean $\overline{A}$ might be from $\mu$.

In particular, the *95-percent confidence interval* for $\mu$ is defined by the boundaries

$$\overline{A} \pm 1.96\sigma_{\overline{A}}. \tag{7.14}$$

If we collect many samples $A$ of size $t$ from the population and compute the interval in (7.14) from each sample, then about 95 percent of the intervals will contain $\mu$. This describes our confidence in how close $\overline{A}$ is to $\mu$.

Different coefficients can be substituted for 1.96 in (7.14) formula to obtain other sizes of confidence intervals:

| Confidence | 90% | 95% | 99% | 99.99% |
|---|---|---|---|---|
| Coefficient | 1.645 | 1.96 | 2.276 | 3.291 |

Since the standard error $\sigma_{\overline{A}}$ is not known, we estimate it with $se(A) = ssd(A)/\sqrt{n}$. This is a simple approximation and not the best estimator known for the standard error. However, it works reasonably well if (1) the population that generates $A$ is symmetric and approximately normal, and (2) sample size $t$ is at least 30. If one of these conditions fails, there are better ways to estimate $\sigma_{\overline{A}}$, and better alternatives for calculating confidence intervals; see [2], [7], or most introductory statistics textbooks, for details.

Increasing sample size $t$ is guaranteed to shrink $\sigma_{\overline{A}}$, as well as the width of the confidence interval. But there is a law of diminishing returns: the difference between confidence intervals at $t = 10$ versus $t = 20$ is much bigger than the difference at $t = 30$ and $t = 40$. Therefore, taking sample sizes much larger than $t = 30$ has little effect on the size of the confidence intervals.

**Guideline 7.6** *Calculate confidence intervals for your sample means.*

### Resampling

Most classical methods of inference follow the general approach illustrated previously: start with an assumption that the sample $X$ is drawn from a normal distribution described by $\mu$ and $\sigma$ and perform a computation on the sample to estimate a parameter (or to perform a hypothesis test). The accuracy of the estimate is assessed via confidence intervals or a similar quantity.

Of course, in many experimental situations the underlying distribution is not normal, and we may be interested in other properties besides $\mu$ and $\sigma$. As a general rule there is no known way to apply inferential statistical methods to general distributions or population parameters, so the basic approach breaks down.

In these cases, *resampling techniques* such as *bootstrapping, jackknifing,* and *permutation tests* can be used to extend inferential statistical methods to non-standard problems. They are sometimes called *computer-intensive methods* of inference because they often require large amounts of computation time.

Resampling can be applied, for example, to estimate the standard error and therefore to calculate confidence intervals for just about any property of just about any distribution. To illustrate this technique, we apply bootstrapping to estimate the median (defined in formula (7.3)) and find a confidence interval for the distribution that produced data sample B in Figure 7.4.

Recall that sample B, containing $t = 50$ points, appears to be uniformly distributed (Figure 7.4), except for six identical points at the high end. The sample median is $\mathrm{Med}(B) = 100.98$.

The bootstrap procedure for calculating a 95-confidence interval for the median of the distribution is as follows.

1. Create $K$ *pseudosamples* of size $t$ by selecting random elements uniformly with replacement from $B$. "With replacement" means that each element is "put back" into $B$ before the next one is drawn. Therefore, the pseudosample may contain multiple copies of any element in $B$. As a rule of thumb, $K$ should be

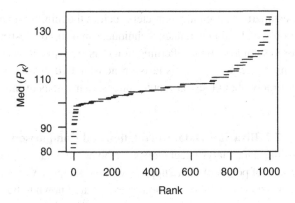

Figure 7.9. Empirical density plot for $K = 1000$ bootstrap medians of sample $B$ with pseudosample size $t = 50$.

at least 200, and more is better: take as large a value as computation time will allow.

2. Compute the statistic of interest (in this case, the median) for each pseudosample. This creates a pool $P_K$ containing $K$ samples of the statistic.
3. Check the distribution of $P_K$ with an empirical density plot. If the distribution looks symmetric and normal, confidence intervals can be calculated directly from the order statistics of $P_K$. In particular, the boundaries of the 95-percent confidence interval may be found at ranks $p_{(.025K)}$ and $p_{(.975K)}$ within the pool.
4. If the distribution does not look symmetric and normal, try again with larger $K$. If that does not work, confidence intervals may still be calculated using more advanced techniques such as the bias-corrected accelerated (BCa) bootstrap: see [9] or [10] for details.

Applying this procedure to sample $B$ with $t = 50$ and $K = 1,000$, we obtain the empirical density plot for the bootstrap medians in Figure 7.9. The data exhibit the propeller shape typical of a normal distribution. With $K = 1000$ we find the $25^{th}$ and $975^{th}$-order statistics, which are [90.24, 119.07].

Thus, we estimate the distribution median with Med(B) $= 100.98$, and we have some confidence that the interval [90.25, 119.07] is likely to contain the true median.

**Guideline 7.7** *Use bootstrapping (and related resampling methods) to generalize inferential methods to nonnormal distributions and nonstandard statistics.*

Bootstrapping can be used for estimating standard errors and confidence intervals for a variety of population parameters and distributions. The procedure is less effective for estimating extremal parameters such as the minimum and maximum of a distribution. Jackknifing, a related technique, can be used to estimate bias and standard error in sample statistics. Permutation tests are typically used to measure statistical significance in hypothesis tests on nonstandard distributions. See [7], [10], or [9] for more about these computer-intensive methods of inference.

## 7.2 Bivariate Data: Correlation and Comparison

Now we consider data analysis techniques for bivariate data samples, which are presented as pairs of points $(X, Y)$. Suppose we have samples $X = x_1, x_2 \ldots x_n$ and $Y = y_1, y_2, \ldots y_n$, such that the paired points $(x_i, y_i)$ are known to be related in the experiment.

In algorithmic experiments the pairs may represent some type of cause-and-effect relationship; for example, $X$ is input size and $Y$ is algorithm performance. Or, in tests of an iterative algorithm, $X$ may represent computation time and $Y$ solution cost. Or, the data may represent two outcomes measuring the costs of algorithms $X$ and $Y$ when run on common input instances.

The sample $(X, Y)$ is presumed to have been generated according to some *joint probability distribution*. This distribution is defined by a two-dimensional probability density function of the form $f(x, y)$, which describes the probability that a given pair $(x_i, y_i)$ will be in the sample. Data analysis is used to describe the relationship between $Y$ and $X$ and to understand properties of the underlying joint distribution.

This section surveys techniques for describing the relationship between paired elements $(x_i, y_i)$. Section 7.3 presents analysis techniques for understanding $Y$ as a function of $X$.

We turn once again to Move-to-Front and Transpose, the two sequential search algorithms described in Section 6.1.1. When the samples M1, M1001, T1 and T1101 were compared in Figure 7.7, they were treated as four independent univariate data sets.

In fact, the experiment that produced these samples measured the costs of MTF and TR when initialized the same way and run on identical inputs. Because of this relationship we can treat (M1, T1) as a bivariate data sample at the design point $m = 1$, and (M1001, T1001) as a bivariate sample at $m = 1001$. What can we learn about the relationship between these two algorithms?

*Correlation and Covariance.* We say that $M$ and $T$ are *positively correlated* when $m_i$ and $t_i$ move together, in the sense that $m_i$ is high when $t_i$ is high, and vice versa. The sample is *negatively correlated* if high values of $m_i$ are matched with low values of $t_i$, and vice versa. If $m_i$ and $t_i$ appear to have no such relationship

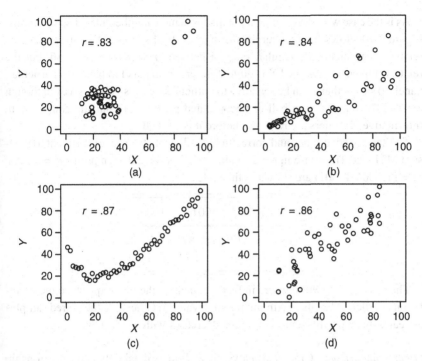

Figure 7.10. Correlation. Each panel shows 50 paired measurements of $(x_i, y_i)$. The value of the correlation coefficient $r$ is about the same in each panel, even though the paired relationships are very different.

– as if they were generated independently of one another – then we say $M$ and $T$ are not correlated.

Correlation statistics can be defined in different ways; two common statistics are described here. Recall that $\overline{M}$ denotes the sample mean (formula (7.2)), and $sd(M)$ is the sample standard deviation (formula (7.5)). The sample *covariance* is defined by

$$\text{Cov}(M, T) = \frac{1}{t-1} \sum_{i=1}^{t} (m_i - \overline{M})(t_i - \overline{T}). \tag{7.15}$$

This statistic is positive when the samples are positively correlated, and vice versa.

The sample *correlation coefficient*, typically denoted $r$, is the covariance, scaled so that it takes values in the range $[-1, 1]$.

$$r = \text{Cor}(M, T) = \frac{\sum_{i=1}^{t} (m_i - \overline{M})(t_i - \overline{T})}{(t-1)sd(M) \cdot sd(T)}. \tag{7.16}$$

As is the case with most summary statistics, a mere number may obscure details. Figure 7.10 shows four scatterplots of hypothetical samples $X$ and $Y$. The correlation coefficients are similar, ranging between $r = .84$ and $r = .86$, but the relationship between $X$ and $Y$ is quite different from panel to panel. In particular, panel (a) shows that $r$ can be sensitive to outliers, since $r$ is quite high even though most of the data are in a ball of uncorrelated points. This statistic can be more informative if outliers are removed before it is applied.

The sample covariance and correlation coefficients from an experiment to measure MTF and Transpose in $t = 25$ paired trials at three design points $n = 50$ and $m = (1, 5001, 10001)$ are shown in the table.

|      | 1      | 5001   | 10001  |
|------|--------|--------|--------|
| Cov  | 225.79 | 189.87 | 107.08 |
| $r$  | 1.00   | 0.72   | 0.53   |

The costs of the two rules are in fact identical on the first request, so the correlation coefficient has its maximum possible value 1. Otherwise the paired samples appear to have positive correlation that decreases with $m$.

*Other Comparisons.* Graphical analysis reveals more details about the relationship between MTF and TR. Figure 7.11 shows four different graphical views of data samples $(M, \dot{T})$ for our three design points $m = (1, 5001, 10001)$. Here are some things we can learn from these graphs.

* Panel (a) is a scatterplot of paired points $(m_i, t_i)$. The points are *coded* so that symbols (a, b, c) denote design points $m = (1, 5001, 10001)$, respectively. The perfect correlation in the first design point is revealed by the straight line of points marked a. Points b and c have weaker positive correlations and follow a generally upward trend. Most of these points are below the line $y = x$; that means that MTF costs more than TR in most cases. Two outliers, where TR costs significantly more than MTF, appear in the upper left corner.
* Panel (b) shows a *segment pairplot* of the same data. In this graph both $m_i$ (plusses) and $t_i$ (circles) are plotted on the $y$-axis, and matched pairs are connected by short line segments. The perfect correlation at $m = 1$ appears in the horizontal segments in the first data column. We can also observe that these points are fairly evenly distributed within their range (0,50).

    In the middle column ($m = 5001$), most segments have negative slope, again suggesting that MTF costs more than TR in most cases. The pair with the large positive slope corresponds to the outlier b in panel (a). In the middle and right columns the two distributions appear to be skewed more for TR.

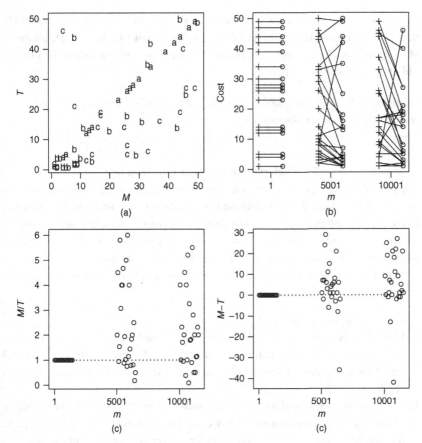

Figure 7.11. Four views of correlation. Panel (a) shows a coded scatterplot $(M, T)$ coded by design point: $a : m = 1$, $b : m = 5001$, and $c : m = 10001$. Panel (b) shows a segment pairplot of the same data (plusses $= M$, circles $= T$). Panel (c) plots ratios $M/T$ for each design point. Panel (d) shows differences $M - T$.

- Panel (c) shows a jittered scatterplot of the cost ratios $(m_i/t_i)$, at each design point. Again the perfect correlation at $m = 1$ is obvious. We also observe that MTF is never more than six times worse than TR and that cost ratios are fairly evenly spread in their range.
- Finally, panel (d) presents a jittered scatterplot of cost differences $(m_i - t_i)$. From this graph we learn that although MTF is more frequently worse than TR, the two outlier points indicate that TR can sometimes be equally bad.

Panels (c) and (d) give somewhat different impressions about the comparative costs of the algorithms. In panel (c), the data above the line $(m_i/t_i \doteq 1)$ occupy more space in the graph than the data below the line; MTF appears to be a lot worse than Transpose in some cases, but Transpose is never that much worse than MTF. But this impression is an artifact of the display: panel (d) shows that, although MTF beats Transpose much less frequently, the cost differences can be equally bad above and below the line.

**Guideline 7.8** *Different graphs give different views of relationships in data. Look at many views to learn the full story.*

### 7.3 Understanding $Y$ as a Function of $X$

The most common question asked in algorithm analysis is, *How does algorithm cost depend on input size?* To address this question via experiments, we can run tests of the algorithm at various input sizes $n_i$ and create a bivariate data set $(N, C)$ containing measurements of algorithm cost $c_i$ at input sizes $n_i$. The goal of the analysis is to learn something about the unknown cost function $c = f(n)$.

In statistics this is considered a problem in *modeling*, which involves the following steps:

1. Gather a data sample $(N, C)$.
2. Identify a function family (the *model*) that describes the general shape of the relationship between paired data samples $(N, C)$. For example, the model might be the family of linear functions $c_i = f(n_i) = an_i + b$, with unknown coefficients $a, b$.
3. Apply inferential techniques to *fit* the model to the data. This involves finding values for model parameters, in this case, the coefficients $a$ and $b$, that yield the best fit between model and data under a given definition of fit quality.
4. Apply inferential and graphical analyses to *validate* the model by comparing the fit to the data. Some validation techniques provide insights about how to improve the model: when appropriate, adjust the model and go to step 1.

When this procedure is applied to questions in algorithm analysis, the result can be resounding success or abject failure. Modeling is easy when (a) the correct function family is easy to identify, or (b) the goal is to find a convenient *descriptive* model for making predictions, with no guarantee of correctness, so the exact function family is not important.

Often in algorithm research, neither of these properties holds: the whole point of the experiment may be to understand the *true* nature of the underlying cost function. Standard modeling techniques of data analysis do not adapt well to this problem.

To make matters harder, the input or the algorithm or both are usually randomized. Therefore, the model $f_n(c)$ defines an unknown probability distribution that is parameterized by $n$, and $c_i$ is a sample from the distribution $f_{n_i}(c)$. The usual goal of the analysis is to understand how the distribution mean varies with $n$: $\mu = g(n)$ of $n$.

This is not a simple modeling problem. The combination of very little a priori knowledge about $f_n(c)$ and $g(n)$, weak or nonexistent tools of data analysis, and high expectations about correctness can yield disappointing results.

To illustrate this point, the next two sections present two case studies, one reasonably successful and one with mixed results. Section 7.3.1 describes a project to find a reasonable descriptive model to predict cost on typical inputs, for a fixed range of input sizes. Section 7.3.2 describes a project with the goal of analyzing the data to support (or refute) a conjecture about asymptotic growth.

### 7.3.1 Building a Descriptive Model

The Markov Chain Monte Carlo (MCMC) algorithm for random text generation is described in the case study of Section 3.1. This algorithm reads an input text $T$ containing $n$ words, together with parameters $m$ and $k$. It generates a random text of $m$ words, based on frequencies of $k$-word phrases in $T$. If $k = 1$, the frequencies are computed for single words; if $k = 2$, the frequencies are based on two-word phrases, and so forth. Here we restrict the analysis to the case $k = 1$.

The algorithm comprises three steps, two of which are straightforward to model. The third, the random selection step, is more challenging. In this case study we develop a function to model the cost of random selection in the MCMC algorithm.

Let rcount denote the total (comparison) cost of this step measured in one trial at a given design point $(T, n, m, k)$. The step is performed once per output word; let rcost = rcount/m denote the average cost per output word in that trial. This average rcost is a random outcome because the algorithm generates a different sample of words in each trial.

The goal is to find a function $g(n)$ that describes the expected value of rcost as a function of $n$. This function corresponds to the average number of word duplicates (for example, the may have 123 duplicates, and may have 45 duplicates, and so forth) in a sample of $m$ words selected at random from the $n$ words in $T$, such that words with more duplicates have a higher probability of being selected. We expect $g(n)$ to increase with $n$, since large texts are likely to have more duplicates per word; otherwise little is known about its general shape.

To build $g(n)$, we apply the modeling process outlined at the beginning of this section.

*Step 1: Gather Data.* The first step is to gather a data sample $(N, R)$. Figure 7.12 shows the results of an experiment to measure rcost using eight files described

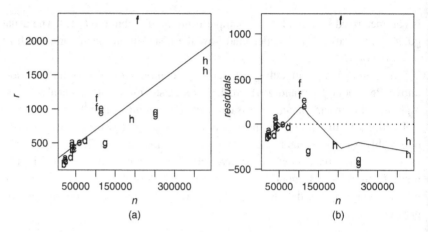

Figure 7.12. Modeling rcost. Panel (a) shows a scatterplot of sample $(N, R)$, with a least-squares regression line $g(n) = .004n + 254$ superimposed. Panel (b) shows residuals from the linear fit, with a horizontal sight-line and a lowess curve superimposed.

in the following table. For each file, two random trials are run using the full file size $n$, and two trials are run using the first half of the file (by line count), $n_h \approx n/2$. This creates 16 levels of $n$, and measurements for 2 trials at each level, totaling $t = 32$ data points in the sample. Let $(n_i, r_i)$ denote the measurement of input size and rcost, respectively, in the $i^{th}$ trial.

| Key | Text | $n$ | $n_h$ |
|-----|------|-----|-------|
| a | *Constitution of the United States* | 39,960 | 21,997 |
| b | *Aesop's Fables* | 40,863 | 19,439 |
| c | The Book of Psalms | 45,146 | 23,950 |
| d | Twain, *Tom Sawyer* | 72,989 | 37,003 |
| e | Twain, *Huckleberry Finn* | 112,493 | 58,109 |
| f | Darwin, *Voyage of the Beagle* | 207,423 | 103,596 |
| g | Shakespeare tragedies | 251,181 | 123,434 |
| h | Shakespeare comedies | 377,452 | 191,281 |

Panel (a) shows a scatterplot of $n_i$ versus $r_i$ at each design point. The points are coded by file as shown in the table. We can make several interesting observations about this data: $N$ and $R$ are positively correlated, as expected; the joint distribution is skewed, with points clustered in the bottom-left corner and spread out toward the top-right corner; in many cases pairs of letters are superimposed, indicating that two random trials at the same design point returned nearly identical measurements of $r_i$; and there is one outlier file $f$ (Darwin) that contains an unusually high number of duplicates per word.

*Step 2: Choose A Model.* The data in panel (a) have a generally linear trend, so we start with a linear model $r_i = g(n) = an_i + b$.

*Step 3: Fit the Model to The Data.* A *least squares regression line* is superimposed on the points in panel (a). The regression line $g(n) = 0.004n + 253$ represents the *least squares fit* of the linear model to the data, which corresponds to the coefficient pair $(a,b)$ that minimizes the following sum:

$$S(a,b) = \sum_{i=1}^{t} s_i^2 \text{ where} \tag{7.17}$$

$$s_i = y_i - (a \cdot n_i + b). \tag{7.18}$$

The values defined by (7.18) are called the *residuals* from the fit: $s_i$ is equal to the vertical distance between the line $g(n_i)$ and the point $y_i$ in the sample.

This fit may be perfectly adequate for predicting rcost as a function of n in many cases: except for the outlier $f$, the points in panel (a) appear to be fairly close to the line, and given the amount of file-to-file variation, we could argue that this fit is likely to be as good as any other. But better models do exist, as illustrated in the next step.

*Step 4: Validate the Model.* To validate the linear model we start by plotting $n_i$ versus the residuals $s_i$, as shown in panel (b). A horizontal sight line is drawn on the graph at $y = 0$.

The solid curve is called a *locally weighted scatterplot smooth* (lowess) curve. A lowess curve is built by computing weighted averages in a sliding window of the data points $(n_i, s_i)$. This handy tool of graphical analysis "smooths" the data to show the general trend of the point set. We observe here that the residuals have a generally concave shape: the extreme points are below the horizon and the middle points are above it. This indicates that the points are curving downward compared to the regression line and that a better fit to the data could be obtained with a sublinear model.

**Guideline 7.9** *Let the trend in residuals guide the search for a better model for your data.*

We can consider a few different approaches to improving the model on the basis of the information in panel (b). The goal is to find and fit a model so that the residuals are generally flat, with no obvious concave or convex trend.

One simple idea is to remove the outlier points f and try again with linear regression. Omitting these points would move the least squares fit closer to the center of the remaining points and flatten out the lowess curve. Here, however, we make the choice to keep the outliers because they represent events that do occur in practice.

Another idea is to apply a power transformation as described by formula (7.11). The transformation "straightens out" the data trend so that a linear model fits better. Tukey's [16] *ladder of transformations* provides a systematic way to look for power transformations. Here is a portion of the transformation ladder, for a bivariate sample $(X, Y)$ modeled by $y = f(x)$ and $y > 0$. The idea is to apply a function to $y$ so that the transformed data $(X, Y')$ form a straight line on a scatterplot. The center of the ladder is the identity transformation $y' = y$. Negated terms are used on the left side so that the transformed data are increasing (or decreasing) to match the original data, which simplifies analysis.

$$\ldots, \quad -1/y, \quad -1/\sqrt{y}, \quad \ln y, \quad \sqrt{y}, \quad y, \quad y^2, \quad y^3, \quad \ldots$$

Use the ladder as follows:

- if the data trend is convex upward (superlinear), apply a transformation $y' = t(y)$ using a function from the left of center, to bend the curve downward toward a straight line.
- if the trend is concave (sublinear), apply a transformation from the right of center to bend the curve upward.

The transformations farther away from center are more extreme. These transformations can also be applied to $x$, working in the opposite direction – that is, to bend a curve downward, apply functions from the right – or to both $x$ and $y$. See [7] or [16] for more about this approach to modeling.

The *Box-Cox procedure* combines this ladder-of-transformation idea with statistical analysis, by identifying a transformation on $Y$ described by parameter $\lambda$ (e.g., $\lambda = 2$ corresponds to $y^2$) that best straightens out the sample. The best choice of $\lambda$ is defined as the one that minimizes the *sum of squared errors*, a statistic computed on the residuals from a linear regression fit to the transformed points $(X, Y^\lambda)$. The Box-Cox transformation scales the points so that residuals are comparable across different values of $\lambda$. For more information about this approach see [5] or [11].

Yet another approach to finding a better model is to apply a *power transformation*, described next.

## Power Transformations

Panel (a) of Figure 7.13 shows our cost data after applying a logarithmic transformation to both $N$ and $R$: $r' = \ln(r)$ and $n' = \ln(n)$. This has the effect of replotting

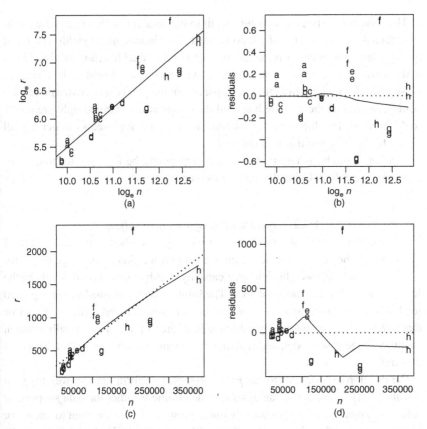

Figure 7.13. Modeling `rcost`. Panel (a) shows $(N, R)$ under log-log transformations $n' = \ln n$ and $r' = \ln r$, together with a linear regression fit $r' = 0.7n' - 14$. Panel (b) shows residuals from the fit to the log-log data. Panel (c) shows this regression fit translated back to the original scale, $g(n) = 0.22n^{0.7}$. The linear regression fit computed earlier is also shown (dotted line). Panel (d) shows the residuals from this fit on the original scale.

the points on a log-log scale. Logarithmic transformation improves our view of the data by spreading out the points more evenly in their range and moving the outliers f closer to the center. A least squares regression line $r' = 0.7n' - 1.5$ is superimposed in panel (a). The residuals in panel (b) show a slightly downward trend, but the lowess curve is much straighter than before, indicating that the regression line nicely matches the growth in the data.

Our next step is to apply a reverse transformation to map this regression line back to the original scale. The *power law* states that if $\ln y = f'(x) = k \ln x + \ln a$, then $y$ and $x$ are related by $y = f(x) = ax^k$, Therefore, the fit $r' = 0.7n' - 1.5$ becomes $r = .22n^{0.7}$ in the original scale (with $.22 = e^{-1.5}$).

The solid line in panel (c) shows this fit to the data; the dotted line is the linear fit obtained previously. The slight downward curve in this model yields a better fit to the data points at the extreme left and right ends. Panel (d) shows the residuals and a lowess curve from the new fit, also mapped to the original scale. Compare these residuals to those in Figure 7.12 panel (b): the points at the extreme left are better centered on the horizon line, and the points at the extreme right are closer to the horizon. The differences are subtle, but this curve represents a better overall match to the data, and that was the goal.

If a better model is required, the next step would be to apply techniques of *nonlinear modeling*. Cohen [7] has a good survey.

### 7.3.2 Experimental Asymptotic Analysis

Recall the *first fit* (FF) algorithm for bin packing described in the case study of Section 3.2. The algorithm takes as input a list of $n$ weights in the range $(0, u)$, for $u \leq 1$, and packs the weights into unit-capacity bins by placing each weight in the first (leftmost) bin that can contain it. The solution cost is defined as the expected total amount of *empty space* left in the tops of bins, denoted $E(n, u)$. We know that if $E(n, u)$ is asymptotically sublinear in $n$, then FF is asymptotically optimal in this average case model, and if $E(n, u)$ is asymptotically linear, then FF is not optimal.

We develop experiments to run FF on lists of $n$ uniform random weights with $0 < u \leq 1$. The goal of data analysis is to determine whether the data support, or refute, a conjecture of asymptotically linear growth. That is, we want to know, for given $u$, whether there is a $k < 1$ such that $E(n, u) \in O(n^k)$. For fixed $u$, let $(N, E)$ denote a sample containing pairs of input sizes $n_i$ and measurements of empty space $e_i$.

### The Power Law

First we try the power transformation procedure illustrated at the end of Section 7.3.1: apply log-log transformation to the $(E, N)$ data and use linear regression on the transformed data set. A linear fit $y' = ax' + b$ on the transformed data corresponds to a fit to the model $bx^a$ in the original scale. What can we learn about $a$?

Figure 7.14 shows results of an experiment to measure FF in three random trials each at design points $u = (1, 0.8)$ and $n = (10000, 20000, 30000 \ldots 200000)$.

Panel (a) shows a scatterplot $(N', E')$ after log-log transformation, with a least squares regression line superimposed. The slope of the line is $a = 0.69$. Panel (b) shows the residuals from that regression fit, with a lowess curve and a horizontal sight line. The lowess curve gives slight indications of concavity in the residuals,

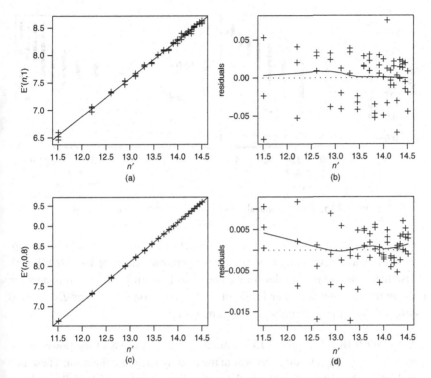

Figure 7.14. Asymptotic analysis of the first fit algorithm on lists of *n* random weights drawn uniformly on $(0, u)$. Panel (a) shows measurements of empty space when $u = 1$. The power rule is applied and the regression fit has slope $a = 0.69$. Panel (b) shows the residuals from this fit. Panel (c) shows the same analysis for $u = 0.8$; here the line has slope $a = 0.9883$. Panel (d) shows residuals from that fit. The slight concavity in the lowess curve suggests the data are growing faster than the fit.

which suggest that the line is growing slightly faster than the data. This gives strong support for a conjecture that, in the original scale, the data grow *more slowly than* the function $e = cn^{0.69}$ (for constant $c$ that can be calculated from the fit). This suggests that $E(n, 1) \in O(n^{0.69})$: therefore FF is asymptotically optimal.

This experimental observation was first published in [4] together with a conjecture that $E(n, 1) \in O(n^{0.7})$: an asymptotic bound of $O(n^{2/3} \log n)$ was subsequently proved [15]. Note that the asymptotic bound $O(n^{2/3} \log n)$ is slightly below the conjecture of $O(n^{.7})$. Data analysis suggested an upper bound that was both correct and low enough to suggest sublinear growth. This is an example of a successful asymptotic analysis of a finite data set.

Panels (c) and (d) show the same analysis applied to measurements of $E(n, 0.8)$. In this case the observed slope $a = 0.9883$ is very close to 1, and the residuals

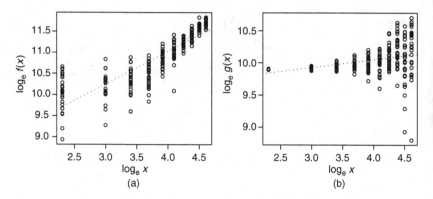

Figure 7.15. Power law analysis of two quadratic functions $f(x)$, $g(x)$.

curve upward. This time the analysis is inconclusive: $E(n, 0.8)$ might be asymptotically linear in $n$, or it might be $O(n^{1-\epsilon})$ or perhaps something like $O(n/\log n)$. These functions are too similar for data analysis to distinguish one from another, even in tests on much higher levels of $n$. The question of whether $E(n, 0.8)$ is asymptotically linear or sublinear in $n$ remains open.

*Why Didn't It Work?* Figure 7.15 illustrates some limitations of the power transformation when used to study growth in the leading term of a function. These two panels show the results of applying the power transformation to the following two random functions.

$$f(x) = 10x^2 + x + 25{,}000 + \epsilon(10{,}000)$$

$$g(x) = x^2 - 10x + 20{,}000 + \epsilon(x^2)$$

The last term $\epsilon(s)$ denotes a random noise variate generated according to a normal distribution with mean $\mu = 0$ and standard deviation $\sigma = s$. The data samples each contain 25 random points at levels $n = 10, 20, \ldots 100$. In both cases the leading term is quadratic.

Panel (a) shows log-log plot of $(x, f(x))$, and panel (b) shows a log-log plot of $(x, g(x))$. The coefficients $a$ from linear regression fits to the transformed points are $a = 0.73$ and $a = 0.12$, implying that $f(x) \approx cx^{0.73}$ and $g(x) \approx cx^{0.12}$, respectively. These results are well off the mark, since we know that both functions are $O(x^2)$. (Inspection of the residuals does at least indicate correctly that these are lower bounds on the order of the leading term.)

Here the analysis is sabotaged, first, by the presence of large secondary terms in the functions, and, second, by random noise in the data. In panel (a) the nonlinear shape in the transformed data is due to the huge constant term in $f(x)$. In this case, we can get a better estimate of $a$ by fitting a line to the two highest sample points. That fit yields a slope of $a = 1.4$, which is closer to the true bound of 2, but still a significant underestimate. In panel (b) the negative second term produces an initial decrease in the data at small $x$, which, together with growth in the random term, completely obscures the quadratic term of $g(x)$.

The experimental remedy for an analysis marred by large low-order terms is to run more trials at higher levels of $x$, so that the leading term has a better chance to dominate. The remedy for random noise is to run more trials at the same design points, to reduce variance. These remedies may or may not be feasible to apply in a given experimental situation, and there is no guarantee in general that the result will be sufficient for the analysis problem at hand.

In fact, any data analysis technique that returns an asymptotic bound based on a finite data sample cannot guarantee to be correct (see [12] for details). The basic argument is, since the sample contains at most $d$ design points (distinct values of $n_i$), data analysis cannot distinguish among models of degree $d$ or higher. For example, two design points $(n_1, n_2)$ can be used to find a best fit to a linear model, but not a quadratic model. But the underlying function $f(n)$ could be of arbitrarily high degree.

Even when there is some confidence that the design has enough levels to capture the degree of $f(n)$, the standard techniques for *fitting* a function to data are not well suited for *bounding* the leading term of the function. This is considered a type of *extrapolation* – extending an analysis beyond the range of the sample – that is usually only mentioned in the data analysis literature in warnings against trying it:

- *It would be a serious error to extrapolate the fitted function very far beyond the range of the data.* [3]
- *It is not always convenient to remember that the right [asymptotic] model for a population can fit a sample of data worse than a wrong model.* [17]

On the other hand, given that asymptotic analysis is the main goal of algorithm research, the payoff for a successful data analysis can be a bona fide advance of the discipline, as in our first example with $E(n, 1)$: sometimes everything works.

**Guideline 7.10** *Any data analysis technique applied to answer an asymptotic question about a finite data set must be considered a heuristic that provides no guarantees. Insight, rather than certainty, must be the goal.*

## The Ratio Test

The *ratio test* is an alternative to the power law procedure that can help build insight about the leading term in a function. Given a covariate sample $(X, Y)$ that is assumed to be related by an unknown function $y = f(x)$, this approach involves

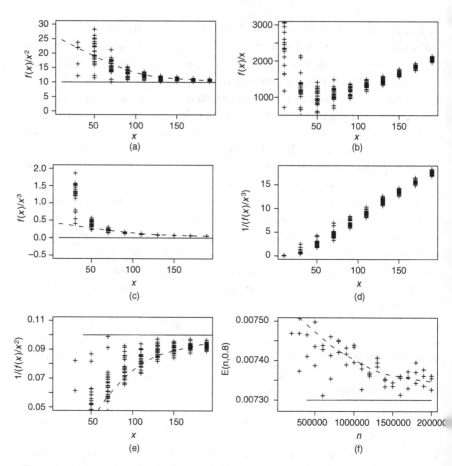

Figure 7.16. Ratio Test. Panels (a) through (e) show ratio tests for five guess functions $g(x)$, compared to $f(x)$. Panel (f) shows the result of the ratio test applied to the function $E(n, 0.8)$.

guessing the first term $g(x)$ of function $f(x)$ and evaluating the results of the guess.

The procedure is based on the following rationale. If $g(n)$ has the same order as the first term of $f(x)$ – that is, if $g(x) \in \Theta(f(x))$ – then the ratio $r(x) = f(x)/g(x)$ as $x \to \infty$ approaches a constant $c_g$ as $x \to \infty$. If the guess $g(x)$ is too low (that is, if $(f(x)) \in O(g(x))$), then the ratio $r(x) = f(x)/g(x)$ increases in $x$; if the guess is too big, the ratio $r(x) = f(x)/g(x)$ approaches 0. The ratio test uses graphical analysis to evaluate the trend in a plot of the *ratio data* $Y/g(X)$ against $X$.

Figure 7.16 shows the results of applying the ratio test to our example function $f(x)$ from the previous section. Note that in some panels the $y$-scale is restricted so that convergence in $x$ is easier to see, so some data points are not plotted.

Panel (a) shows a plot of $x$ versus the correct guess $g(x) = x^2$, together with a lowess curve showing the general trend and a horizontal sight line at $y = 10$. From visual inspection it is difficult to tell whether the ratio data approach a constant near 10 or will continue to decrease toward 0 at higher values of $x$. But, on the other hand, there is no suggestion that $f(x)$ grows more slowly than $n^2$, so we may take the guess $g(x) = n^2$ as a tentative lower bound on the first term of $f(x)$. Panel (b) supports this conclusion: the guess $g(x) = x$ is clearly too low, since the ratio data increase.

Panel (c) shows ratio data for the guess $g(x) = x^3$. Again, it is difficult to tell from visual inspection whether the ratio data decrease toward 0 or simply approach a constant $\epsilon$ near zero. However, a look at the *inverse ratio data* in panel (d) settles the question.

The rationale is that $f(x)/g(x)$ approaches 0 when $1/(f(x)/g(x))$ grows without bound, and that $f(x)/g(x)$ approaches a constant $c$ when $1/(f(x)/g(x))$ approaches a constant $1/c$. Applying this principle to the guess $g(x) = x^3$, panel (d) shows a plot of $X$ vs $1/(Y/n^3)$. Since the ratio data grow without bound, we can conclude that the guess $g(x) = n^3$ is too high, and that the data in panel (c) are indeed converging to 0.

Now apply this principle to the guess $g(x) = x^2$ from panel (a). Panel (e) shows a plot of $X$ vs. the inverse $1/(Y/n^2)$. As with panel (a) it is difficult to tell whether this function approaches a constant near 1.0 or continues to increase. But because one is an inverse of the other, we know that either (1) both data sets approach a constant and the guess is correct or (2) one set approaches 0 and the other approaches a (slowly increasing) function of $x$. This observation narrows our range of guesses.

Like the power law, the ratio test is inconclusive on the question of whether $f(x)$ is asymptotically $\Theta(n^2)$, or perhaps in some nearby class such as $\Theta(n^2 \log n)$ or $\Theta((n^2)/\log n)$. On the other hand, the ratio test has narrowed down the range of possibilities with convincing evidence that $f(x)$ is in neither $O(x)$ nor $\Omega(x^3)$.

Panel (f) shows the application of the Ratio Test to our difficult data set $n$ vs. $E(n, 0.8)$, from the previous section. Recall that the open question is whether the function describing $E(n, 0.8)$ is linear or sublinear in $n$. The panel shows the ratio data $E(n, 0.8)/n$: once again the results are inconclusive. Like the power law procedure, the ratio test can be very sensitive to low-order terms, and in the presence of noise one guess cannot be distinguished from another.

See the paper by McGeoch et al. [12] for detailed discussion of the power law, the ratio test, and other analysis techniques for inferring asymptotic performance from finite data sets.

**Guideline 7.11** *Try using the power law or the ratio rule to find the leading term in the unknown function relating X and Y.*

## 7.4 Chapter Notes

Plenty of data analysis techniques useful to algorithmic experimenters are omitted from this chapter. One omission worth noting is a discussion of analysis techniques for trivariate data samples $(X, Y, Z)$, as well as data in higher dimensions, which are common in algorithm studies.

In fact, most of the case study experiments in this text generated multivariate data samples. Here are just two examples: first, the Move-to-Front and Transpose experiments described in Sections 6.1 and 7.2 created six-dimensional data samples of the form $(n, m, Rm, Rt, MTF, TR)$: $n$ and $m$ are input parameters, $Rm$ and $Rt$ are requests generated at time $m$, $M$ and $T$ denote the algorithm costs. Higher-dimensional samples were created in the variance reduction experiments that reported alternative cost measurements. Second, the first fit experiments discussed in Sections 3.2 and 7.3.2 created four-dimensional data samples of the form $(n, u, S, B)$, where $n$ and $u$ are input parameters, $S$ denotes the sum of the list weights, and $B$ denotes the number of bins used by first fit.

Although the discussion of data analysis techniques for these data samples focused on questions about one- and two-dimensional relationships, the graphical displays in Figures 7.11 and 7.14 depict three- and four-dimensional relationships. These figures illustrate basic principles for plotting higher-dimensional point sets in two-dimensional graphs. First, use the $x$ and $y$ dimensions in the graph to highlight the relationship between the two data dimensions of main importance. The third data dimension of interest can be treated by the one of the methods in the following list; higher-dimensional point sets can be treated with combinations of these techniques.

- Identify the third dimension by *coding* data points with different symbols. For example, Panel (a) in Figure 7.11 plots cost $M$ against cost $T$ and codes the points according to input size $(a, b, c)$.
- The third dimension can be identified by using a *subscale* on the $x$-axis. Panel (b) of Figure 7.11 shows problem size $m$ on the main scale of the $x$-axis, but each $m$ level has a subscale (left, right) corresponding to the $M$ and $T$ costs, which are coded with plusses and circles. Corresponding points from each sample (a fourth dimension corresponding to trial index) are joined by line segments.
- Two dimensions can be combined into one using an arithmetical formula. Panels (c) and (d) in Figure 7.11 show problem size $m$ on the $x$-axis and functions $M/T$ and $M - T$ on the $y$-axis, respectively.
- If the preceding methods do not work because the data set is too complex for one panel, use *coplots*, which are panels plotted side by side, for the third dimension. Grids of panels can be used for four-dimensional data. For example, Figure 7.14

shows coplots of the $u = 1$ versus the $u = .8$ data for FF (reading top to bottom), and coplots of fits versus residuals for these two samples (reading left to right).

Consult the following sources to learn more about the data analysis techniques surveyed here.

- Descriptive statistics and inferential methods are discussed in most introductory data analysis textbooks. Two introductory texts, by Baron [2] and Cohen [7], are written explicitly for a computer science audience.
- To learn more about exploratory data analysis, consult Tukey's classic text [16]. See Mosteller and Tukey [13] for an introduction to regression analysis and model validation.
- Chambers et al. [6] and Cleveland [8] present good introductions to graphical methods of data analysis. Both texts contain discussions of graphical techniques for coping with higher-dimensional data samples.

The graphs throughout this text were created using the R statistical package [14], which is a freeware implementation of the S data analysis language. Visit www.r-project.org to learn more about R. The R source code for the graphs in this text can be found in the *GraphicsLab* section of *Alglab*.

Here are the guidelines presented in this chapter.

*7.1 Test programs should report outcomes as ratio data whenever possible, but not at the price of lost information.*

*7.2 Location and dispersion are the yin and yang of data summaries; do not report one without the other.*

*7.3 The empirical rule: in a sample from a normal distribution, 68 percent of the data fall within $\pm\sigma$ of the mean, 95 percent fall within $\pm 2\sigma$ of the mean, and 99.7 percent fall within $\pm 3\sigma$. Check that your data are indeed normally distributed before applying this rule.*

*7.4 Apply logarithmic transformation, or more generally a power transformation, to impose symmetry in a skewed data sample.*

*7.5 Consider these properties when deciding how to summarize a data sample: symmetry, outliers, skew, bi- or multimodality, kurtosis, and data censoring.*

*7.6 Calculate confidence intervals for your sample means.*

*7.7 Use bootstrapping (and related resampling methods) to generalize inferential methods to nonnormal distributions and nonstandard statistics.*

*7.8 Different graphs give different views of relationships in data. Try many views to learn the full story.*

*7.9 Let the trend in residuals guide the search for a better model for your data.*

*7.10* Any data analysis technique applied to answer an asymptotic question about
a finite data set must be considered a heuristic that provides no guarantees.
Insight, rather than certainty, must be the goal.

*7.11* Try using the power law or the ratio rule to find the leading term in the
(unknown) function relating X and Y.

### 7.4.1 Problems and Projects

1. Go back to an experiment from a previous chapter and reexamine the data
   distribution. What properties does it have that are relevant to the choice of
   summary statistics?
2. How would you extend the analysis of correlation in the Move-to-Front and
   Transpose algorithms to incorporate changes in both $n$ and $m$?
3. Can you find a better fit to the rcost data? Start by running experiments on
   more test files and varying problem sizes to generate a larger pool of data. Try
   the two modeling techniques illustrated here: remove outliers and reapply the
   linear and $O(n^{0.7})$ model; and apply Tukey's transformation ladder to straighten
   out the plot.
4. Apply the techniques for finding a descriptive function to the problem of predicting the crossover point $m^c$ (described in Section 6.1 for MTF and TR as a
   function of $n$ and $m$).
5. Find a large table of experimental data from a research paper in experimental algorithmics. Download this multidimensional data set and use graphical
   exploratory analysis to find relationships that are not apparent from the numbers.

### Bibliography

[1] Ackoff, Russell, "From data to wisdom," *Journal of Applied Systems Analysis,* Vol 16,
    Issue 1, pp. 3–9, 1989.
[2] Baron, Michael, *Probability and Statistics for Computer Scientists,* Chapman &
    Hall/CRC Press, 2007.
[3] Bennet, C. A., and N. L. Franklin, *Statistical Analysis in Chemistry and the Chemical
    Industry,* Wiley, 1954. (Quoted in [6], p. 280.)
[4] Bentley, J., D. S. Johnson, T. Leighton, C. C. McGeoch, and L. A. McGeoch, "Some
    unexpected expected behavior results for bin packing," STOC pp. 279–288, 1984.
[5] Box, George, Stuart Hunter, and William G. Hunter, *Statistics for Experimenters: An
    Introduction to Design, Data Analysis, and Model Building,* Wiley & Sons, 1978.
[6] Chambers, John M., William S. Cleveland, Beat Kleiner, and Paul A. Tukey, *Graphical
    Methods for Data Analysis,* Wadsworth International Group/Duxbury Press, 1983.
[7] Cohen, Paul R., *Empirical Methods for Artificial Intelligence,* MIT Press, 1995.
[8] Cleveland, William S., *Visualizing Data,* Hobart Press, 1993.
[9] Davison, A. C., and D. V. Hinkely, *Bootstrap Methods and Their Application,*
    Cambridge University Press, 1997.

[10]  Efron, Bradley, and Robert, J. Tibshirani, *An Introduction to the Bootstrap*, Monographs on Statistics and Applied Probability No. 57, Chapman & Hall, 1993.

[11]  Law, Averill M., and W. David Kelton, *Simulation Modeling and Analysis*, 2nd ed., McGraw-Hill, 1991.

[12]  McGeoch, Catherine C., Peter Sanders, Rudolf Fleischer, Paul R. Cohen, and Doina Precup, "Using finite experiments to study asymptotic performance." Dagstuhl Seminar on Experimental Algorithmics, LNCS 2547, pp. 93–126, 2002.

[13]  Mosteller, Frederick, and John W. Tukey, *Data Analysis and Regression: A Second Course in Statistics*, Addison Wesley, 1977.

[14]  *The R Project for Statistical Computing*. Available from: www.r-project.org, sponsored by the R Foundation for Statistical Computing.

[15]  Shor, Peter, "The average-case analysis of some on-line algorithms for bin packing, *Combinatorica*, Vol 6, No 2, pp 179–200, 1980.

[16]  Tukey, John W., *Exploratory Data Analysis*, Addison Wesley, 1977.

[17]  Wilkenson, Leland, *The Grammer of Graphics (Statistics and Computing)*, Springer, 1999.

# Index

Printed in the United States
by Baker & Taylor Publisher Services